Take a trip to
WEST GERMANY

Text and photographs by
Chris Fairclough

General Editor
Henry Pluckrose

Franklin Watts
London   New York   Sydney   Toronto

Words about West Germany

Alps
Autobahn

Bavaria
beer
Ludwig van
   Beethoven
East Berlin
West Berlin
Bierfest
Bonn
Bundeshaus

chemicals
clocks
coal
Cologne (Köln)

Danke
Deutschmark
Dom
Dortmund

Elbe
electrical goods
Essen

flower market
Frankfurt
frankfurters

Hamburg

iron

Moselle
Munich
   (München)

Pfennig

Rhine
Ruhr

steel

trams

vineyards
Volkswagen

wheat

Franklin Watts Limited
12a Golden Square
London W1

ISBN UK edition: 0 85166 927 1
ISBN US edition: 0 531 04320 7
Library of Congress Catalog Card No:
81–50032

© Franklin Watts Limited 1981

Reprinted 1983

Printed in Great Britain by
E. T. Heron, Essex and London

Maps by Brian and Constance Dear, and
Tony Payne.
Design by Tim Healey.
The author and publisher would like to
thank the following for kind permission to
reproduce photographs: Goethe Institute,
London (cover, 12, 13, 14, 17, 19, 24, 28);
Ian Goodwin (3); The Crafts Council of
Great Britain (18); Stephen Emmerson
(31); Frieder Blickle (11).
The author will also like to thank C.D.G.

West Germany is a large country in the middle of Europe. It stretches from the mountainous Alps in the south to flat coastlands in the north. There are many thriving industrial cities and small villages too, set in beautiful countryside.

West Germany was formed after World War II, when the old Germany was divided into two new countries: East Germany and West Germany. Bonn is the capital of West Germany. The West German parliament is called the Bundeshaus.

The German people are famous for their love of music. One of the world's greatest composers, Ludwig van Beethoven, was born in Bonn. His house still stands in the old part of the city.

This shows West German stamps and money. There are 100 Pfennigs in each Deutschmark.

6

WORLD MAP

West Germany

DENMARK

BALTIC SEA

NORTH SEA

Hamburg

Elbe

HOLLAND

Berlin

Dortmund

Essen

EAST GERMANY

Düsseldorf

Cologne (Köln)

Bonn

BELGIUM

Rhine

Frankfurt

CZECHOSLOVAKIA

LUX

WEST
GERMANY

FRANCE

BAVARIA

Stuttgart

Rhine

Munich
(München)

AUSTRIA

SWITZERLAND

7

The River Rhine flows through West Germany from south to north. It has always been an important link between regions, and there are many historic castles on its banks. Some of the finest were built over 200 years ago by rich noblemen.

8

The Rhine is still a major
transport link. Barges and larger
vessels carry goods between West
Germany's inland cities and the
mouth of the river in Holland on the
North Sea.

Cologne is a beautiful city on the Rhine. Its German name is Köln. The cathedral is over 700 years old, and is one of the largest in Europe. It is called the Dom, and its spires are nearly 160 m. (525 ft) high.

Artists draw pictures with chalk on the pavements near Cologne Cathedral. Here, the artist has copied a work by a great painter. Tourists give him money. The artist has written "Danke" (thank you).

North of Cologne lie the industrial regions of Dortmund and Essen in the rich coalfields which are in the river Ruhr district. The coal is used for smelting iron and steel at many great works nearby.

12

West German industries are very efficient. The people have a reputation for hard work. Cars are a major export. Motor companies such as Volkswagen, Opel and Mercedes export cars and vans to almost every country in the world.

The northern region of West Germany contains much flat farming land. The farmers raise dairy cattle, and grow cereal crops such as wheat, rye, barley and oats. Here you can see a combine harvester at work.

West German exports, such as
cars, electrical goods and chemicals
are shipped all over the world.
Hamburg is at the mouth of the
River Elbe on the North Sea coast.
It is one of the biggest and busiest
ports in Europe.

15

The southern part of West Germany rises towards the Alps, the great mountain range in the heart of Europe. The southern region is called Bavaria. In winter, the mountains are covered with snow.

Munich is the largest city in Bavaria. It is called München in German. The city is famous for brewing beer. There are Bierfests (beer festivals) every year. Visitors come to sample the various types of beer.

Holidaymakers flock to Bavaria.
The tourists buy local handicrafts.
Bavaria is famous for its ironwork.

The West Germans are keen
sports fans. Football is one of the
most popular sports. The Olympic
Games were held in Munich in 1972.
This stadium was built specially for
the Games. It holds 80,000 people.

Flower markets are a common sight in many West German towns. The stall holders arrive early in the morning. They hope to sell their flowers before it gets too hot and the flowers start to wilt.

People use trams to get about in many cities. The trams run on a fixed track and stop at stations in the street. Some streets are completely closed to traffic, making shopping easier and more enjoyable.

Most West German city-dwellers
live in flats. Many modern blocks,
like this one in Cologne, are built on
the edge of the city, and are
surrounded by parks.

Flats usually have large windows and balconies. Furniture is generally modern and very carefully chosen. Indoor plants are very popular and some flats have balcony gardens.

On their first day at school, children take cones filled with sweets and presents from their parents. The primary school is called a "Grundschule" (ground school).

West German children only go to primary school in the mornings. They begin their lessons at 8.30 and finish at 1.30. However all pupils are expected to do homework in the afternoon. They carry their books in large satchels.

West Germany borders nine other countries. Some children grow up speaking two languages: For example, children living near the French border may speak French as well as German. English is the main foreign language taught in schools.

West Germans are fond of good food. Sausages, called Würst, are particularly liked. There are over one hundred types. Some are named according to region. For example, frankfurters come from Frankfurt.

Most West German wines are white. The grapes are grown especially in vineyards in the valleys of the Rhine and the Moselle rivers. Local villagers hold annual festivals to celebrate the grape harvest.

28

West Germany is a large country so it needs good communications. Most of the railways are electric. Inter-city trains can travel at 200 km (144 miles) per hour.

West Germany's roads are fast and modern. Motorways are called Autobahns. Some of them hold ten lanes of traffic. A network of Autobahns covers the country and you can go right across West Germany on them.

Before World War II, Berlin was
the capital of Germany. Today,
Berlin is inside East Germany.
However, the city is divided. East
Berlin is part of East Germany, but
West Berlin belongs to West
Germany. A wall separates them.

Index

Alps 3,, 16

Bavaria 16, 17, 18
Beethoven, Ludwig van 5
Berlin 31
Bierfest 17
Bonn 4, 5
Bundeshaus 4

Cologne (Köln) 10, 11, 12, 22

Deutschmark 6
Dom 10
Dortmund 12

East Berlin 31
East Germany 4, 31
Elbe River 15
Essen 12
Exports 13, 15

Festivals 17, 28
Frankfurt 27

Hamburg 15

Money 6
Moselle River 28
Munich (München) 17, 19
Music 5

Olympic Games 19

Railways 29
Rhine River 8, 9, 10, 28
Ruhr River 12

Sausages 27
School 24, 25
Sports 18, 19
Stamps 6

Tourists 11, 18
Transport 9

Vineyards 28
Volkswagen 13

West Berlin 31
Wines 28
World War II 4, 31
Würst 27

DATE DUE

CINEMA BY THE BAY

CINEMA BY THE BAY

BY SHEERLY AVNI

INTRODUCTION BY
MICHAEL SRAGOW

A WELCOME BOOK

PUBLISHED BY GEORGE LUCAS BOOKS
AN IMPRINT OF JAK FILMS, INC.

GEORGE
LUCAS
BOOKS

CONTENTS

INTRODUCTION *by Michael Sragow*   12

THE STUDIOS
American Zoetrope   24
The Saul Zaentz Company   74
Lucasfilm Ltd.   98
Pixar Animation Studios   146
Pacific Data Images   168

THE DIRECTORS
Carroll Ballard   186
Joan Chen   192
Chris Columbus   194
Clint Eastwood   202
Philip Kaufman   212
John Korty   218
Rob Nilsson   222
Michael Ritchie   224
Matthew Robbins   228
Henry Selick   232
Wayne Wang   236
Terry Zwigoff   240

FILMOGRAPHIES   244

INDEX   260
CREDITS   268
ACKNOWLEDGMENTS   271

INTRODUCTION

From cinema's beginnings, San Francisco was Athens for moviemakers—the place that encouraged open-ended explorations of comedy and drama and technique. Los Angeles was Sparta—the place where moviemakers majored in aggression, especially when it came to dealmaking or marketing.

Northern California has been at the forefront of experiments in color, sound, and digitalization, of attempts to film literary works considered unfilmable, from Frank Norris' *McTeague* to Milan Kundera's *The Unbearable Lightness of Being*. It has become known for pulling off special-effects feats judged beyond any moviemaker's reach, such as scarily believable computer-generated dinosaurs for the *Jurassic Park* movies. But it has also attracted moviemakers because of its social and theatrical ferment. The first movie stars arose here. The greatest movie star in history perfected his persona here.

The San Francisco Bay Area's tradition of risk-taking and innovation has continued to attract adventurous and individualistic filmmakers who've settled in every pocket of Northern California: Carmel and Redwood City, Emeryville and Berkeley, Marin County, and, of course, San Francisco itself.

Not just California films, but all films, started in Northern California, with the inspired tinkering of transplanted Englishman Eadweard Muybridge. In the 1870s, under the sponsorship of former California governor and Central Pacific Railroad president Leland Stanford, who had a passion for horses and hoped he could capture precise images of them in action, Muybridge pioneered stop-action photography and invented a forerunner of the modern motion-picture projector, the Zoopraxiscope. Then Muybridge moved on from horses to humans. San Francisco film historian

Geoffrey Bell has called his model human athlete, S.F. Olympic Club gymnast William Lawton "the world's first movie 'star'," and Lawton's first onscreen somersault "the initiation of motion picture drama."

When you look at Muybridge's pictures, Lawton does appear, as Bell says, "aglow with the vitality of youth." And there's a straight line from Lawton's virile poses to those of S.F. filmmaking's next significant influence—Gilbert M. Anderson, the creator of Broncho Billy, the first cowboy icon of the movies and the first screen personality to be a box-office draw. Born Max Aronson, Anderson was a vaudeville performer, model, moviemaker, and entrepreneur from Little Rock, Arkansas, who ended up in the Bay Area by way of New York and Chicago. He played bit parts in Edwin S. Porter's 1903 *The Great Train Robbery* and continued to act before joining forces with theatre-owner George K. Spoor in 1907 to form the Essanay Film Manufacturing Company in the Windy City. In 1909 Anderson took his cameraman and a few members of his company and moved West, eventually establishing an Essanay studio in Niles (now part of the city of Fremont) and turning out hundreds of Westerns over the next few years.

In Essanay's happiest coup, it signed Charlie Chaplin, who made a handful of films at the Niles studio, including his breakthrough, *The Tramp* (1915), where he seamlessly merged the Tramp's kick-in-the-pants pluck and slapstick pathos. Chaplin's "little fellow"—the most popular human movie character of all time (only Mickey Mouse rivals him), and arguably the most anti-establishment and subversive—found his footing in eclectic, iconoclastic Northern California.

In 1914 another Bay Area movie company, the California Motion Picture Corporation, built production facilities on open ranch land near Marin County's San Rafael. Surrounding its opera-singer leading lady, Beatriz Michelena, with actors from S.F.'s burgeoning theater community, it made a series of adaptations of well-known properties, from Bret Harte's *Salomy Jane* to Mrs. Wiggs of the *Cabbage Patch* and *Mignon*. By the end of 1916 Essanay and the CMPC lost their biggest stars and went into decline. Still, San Francisco continued to make its presence felt with discoveries that rippled throughout the world of filmmaking. S.F.-based inventor Leon F. Douglass devised the first practical color film and shot the first color feature, *Cupid Angling*, in the Bay Area, hosting its world premiere in San Francisco on June 16, 1918.

Producers who prized the constant sunshine in Los Angeles began to consolidate their studios and gear up for mass production after World War I. San Francisco, however, served as a magnet for Hollywood filmmakers like Erich Von Stroheim, who wanted to keep their imaginations free of executive influence. San Francisco drew movie people partly because it was a real city when L.A. was a sleepy desert town.

What Frank Norris (1870–1902) wrote about the appeal of San Francisco for fiction writers over a century ago would go on to apply to S.F. films as well as S.F. novels: "Things can happen in San Francisco, Kearny Street, Montgomery Street, Nob Hill, Telegraph Hill, of course Chinatown, Lone Mountain, the Poodle Dog, the Palace Hotel and the What Cheer house, the Barbary Coast, the Crow's Nest, the Mission, the Bay, the Bohemian Club, the Presidio, Spanish town, Fisherman's Wharf. There is an indefinable air about all these places that is suggestive of stories at once. You fancy the name would look well on a book's page. The people who frequent them could walk right into a novel and be at home."

Norris' own novels provided the basis for the 1922 Rudolph Valentino vehicle, *Moran of the Lady Letty*, and for Von Stroheim's 1923 *Greed*, the movie that set the tone for relations between San Francisco-based filmmaking and Hollywood studios. Von Stroheim did more than film Frank Norris' 1899 novel, *McTeague*, chapter by chapter. He added scenes merely implied in Norris' descriptions and flashbacks. Von Stroheim's mix of actual locations (it's a valuable document of the Bay Area in the early 1920s), veracious action, and novelistic details anticipated epic film adaptations like Luchino Visconti's *The Leopard* by four decades. The director envisioned the movie as a special two-night presentation.

But Von Stroheim, who continued to call Hollywood home, produced *Greed* for L.A.'s Samuel Goldwyn Company, which merged with Metro Pictures before the film was completed. Irving Thalberg, production chief for the resulting corporation, Metro-Goldwyn-Mayer, insisted that Von Stroheim truncate the film to normal feature length. Hoping to compromise with MGM, the director himself reduced and polished his nine-hour-plus first cut, arriving at a print that ran between four and five hours. This version, too, was deemed unacceptable. Then he asked for help from his fellow epic filmmaker, Rex Ingram, who assigned editor Grant Wytock to whittle the running time to three-and-a-quarter hours. MGM ignored their efforts and got *Greed* down to two hours and ten minutes. Von Stroheim disowned (and never saw) the MGM edition.

Von Stroheim's battle presages the fights George Lucas (as director) and Francis Coppola (as executive producer) lost with Warner Bros. on *THX 1138* and with Universal on *American Graffiti*—and the fights Coppola won with Paramount (or at least came out even on) during the making of *The Godfather*.

After *Greed* few producers or studio heads would let their moviemakers base entire productions in San Francisco. But San Francisco natives who'd gone Hollywood would keep sneaking propaganda for their favorite town into their movies. The San Francisco screenwriter, Anita Loos, wrote that she and her cowriter, Robert Hopkins, "happened to share a particular distaste for Southern California, one which is the heritage of all natives of San Francisco. We delighted in memories of the city of our youth; its brisk Northern climate generates energy, just as the tepid air of Southern California dissipates it…" Spurred on by the nostalgia of writers like Loos and directors like Lloyd Bacon (who made *The Frisco Kid*), Hollywood minted an image of San Francisco as the Peter Pan of pleasure spots, a metropolis that would never grow up—or at least would age without losing its spunk.

San Francisco permeated Hollywood movies even when it appeared only in file or newsreel footage or second-unit shots. It became the focus of another classic tale of greed—this time treated as tense comic melodrama—in John Huston's enduring 1941 adaptation of Dashiell Hammett's *The Maltese Falcon*. As the years went by, it alternated between being a picture-book backdrop for escapist frolics (from 1943's *Hello, 'Frisco, Hello* to 1979's *Foul Play*) and a stylized setting for despairing melodramas (like Orson Welles' 1948 *The Lady from Shanghai*). There were tributes to San Francisco Irish in Raoul Walsh's 1941 biography of boxer Jim Corbett, *Gentleman Jim*, and to San Francisco Norwegians in George Stevens's 1948 *I Remember Mama*, and to the city's saloon culture in James Cagney's 1948 production of William Saroyan's *The Time of Your Life*.

Northern California reclaimed its identity as a lodestone for alternative creativity when filmmakers began using it to conjure fantasies that drew stubble on the smiley face of late-1940s and 1950s popular culture. In one of the darkest of all film noirs, *D.O.A.* (1949), a Banning businessman goes to S.F. and becomes the victim of a slow, fatal poisoning. Director Rudolph Mate uses real S.F. locations in exaggerated ways to express the anti-hero's frenzy: Whenever we see the St. Francis Hotel, it's overrun with conventioneers. San Francisco was at its dreamiest—and also most hallucinatory—in Alfred Hitchcock's 1958 tale of romantic obsession, *Vertigo*. Hitchcock gave a tenebrous underglow to the most luminous settings, like the Mission Dolores or the Palace of Fine Arts, as he turned a metropolitan reverie into a nightmare. Also in 1958, in *The Line-Up*, Don Siegel began to chart new and controversial sorts of anti-heroes making their way through amoral environments—a course that would bring Oakland-bred Clint Eastwood back home as the star of Siegel's *Dirty Harry* (1971).

San Francisco became the centripetal force for artists who wanted to say no when everyone else was saying yes, or who thought that Americans should explore frontiers of the mind and emotions as well as new technology. Poetry and avant-garde filmmaking sprung up simultaneously around the late James Broughton. Pauline Kael had a relationship with him (he is the father of her daughter) before she cofounded the Berkeley Cinema Guild and Studio, the first twin art-movie house in the U.S., where she trailblazed adventurous revival programming, complete with legendary program notes. (Even filmmakers who'd later suffer her critical barbs admitted that she motivated them at the Cinema Guild and Studio.) Urged on by his high school pal, Beat poet Michael McClure, collage artist Bruce Conner went to San Francisco in 1957 and became a member of an anti-Establishment art movement he called the "Ratbastard Protective Association." Conner continued to work with "found" material as a moviemaker, ranging from simple film leader to stag-film footage of Marilyn Monroe. Conner's teacher, Stan Brakhage, flooded screens with colorful abstractions, while Jordan Belson, who began as a painter, toyed with mystical, cosmic graphics that writer-director Philip Kaufman was wise enough to incorporate into *The Right Stuff* (1983).

The Bay Area also became a center for documentary-makers. They ranged from Les Blank (1969's *The Blues Accordin' to Lightnin' Hopkins*, 1982's *Burden of Dreams*) and Rob Epstein and Jeffrey Friedman (1989's *Common Threads*) to Terry Zwigoff, who was a master of factual funk in films like *Louie Bluie* (1985) and *Crumb* (1994) before he became a master of feature-film funk with *Ghost World* (2001) and *Bad Santa* (2003).

The tremendous box-office success of Steve McQueen's 1968 production *Bullitt* (directed by Peter Yates) boosted on-location feature filmmaking, as others vainly tried to match that movie's famous car chase. *Bullitt* updated S.F.'s traditional progressive image in its portrait of an idealistic cop: The film was like Bogart for bohemians, and his sport-jacket-and-turtleneck style established police-detective chic. The one fascinating aspect of the otherwise lame Sidney Poitier vehicle, his 1971 Virgil Tibbs movie *The Organization*, was that it hinged on a multi-cultural, vaguely countercultural, and militant group that was trying to force S.F. cops (through detective Tibbs) to bust the drug rackets preying on the neighborhoods.

San Francisco is used more for discord than for harmony in most films from this period, whether *Dirty Harry* or that haunting example of non-conformist "kook" movies, Richard Lester's 1968 *Petulia* (with Julie Christie and George C. Scott). Director Richard Rush (*The Stunt Man*) shot *Psych-Out* right after the *Summer of Love*, partly in the hippie capital Haight-Ashbury; as a deaf girl (Susan Strasberg) searches the Haight for her deranged brother (Bruce Dern), she crashes with a sly guitarist played by Jack Nicholson. His killer smile is in full gleam, but Nicholson isn't the only future actor/writer/director to make his mark here: Henry Jaglom is a drug-crazed graphic artist, and Garry Marshall is a cop who's sick of the whole psychedelic scene. Dean Stockwell, in long hair and headband, coins be-true-to-yourself aphorisms, while the Seeds and the Strawberry Alarm Clock deliver music to burn incense by. With cinematographer Laszlo Kovacs (who would soon do *Easy Rider*), Rush pioneered the kind of complex, focus-shifting shots that can make viewers feel as if they're bobbing and weaving through a commune.

San Francisco Chronicle columnist Herb Caen conducted an ongoing campaign against the Hollywood invasion of San Francisco. Hollywoodians could display a cavalier attitude toward local landmarks—for example, Peter Bogdanovich's Barbra Streisand-Ryan O'Neal slapstick smash, *What's Up, Doc?*, chipped a couple of steps at Alta Plaza Park. What's worse, the low-style movies that often resulted tarnished the area's luster. Out-of-towners actually liked to film here because it was so humane. Woody Allen made his 1969 directorial debut, *Take the Money and Run*, in San Francisco, even though it was set elsewhere. Said Allen: "I'd rather spend ten weeks here than in Gary, Indiana."

Moviegoers might have thought that following the Haight-Ashbury era, the Berkeley protests, and all these frantic, bloody movies, S.F. was a center of urban unrest. Yet the invasion of these Spartan entertainments helped Athens to rise again, heightening S.F.'s visibility as a film town and seeding local crews.

Filmmaker/animator John Korty had already shown the way to Bay Area independence both by shooting his 1965 *The Crazy Quilt* in and around Stinson Beach and his 1967 *Funnyman* in San Francisco, and by doing post production at his own personal facility in a barn near Stinson Beach. While Korty was setting up a third feature, George Lucas was befriending Francis Ford Coppola (then the youngest director in Hollywood), while observing him on the set of *Finian's Rainbow*; Lucas then joined the Coppola caravan that was filming *The Rain People* across the country. (Lucas was writing *THX-1138* and filming a documentary about *The Rain People* experience.) Lucas met Korty at a convention in San Francisco and spread the word of Korty's one-man rebellion against Hollywood to Coppola. When the movie Laszlo Kovacs shot a year after *Psych-Out*—1969's *Easy Rider*—upended Hollywood and opened the studios, however briefly, to original ideas, Coppola seized the day. Knocked out by Korty's setup, Coppola and Lucas decided to establish a San Francisco production company with money from a Hollywood desperate for youth, and stack it with the seminal talents of their generation.

Coppola named the company American Zoetrope—a reference to a device that produced an illusion of movement similar to Muybridge's Zoopraxiscope. Walter Murch soon joined them, and turned his genius for synesthesia—making a movie's sound enlarge or color its imagery (and vice versa)—into a Northern California specialty. Carroll Ballard (*The Black Stallion*), Matthew Robbins with Hal Barwood (*Dragonslayer*), Robert Dalva (*The Return of the Black Stallion*), and Korty himself, among others, filled the ranks. Many more passed through to use Zoetrope's offices and equipment.

What follows is a history of that creative explosion, fragments of which extend all the way to the phenomenal success of later companies, such as Lucasfilm, Ltd., Industrial Light and Magic, and Pixar Animation Studios, which started at Lucasfilm, then split off. It's also the story of other, non-Zoetrope filmmakers, including: writer-director Philip Kaufman (*Henry and June*), who jolted the industry by filming *The Right Stuff* almost entirely in the Bay Area; director Michael Ritchie, who did much of his finest work (*The Candidate*, *Smile*) in Northern California; and Chris Columbus (*Nine Months*, *Mrs. Doubtfire*, the first two *Harry Potter* films). It's about stars with Northern California roots who became filmmakers and did their best work with Bay Area writers, such as Joan Chen directing Geling Yan's *Xiu Xiu*, *The Sent-Down Girl*; Eastwood directing Kaufman's script for *The Outlaw Josey Wales*; and David Webb Peoples' script for *Unforgiven*. It's about a music company called Fantasy that went into films and made *Payday* and *One Flew*

Over the Cuckoo's Nest and then, as the Saul Zaentz Company, made *Amadeus* and *The Unbearable Lightness of Being*. It's about computer animation like PDI's *Shrek* films and Pixar's *The Incredibles* and *Finding Nemo*, and a stop-motion genius like Phil Tippett bringing his instincts into virtual reality in films like *Starship Troopers*. It's about director Wayne Wang, who goes back and forth between the indie and big-studio worlds, from the graphic sex of *The Center of the World* to the big-star romance of *Maid in Manhattan*. And it's about the totally indie filmmaker Rob Nilsson, whose *Signal 7* might have pleased the Frank Norris who declared, "It's the Life that we want, the vigorous, real thing, not the curious weaving of words and the polish of literary style. Damn the 'style' of a story, so long as we get the swing and rush and trample of the things that live."

Of course, other regions have given birth to distinctive styles and modes of cinema. New York filmmakers from Elia Kazan, John Cassavetes, and Sidney Lumet to Martin Scorsese, James Toback, and Spike Lee have drawn on the city's wealth of acting talent and the vitality of its streets, just as Woody Allen became the comic laureate of its educated upper-middle class. For thirty-five years John Waters has tapped into the funky strain of his hometown, Baltimore, even in his family-friendly *Hairspray*—just as Barry Levinson, a sometime Bay Area resident (now living in Connecticut), has chronicled his native Baltimore's changing middle class for a quarter-century, along the way leading Baltimorean David Simon to produce the most persuasive street dramas ever put on TV (*Homicide: Life in the Street*, *The Corner*, *The Wire*). John Hughes deepened high-school dramedy (*Sixteen Candles*, *The Breakfast Club*) partly by staying put in suburban Chicago; Gus Van Sant's work (*Mala Noche*, *Drugstore Cowboy*, *Last Days*) has exposed corners of longing and malaise in the verdant Pacific Northwest. Robert Rodriguez and Richard Linklater have helped turned Austin into a regional hub, complete with cutting-edge production facilities. But Coppola and Lucas set examples for them and directly mentored Rodriguez.

No other group of filmmakers has done as much as those in the Bay Area to change the way all movies are produced, distributed, and perceived, or to pass their hard-won lessons down to younger generations, like Walter Murch telling Terry Zwigoff to add just three seconds to *Crumb*, then offering to mix the film for free. From American Zoetrope at 827 Folsom Street to Lucas companies expanding into S.F.'s former army base, the Presidio, it's beginning to look like a permanent revolution.

MICHAEL SRAGOW, lead film critic for the *Baltimore Sun*

"I had always wanted to be part of that type of artistic scene like you hear about in Paris. What might it have been like to be there? There's Hemingway in the Ritz Bar, and F. Scott Fitzgerald, and Sartre, and these wonderful people.

When we were in San Francisco, broke, trying to figure out how to pay for anything, little did I realize that in effect, that's what that was. All those people were to go on and become wonderful artists."

— Francis Ford Coppola

AMERICAN
ZOETROPE

F rancis Coppola adored movies from an early age, and when a bout with polio left him bedridden for a year at age ten, he also developed a love for puppetry and ventriloquism. He grew up surrounded by the arts. His father Carmine was a classical flutist, musical arranger, and composer. His mother Italia had been an actress, and his older brother August, whom he worshipped, was determined to be a writer. But it wasn't until college at Hofstra University that he discovered his talent as a director. By all accounts, Coppola assumed full control of the theater department while he was there, turning it into a student-run "regime." By the time he came out to Southern California for film school, he had already experienced the joys of working with and ruling over a talented group of like-minded artists. "I left Hofstra as really the top guy," he says. "We got lots of things done, lots of imaginative, crazy things—and lots of stuff that failed."

Coppola's experience at UCLA was less inspiring. The film school was all male at the time, heavy on theory, light on practical training. But he wanted, essentially, to make movies, not theorize about them. And make movies he did, first as an assistant to B-movie director Roger Corman, and then as the only student in his class who managed to get his thesis film produced by a major studio. That film, a charming coming-of-age romp called *You're a Big Boy Now*, garnered him enough respect to get funding for the film he was working on when he first met George Lucas—the Fred Astaire vehicle *Finian's Rainbow*.

Coppola did not enjoy Warner Brothers, but his harrowing stint in what he would later refer to as "the belly of the beast" did introduce him to Lucas, who impressed Coppola so much that he brought him on to his next project *The Rain People*, a road movie starring Shirley Knight, Robert Duvall, and a handsome young New York actor named James Caan. *The Rain People* was made over a four-month trip through eighteen states, in a makeshift caravan of station wagons and vans, one of which contained an editing table. The thrill of making a film on the run, with a small crew, shooting during the day and editing at night, lit a fire under Coppola to start a studio of his own. "We began to feel like Robin Hood," he recalls. "We really had the filmmaking machine in our hands, and it didn't need to be in Hollywood—it could be anywhere."

PORTFOLIO

AMERICAN ZOETROPE

Academy Award Nominations	**59**
Academy Awards	**16**
Golden Globe Nominations	**43**
Golden Globe Awards	**11**
Cannes Film Festival Awards	**2**
Films Listed on the AFI Top 100	**3**

JOINT PRODUCTIONS OF FRANCIS FORD COPPOLA AND GEORGE LUCAS

Academy Award Nominations	**10**
Golden Globe Nominations	**6**
Golden Globe Awards	**3**
Cannes Film Festival Awards	**2**
Films Listed on the AFI Top 100	**1**

MILESTONES

1968

The Rain People begins shooting on location. In July the decision is made to create a film company in Marin. Later that year Francis Coppola travels to the Photokina 1968 trade show in Cologne, Germany to buy a KEM and other filmmaking equipment. He visits Mogen Skot-Hansen's Lanterna Films, housed in a mansion near Copenhagen. There the producer gives him an antique zoetrope from his collection and Coppola dubs his new company "American Zoetrope."

1969

Francis Coppola, George Lucas, and Walter Murch set up offices at 827 Folsom Street in San Francisco in a warehouse located by Coppola. John Korty rents an office and edit room but keeps his own film company. Robert Dalva joins American Zoetrope making Office of Economic Opportunities documentaries. Coppola hires John Milius to work on *Apocalypse Now* script with Lucas. Matthew Robbins and Hal Barwood join as writers on other projects. Woody Allen uses American Zoetrope to screen rushes on his film *Take the Money and Run*.

The San Francisco Bay Area.

Walter Murch, Francis Ford Coppola with
one of his antique cars, and a group of kids in
Northern California.

"Anywhere" turned out to be San Francisco, at the time the epicenter of a nationwide countercultural youth movement. San Francisco was beautiful, it was affordable, it was close enough to Hollywood to make trips possible—and there were already filmmakers up there doing what Coppola dreamed of doing. John Korty, for example, a quirky, well-appreciated independent director in Marin, had a mini-studio of his own, which he kept in a barn in Stinson Beach. George Lucas, who had been born in Modesto and had always loved the "big city" by the Bay, had flown to San Francisco to substitute for Coppola at a national teacher's convention. After meeting Korty, Lucas called Coppola in Nebraska and said "you gotta see this." The two immediately fell in love with Korty's studio by the water, and took the inspiration of Korty's success as a sign that they could make their dream of building an independent studio a reality. Once they had agreed on the location, it was now just a question of doing what Francis Ford Coppola was best at—amassing his troops.

"You ask why there are movements in movie history," Coppola would say much later. "Why all of a sudden there are great Japanese films, or great Italian films, or great Australian films, or whatever. And it's usually because there are a number of people that cross-pollinated each other." The two groups that did the most cross-pollinating in San Francisco were the enchanted classes of 1966 and 1967 from the University of California, Los Angeles, and from the University of Southern California. During the late

The doors to the first American Zoetrope office at 827 Folsom Street.

sixties and early seventies, UCLA boasted the likes of Carroll Ballard, Paul Schrader, and Gregory Nava. Out of USC, there was George Lucas, as well as John Milius, Caleb Deschanel, Bob Dalva, Matthew Robbins, Michael Ritchie, and Walter Murch.

These were the talents. But the crack in the wall that made possible the studios' sudden interest in tapping into their talent pool, owed a great deal of its success to one film: The surprise 1969 hit *Easy Rider*.

Easy Rider, the now classic road movie written by Dennis Hopper, Peter Fonda, and Terry Southern, cost less than $400,000 to make but grossed between $50 million and $60 million worldwide. It was also an exhilarating, high-octane evocation of young America's conflicted uncertainty and idealism. But that is not what impressed the Hollywood studios. What they cared about was that this small out-of-nowhere film had succeeded where their own recent big-budget productions had failed: It had lured the next generation of ticket buyers away from their television sets and rock concerts and back into the theaters. Suddenly the search was on for the next hot director, the young guy who could reproduce *Easy Rider*'s success. It was easy for Coppola to cast himself in that role. (As John Milius wryly observed much later, it was enough for them to know he had a beard, and knew hippies.)

Francis Ford Coppola doing more than executive producing on *THX 1138*.

"It was a time," says Carroll Ballard, "when the studio bosses didn't exactly know where the audience was." Coppola convinced them that he would bring them the audiences. Between Coppola's talents and Lucas's award-winning student short, the two directors had—in today's parlance—"the buzz factor." In spades.

Add to that Coppola's charisma. His former classmates speak with almost universal awe about his ability to amass esprit de corps. "You can

1970

Korty cuts his documentary *Imogen Cunningham, Photographer*. George Lucas shoots *THX 1138*. Korty takes his own film to Warner Brothers and gets favorable response. "Black Thursday" occurs in November when Warner Brothers demands repayment of American Zoetrope's $300,000 advance.

1971

American Zoetrope's first film *THX 1138* is released and production begins on *The Godfather*. Francis Ford Coppola shares the Academy Award for Writing (Story and Screenplay—based on factual material or material not previously published or produced) for *Patton* with Edmund H. North. George Lucas incorporates Lucasfilm Ltd. and begins work on the Lucasfilm/Coppola production *American Graffiti*.

1972

Coppola moves his offices into the landmark Sentinel Building on Kearny Street in San Francisco. *The Godfather* premieres in New York. Shooting begins in San Francisco on *The Conversation*.

1973

The Godfather is nominated for ten Academy Awards and seven Golden Globes. Of the three Academy Award wins, Marlon Brando refuses his award for best Actor in a Leading Role to protest Hollywood's treatment of Native Americans. Shooting begins on *The Godfather Part II* in Lake Tahoe, California. Richard Tong, now accountant for Korty, Coppola, and Lucas, is instrumental in the sale of the Sentinel building from his clients The Kingston Trio to Coppola/Zoetrope.

1974

The Conversation is released on Francis Coppola's birthday, April 7, in New York. Coppola phones Carroll Ballard from Sicily while filming *The Godfather Part II* to invite him to direct an American Zoetrope production. Fred Roos suggests *The Black Stallion* for Ballard.

1975

The Godfather Part II is nominated for eleven Academy Awards and six Golden Globes, winning six Oscars, including Francis Ford Coppola's wins for Directing, Writing and Best Picture. At the same time, *The Conversation* is nominated for three Academy Awards and four Golden Globes. By the end of the 47th Academy Awards, Coppola has a personal total of five Oscar Statuettes since his first win in 1970. Francis Coppola becomes publisher/editor of *City* magazine. That same year Francis and Eleanor Coppola purchase 1,560 acres of the drop Francis in the middle of the darkest jungle in Africa," says Carroll Ballard, "without any knowledge of anything, and two days later he'll have control of everything of where he's at." As if to prove the point, John Milius, writer of *Apocalypse Now*, says even more bluntly, "I'd have died for him."

And Universal/Seven Arts wrote checks for him. They gave him a total of $700,000 seed money, and in return Coppola promised them seven scripts—all hip, all young, and all new. The first film would be Lucas's feature-length remake of his award-winning student film, *THX 1138*, a movie which Coppola smoothly assured them was almost wrapped up.

The twenty-eight-year-old had indeed secured funding for Zoetrope—and especially, for turning *THX* into a feature film (which was welcome news, since in true, idealist form, and without a penny to his name, the twenty-three-year-old director Lucas had already started scouting locations and holding auditions.)

Even with the seed money, Coppola couldn't afford the rural estate in Marin that he and Lucas had dreamed of. Instead they found and renovated a huge warehouse in San Francisco's rugged industrial district south of Market Street, and outfitted it lavishly: seven editing rooms, state-of-the-art equipment, a pool table, and an espresso machine. American Zoetrope's all-night opening party was an evening of decadence and excitement that would put a late-nineties dot-com launch to shame. 827 Folsom was right around the corner from the offices of the new music magazine, *Rolling Stone*, and guests included Bill Graham, The Grateful Dead, and Ken Kesey, as well as every beautiful woman under the age of 23 from Haight Street to The Presidio. One could call it an unforgettable night, if any of the principals could remember it.

And it was just the beginning. Woody Allen, Akira Kurosawa, and Sidney Poitier were all known to drop in at the studio. And always, there was a sense of creative energy and openness. It was all "very utopian," according to Caleb Deschanel, "an extension of our experiences at film school." Coppola's son Gio helped build, his wife Eleanor did the interior design, and the entire entourage pitched in to create a dream collaborative environment. They had already successfully brought one film project to completion, in a four-day marathon stretch to finish up *The Rain People* in time for its showing at the Mill Valley Film Festival. Not only did they finish in time, but the film took first prize. It

> ## "I'd have died for him."
> — John Milius, *writer/director*

George Lucas and Francis Ford Coppola on the *THX 1138* set.

American Zoetrope December 1969. Back row, left to right: Barry Beckerman, Robert Dalva, Walter Murch (with pitchfork), George Lucas, Al Locatelli, Lawrence Sturhahn, John Korty; On Ladder: Carroll Ballard, Francis Ford Coppola (with Zoetrope); Front row, left to right: Steve Wax, John Milius (in sombrero), Dennis Jakob, Tim Huntley.

seemed that the dream was going to come true, and at first, according to Lucas's classmate and sound editor extraordinaire, Walter Murch, "The clatter of film was heard twenty-four hours a day."

Even then, the environment was chaotic. This was, after all, San Francisco in 1970, with all its frenzied psychedelic energy. As Lucas explains now, a bit euphemistically, "Everybody was a little bit out of it." There were political activists "borrowing" the state-of-the-art equipment without returning it, couch-surfing bohemians sleeping on editing machines, and of course, lots of money going out—and none coming in. Lucas and Murch finished the edits of *THX* in the relative quiet of an attic in Mill Valley.

By June 1970, Coppola was ready to present Universal Studios with a return on their investment. He sent them seven scripts, and he also brought George Lucas down for a Los Angeles screening of *THX 1138*. He was in the red financially, but confident that with the combined creativity of his fellow filmmakers, he would prove that he and American Zoetrope were firmly in the black in terms of talent. The results of this adventure were black indeed, but not in the way he had hoped. With the remarkable foresight and acumen for which they are so well known, the Hollywood moneymen threw their hands up at the future director of the blockbuster *Star Wars* series. They had wanted far out, they had wanted imagination, but when hit with *THX*, they didn't know what to do with it. Not only did they take over and insist on recutting the film, but they also rejected the other scripts out-of-hand, and began calling their initial seed money a "loan." The rejected scripts included early versions of both *Apocalypse Now* and *The Conversation*.

With the money gone, 827 Folsom lost momentum and began to fall apart. Its original members, most of them still under 30, found them-

Inglenook Estate including the Niebaum residence naming it the Niebaum-Coppola Estate Winery.

1976
Coppola closes *City* magazine and transfers all resources to the *Apocalypse Now* production. The entire Coppola family goes on location to Lake Caliraya in the Philippines. Typhoon Olga destroys the *Apocalypse Now* set and lead actor Martin Sheen has a heart attack. Carroll Ballard and Tom Sternberg head to Malta with cast and crew to shoot *The Black Stallion*.

1977
Apocalypse Now shoot resumes in the Philippines. American Zoetrope post-production facilities open at 529 Pacific Street. Phil Kaufman begins shooting *Invasion of the Body Snatchers* in San Francisco using Zoetrope's equipment.

1978
Robert Dalva returns to Zoetrope to edit *The Black Stallion*. Post-production is done at Lucasfilm's Parkway facility in Marin while Kaufman's *Invasion of the Body Snatchers* is edited and mixed at Zoetrope in San Francisco, followed by Kaufman's next film *The Wanderers*.

1979
Apocalypse Now is screened as a work in progress and wins the Palme d'Or at Cannes, sharing the prize with *The Tin Drum*.

1980
Coppola purchases the old Hollywood General Studios, a ten-and-a-half acre movie-production lot at Santa Monica Blvd. and Las Palmas Ave. Akira Kurosawa's *Kagemusha, The Shadow Warrior* is released in the U.S. with support from Coppola and Lucas and shares the Cannes Palme d'Or award that year with *All That Jazz*.

1981
Napoleon is re-released with a new score by Carmine Coppola. Coppola discovers a modest forest hunting lodge while traveling in Belize.

1982
Paramount Pictures terminates their distribution deal for Coppola's *One from the Heart*, which is subsequently released to low box office. Filming begins in Tulsa on *The Outsiders*. Coppola files for bankruptcy and sells off various properties. *Hammett* is nominated for the Palme d'Or but later opens to disappointing reviews and box office. *The Escape Artist*, directed by Caleb Deschanel, is released and also does poorly at the box office.

1983
The Black Stallion Returns is released earning less than one-third of the original. *The Cotton Club* begins shooting in August and wraps in December. The second Zoetrope film release based on an S.E. Hinton novel, *Rumble Fish*, comes and goes in only a few weeks.

Among the films collaborated on by the filmmakers who forged close relationships in film school and Zoetrope's early days were *American Graffiti* (top), *The Black Stallion* (above), *Apocalypse Now* (right), and *The Godfather II* (below).

selves once more temporarily dependent on the big studio executives to make their films, some like Lucas's USC classmate Robert Dalva, turned to commercials, and there were times when it was the commercial division which kept the struggling studio afloat. But even as the physical space of Zoetrope disappeared and lost its communal feel, the relationships forged in film school and through the studio's brief shining moment have continued and flourished. Francis Ford Coppola and George Lucas have since collaborated on a multitude of projects, including *American Graffiti*, *Mishima*, *Captain EO*, *Tucker*, *Kagemusha*, and *Powaqqatsi*. To give just a few other examples: Walter Murch worked with Coppola on *Apocalypse Now*, *Captain EO*, *The Conversation*, *The Godfather II* and *III*, *American Graffiti*, and *Apocalypse Now Redux*; Carroll Ballard and Coppola worked together on *The Black Stallion* and *Wind*; and Robert Dalva worked on *The Black Stallion* and directed *The Black Stallion Returns*.

Akira Kurosawa, George Lucas, and Francis Coppola on the set of *Kagemusha*.

As for American Zoetrope, Coppola bought North Beach's historic flat-iron Sentinel Building in 1973. His office is still there, on the eighth floor, just a stone's throw away from other San Francisco treasures like City Lights bookstore, Tosca, and Enrico's. The eight-story building also houses his award-winning literary quarterly, *Zoetrope All-Story*, and offices which have provided space for many other local filmmakers over the years, including Sean Penn, Tim Burton, Agnieska Holland, Wayne Wang, and Christopher Columbus, among others. A state-of-the-art DVD lab and other technical facilities are located next door in a modern bank building called 900 Kearny Street, the DVD facility now run by ZAP

The Sentinel Building.

Zoetrope Aubry Productions LLC. The studio American Zoetrope has released some of the most respected and popular films of the past three and a half decades, including not only those profiled in the following pages but also great work by international filmmakers like Chatrichalerm Yukol, Wim Wenders, Hans-Jürgen Syberberg, and Jean-Luc Goddard.

1984
Zoetrope Studios in L.A. is sold. *The Cotton Club* premieres in New York.

1985
Mishima: A Life in Four Chapters, another Coppola/Lucas production, is nominated for Palme d'Or at Cannes and wins for Best Artistic Contribution. Coppola begins shooting *Peggy Sue Got Married* in Petaluma and Santa Rosa and casts his daughter Sofia as Peggy Sue's younger sister. After seven years in barrel, Niebaum-Coppola's premiere vintage of Rubicon is released.

1986
Captain EO, the 3-D Disneyland attraction starring Michael Jackson, directed by Francis Coppola and executive produced by George Lucas, debuts to great acclaim. At fifteen minutes and a $20 million budget it is the most expensive short made to date.

1987
The Lucasfilm production *Tucker: The Man and His Dream*, directed by Francis Coppola, begins shooting on location in the Bay Area.

1988
The Godfrey Reggio film *Powaqqatsi*, presented by Francis Coppola and George Lucas, is released in April followed by the release of *Tucker* in August.

1989
Clownhouse, a low-budget horror film produced by American Zoetrope's low-budget Commercial Pictures headed by Roman Coppola is nominated for the Sundance Grand Jury Prize for Dramatic Film. Sofia Coppola co-writes and costume designs *New York Stories* ("Life Without Zoe" segment). The short, directed by Francis Coppola with music by Carmine Coppola, is released in March. *The Godfather Part III* goes into production.

1990
The Spirit of '76 has a limited release with Roman as co-writer and executive producer and costumes by Sofia Coppola. *The Godfather Part III* premieres in Beverly Hills.

1991
Hearts of Darkness: A Filmmaker's Apocalypse is screened at Cannes. Directed by Eleanor Coppola, Fax Bahr, and George Hickenlooper, it wins two Emmys for Documentary Direction and Documentary Editing. Niebaum-Coppola receives official appellation designation.

1992
Bram Stoker's Dracula is released with visual effects by Roman Coppola, and wins three Academy Awards.

1993
The Secret Garden is released and *Mary Shelley's Frankenstein* begins production. Coppola opens his Blancaneaux Lodge in Belize to the public.

ABOVE: **American Zoetrope mixing stage at Niebaum-Coppola Estate Winery.**
BELOW: **Winery museum with vintage Tucker car.**

Coppola has saved himself from the edge of bankruptcy at least three times, and his mini-empire continues to produce great films. He is still convinced that Hollywood will always be at odds with the artist. "It has any number of spokes; the unions, the distributors, the entertainment press, the studios, the guilds, etc. And those spokes, they all just roll around and make money together." Making money has never been Coppola's prime directive—instead he has devoted his resources and creativity towards his loves: family, wine, the arts, and, of course, film.

Today, Coppola is philosophical about American Zoetrope's long and colorful history: "Then, it seemed like we were just a bunch of young people who wanted to take over the movie business. And in a way we did, but in a way we didn't, because we wanted better things for it than what really happened."

In one sense, Coppola is right. Hollywood is still Hollywood, with all its compromises, profit worship, and corporate control. Hollywood has not changed—but San Francisco has—as a growing alternative to the commercial madness down south. Coppola and his classmates had the courage to make their own mistakes and carve out their own destinies in the unknown. And they brought that independent rebellious spirit to San Francisco, where

ABOVE: **Niebaum-Coppola Estate Winery, Rutherford, California (Napa Valley).**
BELOW: **Francis Coppola with wife Eleanor and sons Roman (behind) and Gio (in front) in San Francisco, 1969.**

against all odds, it still thrives. As for Coppola's own legacy, his son Roman and daughter Sofia have taken over the reins of American Zoetrope, and continue to add luster to the family name. Like Vito Corleone, Francis Ford Coppola started a family empire—but fortunately, his was one in which his children could flourish.

1994
Mary Shelley's Frankenstein is released in November. This is the second American Zoetrope film starring Robert De Niro, after *The Godfather, Part II* in 1974.

1995
Mary Shelley's Frankenstein wins the Oscar for Best Make-up.

1996
The movie *Jack*, starring Robin Williams, is released.

1997
Francis Ford Coppola launches the magazine *Zoetrope: All-Story* which subsequently receives every major short-fiction award, including the National Magazine Award for Fiction.

1998
The TV drama *Outrage*, executive produced by Francis Ford Coppola, Fred Fuchs, and Kevin Cooper and starring Rob Lowe and Jennifer Grey, is released.

1999
First annual American Zoetrope's short-story writer's workshop is established. American Zoetrope expands post-production facility to include a new DVD lab.

2000
Sofia Coppola's feature-film directorial debut, *The Virgin Suicides*, is released in April. Hayden Christensen, who has a bit part as Jake, is later cast as a young Darth Vader in George Lucas's movies *Star Wars Episode II—Attack of the Clones* and *Star Wars Episode III—Revenge of the Sith*.

2001
Roman Coppola's film *CQ* is screened at the Cannes Film Festival.

2002
No Such Thing starring Helen Mirren is released. Mirren's previous work with a Bay Area studio was her turn in the Saul Zaentz Company's 1986 film *The Mosquito Coast*.

2003
Assassination Tango, written, directed, and starring Robert Duvall, is released. This is Duvall's seventh film with Zoetrope after *The Rain People*, *THX 1138*, *The Godfather Part I* and *II*, *The Conversation*, and *Apocalypse Now*.

2004
Sofia Coppola is nominated for three Academy Awards (Director, Producer & Writer) for the American Zoetrope production *Lost in Translation* and takes home the Oscar for Best Original Screenplay. American Zoetrope closes post-production facility and DVD lab.

2005
First annual American Zoetrope's annual screenwriter's workshop started at Blancaneaux Lodge in Belize.

"If you feel you are not properly sedated, call 348-844 immediately. Failure to do so may result in prosecution for criminal drug evasion."

— The voice in THX's medicine cabinet

THX 1138

THE CAST

THX	**Robert Duvall**
SEN 5241	**Donald Pleasance**
SRT, the hologram	**Don Pedro Colley**
LUH 3417	**Maggie McOmie**
PTO	**Ian Wolfe**

TRIVIA

Lucas named the film after his telephone number while in college: 849-1138. The letters THX correspond to the numbers on the buttons, 8, 4, and 9.

GEORGE LUCAS WROTE THE FULL SCREENPLAY FOR *THX 1138* while working on his documentary for Coppola's film, *The Rain People*, and his script was bankrolled under the deal Coppola had struck with Seven Arts. But even before hearing that he had the money, Lucas had begun casting and scouting Bay Area locations for the movie. His goal was to make a new kind of science fiction film, in sound engineer and script co-writer Walter Murch's words "A film *from* the future, rather than a film of the future."

Robert Duvall is THX (pronounced "Thex"), an obedient worker drone, in a passionless post-holocaust underground society, run by a conformist, commercial ethos. Along with his roommate, and in an ironic twist for a film shot during the height of the hippie era, THX falls out of sync with this society the moment he stops taking his drugs. No longer brainwashed by government pharmaceuticals, THX and his

ABOVE: Director George Lucas and Robert Duvall confer on the set of *THX 1138*.
BELOW: Duvall's character *THX 1138* trying to exit his underground world at the end of the film.

roommate, played by Maggie McOmie, fall in love, and THX suddenly finds himself an outlaw. He is befriended by a hologram and harassed by SEN (in a marvelous turn by Donald Pleasance), and his fight for freedom quickly becomes a dark metaphor for the fight between Man and Society.

Like all important science fiction, the themes of *THX 1138* are existential as much as speculative. The film is visually arresting: a detailed, futuristic horror story reminiscent of Sartre's *No Exit*. The ultimate moral, that it is best to break out of the prison of the known, to choose freedom over safety and commercial coercion, foreshadowed not only themes which Lucas would revisit in *American Graffiti* and in the *Star Wars* saga, but also in his own personal drive to retain control over his creative life—independent of the chokehold of Hollywood's studio system.

Largely because of the studio's unwillingness to back distribution, the movie failed miserably at the box office and was almost forgotten after Lucas's success with *American Graffiti*, but it has been released on DVD, and to watch it now is startling. It is a story told in images, mood, and with Walter Murch's astonishing sound effects. Its chilling vague societal overlord remains as relevant today—if not more so—as it was then. *THX 1138* is also a fascinating film for *Star Wars* fans, as one can see prototypes of some of the classic elements of the trilogy, from the faceless policemen, to the exhilarating chases, to the sense of a used rundown future—think of the cranky, dusty, beat-up characters of C-3PO. It even foreshadows the sound of the *Star Wars* lightsabers. But *THX* is a much darker, grimmer vision of the future, quite possibly the most "adult" film Lucas ever made. It has been a cult-classic favorite since its release, and one hopes that with its new availability on DVD, it will reach the viewership it deserves.

"Never let anyone outside the family know what you're thinking."

— Don Vito Corleone

The wedding of Connie Corleone (Talia Shire) to Carlo Rizzi (Gianni Russo).

THE GODFATHER

"The Godfather is not only a perfect movie; it has become one of America's sacred texts; it should be running on a loop at the National Archives between the Declaration of Independence *and a first edition of* Leaves of Grass.*"*

— Sarah Vowell

A NEARLY FLAWLESS CAUTIONARY TALE OF THE RISE AND spiritual fall of crime boss Michael Corleone, *The Godfather* opened the door to a grand tradition of film and television about organized crime. Without it, would there have ever been a *Scarface*, a *Goodfellas*, a *Miller's Crossing*, or a *Sopranos*? More importantly perhaps, it abounds with transcendent and classic scenes and dialogue: from the horse's head, to the shootings in the restaurant, to Michael's idyllic wedding in Sicily, to the carnage of Sonny Corleone's murder-by-tollbooth on the Expressway, to immortal lines like "Leave the car, take the cannoli," and, finally, to one of the most quoted lines in history: "I'll make him an offer he can't refuse."

Ironically, it was Coppola himself who was initially made an offer he couldn't refuse. While Lucas and Murch were alternating shifts on the edits of *THX 1138* in the relative calm of an attic in Mill Valley, Coppola had been managing, (or mismanaging, depending on whom one speaks to) Universal Pictures'

$700,000 seed money, and the combination of rising rents, the cost of his state-of-the-art equipment, opportunistic hippies, and stoned business managers, had left him in financial dire straits. When the offer came through to direct Mario Puzo's bestselling crime potboiler, Coppola the aspiring auteur told his father. "They want me to direct this piece of trash. I don't want to do it. I want to do art films!"

Fortunately for all concerned, Coppola was broke enough to take the job and to listen to Lucas's insistence that, bottom line, Zoetrope needed the money. He also became drawn to the family drama lurking beneath the lurid sex-and-guns plot, and seized the opportunity to explore the themes of family which were closest to his heart: the rivalry of brothers, and the price of loyalty and ambition. Indeed, as so many of the rest of his films would be, *The Godfather* was a family affair: His father scored music for the wedding sequence; his sister Talia played the only Corleone daughter, his own newborn; Sofia, even had a role as Michael's baby son in the film's climactic and ferocious baptism montage.

Robert Duvall, Francis Coppola, and Marlon Brando.

The shoot was plagued with difficulties from the start. Even though the studios had specifically sought out an Italian director, they still wanted an all-American movie, and had been hoping to cast Robert Redford as Michael, arguing that the Corleones could be from "Northern Italy." Confidence about Coppola's competence on set was low: He recalls holding his feet up in a toilet stall to eavesdrop on two crew members who were complaining bitterly that their "idiot director" knew nothing about how to make a film, and later said that throughout the project he was "always on the verge of being fired."

In one of those Hollywood endings that even Hollywood couldn't have written, *The Godfather* broke several film records, won three Academy Awards, and established Coppola as one of the finest directors of his or any generation. *The Los Angeles Times* critic Charles Champlin, called the film "an instant classic," and Vincent Canby wrote in his rave *New York Times* review: "Francis Ford Coppola has made one of the most brutal and moving chronicles of American life ever designed within the limits of popular culture."

THE CAST

Vito Corleone	**Marlon Brando**
Michael Corleone	**Al Pacino**
Santino "Sonny" Corleone	**James Caan**
Pete Clemenza	**Richard Castellano**
Tom Hagen	**Robert Duvall**
Capt. Mark McCluskey	**Sterling Hayden**
Jack Woltz	**John Marley**
Emilio Barzini	**Richard Conte**
Kay Adams	**Diane Keaton**

TRIVIA

Gordon Willis's dark photography has now been imitated in many other films (The Godfather is regularly taught in professional lighting academies as an example of brilliant lighting), but when the developed film first came back from the lab, Paramount executives assumed that there had been some kind of mistake. As one might expect, Coppola and Willis refused studio demands that the film be retouched.

Fredo Corleone (John Cazale) in shock at the shooting of his father Don Vito Corleone (Marlon Brando).

AWARDS

ACADEMY AWARDS
10 Nominations / 3 Awards
GOLDEN GLOBES
7 Nominations / 5 Awards

TRIVIA

George Lucas put together a key montage sequence for The Godfather, *as a favor to Coppola for helping him fund* American Graffiti. *He asked not to be credited.*

THE CONVERSATION

AWARDS

ACADEMY AWARDS
3 Nominations

GOLDEN GLOBES
4 Nominations

CANNES
Palme d'Or

THE CAST

Harry Caul	**Gene Hackman**
Stan	**John Cazale**
William P. "Bernie" Moran	**Allen Garfield**
Ann	**Cindy Williams**
Mark	**Frederic Forrest**

After *The Godfather*'s unexpected, unqualified triumph, Coppola was finally in a position to return to the vision that had informed the creation of Zoetrope in the first place. *The Conversation*, a very personal script he had written and pitched unsuccessfully to Warner Brothers several years earlier, owed a good deal to some of the young director's early influences—Tennessee Williams, Hermann Hesse, and Alfred Hitchcock. It paid loving homage to Michelangelo Antonioni's 1966 masterpiece *Blowup*, in which a single photograph, enlarged several times over, served as the clue to a stylish murder mystery. The executives at Paramount were no more enthralled with the project than the executives at Warner Brothers had been, but they were thrilled with their new golden boy, and desperate to have him make the sequel to *The Godfather*. Coppola himself was almost as desperate *not* to make it, but he could now leverage his new commercial viability to get financing for *The Conversation*, and he also had a trusted team to help pull it off, among them Fred Roos, Walter Murch, Robert Duvall, Teri Garr, John Cazale, and his own brother-in-law, David Shire. Most importantly, he had signed on Gene Hackman, fresh off his star turn as Detective Popeye Doyle in the wildly successful 1971 thriller, *The French Connection*.

The Conversation was not about the car chases, action, or rising body counts thataudiences would be expecting from either the city that had produced *Bullitt* and *Dirty Harry*, or from the director who had produced the operatic bloodletting of *The Godfather*. Part thriller, part character study, and part exploration of Coppola's own cinematic obsessions, the film would walk a tightrope between its standard suspense story elements—the Jealous Husband, the Young Wife, the Lover, the Murder Plot—and Coppola's own fascination with repetition, surveillance, and isolation. *The Conversation* was told exclusively from the point of view of Harry Caul, an intensely private professional eavesdropper

Harry Caul (Gene Hackman) rigging a listening device.

TRIVIA

The blue Mercedes limousine that Cindy Williams is sitting in near the end of the film was won by Coppola on a bet with Paramount Pictures. Coppola had complained about the station wagon he shared with five other passengers during the filming of The Godfather *and studio execs told him if* Godfather *grossed a certain amount they would spring for a new car. After* Godfather *was a huge hit, Coppola and George Lucas went to a dealer and picked out the Mercedes, telling the salesman to bill Paramount.*

hired by a powerful businessman (Robert Duvall) to spy on his young wife (Cindy Williams) and her lover (Frederic Forrest, who would later co-star in *Apocalypse Now*). Gene Hackman played Harry Caul not as hero but as anti-hero: lonely and paranoid, with a bad comb-over, a slight stutter, and an awkward transparent raincoat which would serve as one of the films most startling images, a constant visual reminder of how easily our protective layers can be penetrated. As Coppola later explained, "In a movie like this, you have a choice. You can follow the principals, or you can follow the guy who does the recording. We wanted to follow him. What happens to him? What's his story?"

Coppola tells Harry Caul's story slowly and gracefully, experimenting with stationary cameras—"I wanted them dead, like a passive eavesdropper"—and following Harry through a banal, deglamourized San Francisco. The cameras trail him from his initial surveillance of the two lovers' not-so-private conversation in Union Square, to his barren apartment and equally barren workshop in San Francisco's then-abandoned warehouse district, just south of Market Street. The audience, forced into the position of eavesdropper on Harry's life, never knows more about the action than he does, and the film never explodes in triumph or clear answers. Popeye Doyle may have survived what was then considered the most exciting car chase in American film, but Harry Caul, diffident, paranoid, suddenly an actor in a drama he had sought only to witness, takes the bus. Popeye

Caul evesdropping.

Doyle got the bad guy; Harry Caul does not even learn for sure who the bad guy is, and neither do we.

The production process was riddled with obstacles. Hackman, then a hot, young action star, settled uncomfortably into his role as nondescript technocrat; a crucial dream sequence had to be cut short because of neighborhood complaints about the fog machines' potential pollution. Finally, Paramount had given Coppola the project, but they didn't give him time to edit it. The task of shaping the film fell largely to Walter Murch, then a first-time editor who wasn't yet even in the union. Murch and Coppola couldn't work side by side in the cutting room, and instead met as frequently as possible to screen new cuts, even as Coppola became subsumed in pre-production and shooting of *The Godfather* sequel. Despite these constraints, or perhaps in part because of them (Hackman's "uncomfortable" performance is considered a highlight of his acting career, and Murch has gone on to become an acknowledged master editor and sound designer), the film was a huge critical success. It was nominated for three Academy Awards, four Golden Globes, including Best Picture, and took the Palme d'Or at Cannes in 1974.

Coppola has since described *The Conversation* as his most personal movie, his first chance to work in the European tradition that had inspired him and George Lucas to start Zoetrope studios in the first place. It would also be his last personal movie for many years to come.

Walter Murch re-mixing the soundtrack for *The Conversation* at Zoetrope's Rutherford mixing studio in 2000.

THE GODFATHER PART II

"I don't feel I have to wipe everybody out, Tom. Just my enemies."

— Michael Corleone

COPPOLA NEVER WANTED TO DIRECT A SEQUEL TO *THE Godfather*. He even offered to find another Italian director, and recommended fellow Roger Corman protégé Martin Scorsese, but the studios wanted their star director. The chance to do *The Conversation*, combined with the money that Coppola still needed to keep his other projects alive, convinced him to take on the sequel, and he decided to approach the Corleone saga from two angles, alternating the story between Michael's continuing fall and his father's early rise to power. Coppola had auditioned young Robert De Niro for the role of Sonny while casting the first *Godfather*. He'd found De Niro electrifying, but almost too psychotic and intense to play Sonny sympathetically. However, the actor's volatile charisma and controlled menace marked him as a perfect choice to play the young Vito Corleone.

The second *Godfather* took an enormous risk, splitting the narrative between Michael's spiral into paranoia and isola- tion, and the story of his father's troubled childhood in Italy and America and his eventual rise to the top of organized

The Godfather novelist, Mario Puzo (center) with Francis Ford Coppola and crew on the set of *The Godfather Part II.*

A young Clemenza (Bruno Kirby) points his gun.

TRIVIA

Lee Strasberg came out of retirement to play Hyman Roth at the request of Al Pacino. He was unwilling at first, but agreed to do it after meeting with Carmine Coppola.

A young Vito Corleone (Robert De Niro) in flames.

crime. We see that Michael has elevated his family to higher and higher levels of respectability and influence, but his ascension has come at a price. He has become ruthless, paranoid, withdrawn, and his loved ones' betrayals seem destined, forced into play by his own paranoia. Much of the film's tension hinges on watching a young, idealistic De Niro building his family, while his most beloved son gradually tears it down more than thirty years in the future. *The Godfather Part II* stands much darker than the first: If the first foretold a son's doom, the sequel both seals it and stamps that doom in his family's past—a modern day House of Atreus.

The only significant member of the original cast who did not appear was Brando himself—his asking price was too high—but in many ways his absence looms over the film like a shadow, especially in the unforgettable last flashback scene, preserving the gravitas he had lent the first film. Talia Shire,

Al Pacino, Robert Duvall, Diane Keaton, John Cazale, and new cast members Lee Strasberg and Michael V. Gazzo turned in devastating performances. Post-production, however, was difficult: The moving back and forth in time was tricky—Walter Murch recalled that there were too many cutbacks from past to present, and after a disastrous first screening, he took it back to the editing room and reduced the number of cutbacks from 20 to 14. Coppola himself, perpetually at odds with the studio heads behind the project, would later lament, "If we had only had two more weeks, it would have been so much better." But when the film finally opened in 1974, it received almost unanimously rave reviews, and became the first sequel ever to win an Academy Award. Indeed, the film won the most Oscars of any Zoetrope film (six in total) including Original Dramatic Score by Nino Rota and Carmine Coppola.

The New Yorker's acerbic, opinionated Pauline Kael, wrote eloquently of the film's added power: "The daring of *Part II* is that it enlarges the scope and deepens the meaning of the first film.... It's an epic vision of the corruption of America."

THE CAST

Don Michael Corleone	**Al Pacino**
Tom Hagen	**Robert Duvall**
Kay Adams	**Diane Keaton**
Vito Corleone	**Robert De Niro**
Connie Corleone	**Talia Shire**
Frankie Pentanagli	**Michael V. Gazzo**
Fredo Corleone	**John Cazale**
Deanna-Dunn Corleone	**Mariana Hill**
Hyman Roth	**Lee Strasberg**

TRIVIA

The Godfather Part II *is the first sequel to win an Academy Award for Best Picture.*

THE BLACK STALLION

"I refuse to make violent movies."

— Caroll Ballard

THE CAST

Alec Ramsay	**Kelly Reno**
Alec's Mother	**Teri Garr**
Snoe	**Clarence Muse**
Alec's Father	**Hoyt Axton**
Jim Neville	**Michael Higgins**
Henry Dailey	**Mickey Rooney**

Alec Ramsay (Kelly Reno) making physical poetry with his horse.

OF ALL THE YOUNG MEN WHO WERE PART OF THE EARLY Zoetrope years, it is Carroll Ballard whose description of the crumbling of the first Zoetrope is the most bitingly candid. Ballard had been a classmate of Coppola's at UCLA, and in later interviews would complain that the fall of the first Zoetrope was due to the young filmmakers' inability (or unwillingness) to back each other, or watch out for each other's best interests. Ideas were easy, he would say, the problem was money. When Coppola first offered him *The Black Stallion*, he almost refused. "I didn't like it," he admits today, but it was a chance to do a movie.

As with *The Godfather*, we can be grateful that the director was driven to ignore his first impulse. The final result was a masterpiece, though none of the crew would have expected it during filming. In a plot point now painfully familiar to the Zoetrope filmmakers, *The Black Stallion* was a nightmare to make; the desert island shots required several last-minute location shifts in Sardinia, and the entire Canadian operation was plagued with horrible weather. The summer of 1977 was one of the rainiest and hottest in Canadian history, with temperatures rising as high as 115 degrees. Much of the shooting on the racetrack was done two feet deep in the mud, which added to the drama and look of the film, but caused enormous production delays.

The Black Stallion tells the story of Alec Ramsay, a young boy who finds himself stranded on a desert island after a shipwreck. He saves the life (and is saved in return) by "The Black" a seemingly savage Arabian horse who was also on the downed ship. The casting was inspired: Kelly Reno, was a nonactor but the son of Colorado cattle ranchers, who at the age of 11 was experienced with horses. His assured presence is part of what made the physical poetry of the interactions between boy and horse so effective.

What was perhaps most astonishing was the degree to which Ballard and his cinematographer, the enormously talented Caleb Deschanel (also one of George Lucas's classmates

TRIVIA

Several of the location shots in Sardinia were also used by Lina Wertmuller's enormously popular 1975 desert island romance, Swept Away.

Ramsay and Henry (Mickey Rooney).

Alec Ramsay taming the Black.

at USC), allowed the story to be told by focusing on the beauty and magnetism of the horse itself. Twenty-five years before Robert Zemeckis would be lauded for the risky and innovative decision to film large stretches of *Castaway* in silence, Ballard dared to devote thirty-two solid minutes of dialogue-free running time as Alec and the Black came together on the island. Their idyll, as shot by Deschanel and scored by Carmine Coppola, is one of the loveliest half hours ever to grace a screen.

The film is most notable for its delicacy and understatement. Alec Ramsay's father has died in the shipwreck, and while it's clear that the grieving boy needs a kind of love and strength that can only come from his relationship with the horse, the film-makers never beat a moral into the viewer's head.

After Alec's physical rescue from the island, his relationship with the stallion, and with the trainer who helps prepare him for professional horseracing, gives him the emotional rescue he still needs. Mickey Rooney is delightful as Henry Dailey, the gruff trainer for whom this race is a second chance. We are never explicitly told why Dailey needs a second chance, yet another example of Ballard's willingness to stick to the bare emotional essentials, without getting bogged down in details: Dailey and Alec need each other, Alec and The Black love each other, that is all that matters.

The film was nominated for three Academy Awards, and Pauline Kael, a critic enthusiastic but certainly not over-generous with her praises, simply wrote, "It may be the greatest children's movie ever made."

AWARDS

ACADEMY AWARDS
3 Nominations / 1 Special Achievement Award
GOLDEN GLOBES
1 Nomination

The natives gather around Kurtz's compound.

APOCALYPSE NOW

When John Milius, a USC graduate and the co-writer of *Apocalypse Now* was asked what he would most like to change about Hollywood, he answered that he'd like to see "trials and executions for executives." Twenty years after the initial release of *Apocalypse Now*, Coppola felt the modern audience would be more accepting of the longer, more surreal, original version and released the movie as it was originally conceived. *Apocalypse Now: Redux* includes 53 minutes of additional film footage, including a long interlude in a last-holdout former French plantation, and several expanded scenes with the Playboy bunnies. The tension in the film, between the literary adaptation and the investigation of Vietnam, becomes even more pronounced in it's new three hour incarnation. As one would have expected, critics either loved or hated the new

version, depending on how they had felt about the first. But Vincent Canby, writing for *The New York Times*, reminds us, "It is fruitless and arrogant to second-guess *Apocalypse Now* especially after Mr. Coppola, with the help of Mr. Murch...has so brilliantly second-guessed himself."

The problems which plagued the set of *Apocalypse Now* are now nearly as legendary as the film itself. First there is the fact that the original script was one of the seven which were rejected by the fortunetellers at Warner Brothers in 1970. The idea for *Apocalypse Now* was originally that of George Lucas, who had in mind a *cinéma vérité* documentary style film, but gave up on it when the *Star Wars* saga gradually took over his life. Then there were the series of disasters which Coppola faced on set, including but not limited to: a last minute recast (from Harvey Keitel to Martin Sheen, fresh off his stunning debut in Terence Malick's *Nebraska*), Martin Sheen's heart attack, a rash of set-destroying typhoons, problems with cooperation from the Philippine Government, and Brando showing up on

THE CAST

Colonel Walter E. Kurtz	**Marlon Brando**
Lieutenant Colonel Bill Kilgore	**Robert Duvall**
Benjamin L. Willard	**Martin Sheen**
Jay "Chef" Hicks	**Frederic Forrest**
Chief Phillips	**Albert Hall**
Lance B. Johnson	**Sam Bottoms**
Tyrone "Clean" Miller	**Larry Fishburne**
Photojournalist	**Dennis Hopper**
Hubert de Marais	**Christian Marquand**
Roxanne Sarrault	**Aurore Clément**
Colonel Lucas	**Harrison Ford**

TRIVIA

Cameos by Francis Ford Coppola as director of a TV crew, Vittorio Storaro as a TV photographer, and Dean Tavoularis, are all uncredited.

> *"My movie is not about Vietnam . . . my movie is Vietnam."*
>
> — Francis Ford Coppola, at Cannes

the set severely overweight but unwilling to be portrayed as fat on film. Eleanor Coppola, who accompanied her husband to the Philippines with their children in tow, kept a notebook the entire time she was there, a fascinating record of the struggle it took to get the film made. By the end of shooting, her husband was hanging onto his sanity by a thread almost as thin as the one Colonel Kurtz is dangling from when Sheen's character finally confronts him up river.

In addition to recalcitrant actors, a Third World government at war with itself, nature's wrath, and his ever escalating budget, Coppola had to contend with the split in the project itself: *Apocalypse Now* was both a Vietnam movie, with narration by the celebrated journalist Michael Herr, and a contemporary rendering of Joseph Conrad's classic novel *Heart of Darkness*. The film was conceived as two metaphors which threatened to gobble each other alive: Conrad's crazed colonialist, driven mad as he plumbed the depths of the African Congo, was to serve as a metaphor for the collective insanity of America's involvement in Vietnam. The Vietnam of the film, however, also served as a modern day metaphor for Conrad's meditation on savagery and civilization, on the darkness within us all. The two separate stories threatened to pull each other apart at every turn in the film's execution.

It is a minor miracle that the film was completed at all, as Eleanor Coppola's book, *Notes*, and subsequent documentary,

Hearts of Darkness attests. But the major miracle is that *Apocalypse Now* emerged with Coppola's vision very nearly intact. The film is mesmerizing, and genuinely feels like a descent into Hell—with Brando mumbling incoherently as the devil in its inner circle. And, with brilliant performances from Martin Sheen, Dennis Hopper, Robert Duvall, Frederick Forrest, and, of course, Brando, the film itself is now considered an American classic; visionary, both as a masterly reading of Conrad, and as one of the first significant feature film commentaries on the senselessness of the Vietnam war and the colonial absurdity which inspired it. It was nominated for eight Academy Awards, including Best Picture and Best Director, and won two.

TRIVIA

Harrison Ford's character, Col. Lucas, is named after George.

Marlon Brando working with the director Francis Ford Coppola.

AWARDS

ACADEMY AWARDS
8 Nominations / 2 Awards
GOLDEN GLOBES
4 Nominations / 3 Awards
CANNES
Palme d'Or

TRIVIA

Apocalypse Now was the first film to use the 70mm Dolby Stereo surround-sound system.

LEFT TO RIGHT: **The patrol boat goes up the Nung river; The photojournalist (Dennis Hopper),**
Willard (Martin Sheen), Chef (Frederic Forrest) going to find Colonel Kurtz (Marlon Brando); Lance (Sam Bottoms) on the boat.

THE BLACK STALLION RETURNS

1983

R OBERT DALVA WAS NOMINATED FOR AN ACADEMY Award for his editing work on *The Black Stallion*, and took over from Carroll Ballard on its highly anticipated sequel. The first film had been slow-paced and evocative, building itself around the emotional resonance of Alec's relationship with the Black, and Dalva wisely chose not to attempt a repetition of the drama of grief and reawakening that had informed the original. Instead he led Alec (once again played by Kelly Reno, now a gangly teenager) on a wild and hair-raising adventure which would take him on another journey across oceans and continents.

This time, as news of the Black's racing prowess spreads throughout the world, Moroccan kidnappers steal him from Alec. Alec sets off on his own to find his horse, stowing away on a ship to Africa and braving desert heat, hostile tribes, and dastardly villains on the trek back to the Black. On the

Alec Ramsay (Kelly Reno) is reunited with the Black.

The desert chase.

THE CAST

Alec Ramsay	**Kelly Reno**
Alec's mother	**Teri Garr**
Kurr	**Allen Goorwitz**
Raj	**Vincent Spano**
Meslar	**Woody Strode**

way, he encounters friendship and romance in the form of Vincent Spano's Raj, a friendly young Arab who helps him on his quest, and Jodi Thelan as Tabari, the proud chieftain's daughter who wishes to ride the Black to victory against a warring tribe. The final race, at least as breathtaking as the Black's victory in the first movie, is set against an astonishing desert backdrop and shot by master cinematographer Carlo Di Palma.

Filmed on location in Algeria and Tunisia, this movie was a kid's adventure story, in some ways a *Raiders of the Lost Ark* for horse lovers. Most critics found that it lacked the emotional grandeur of the original, although there was at least one important dissenting voice. Vincent Canby preferred Dalva's film, calling it "funny, unpretentious, and fast-paced," and applauded Dalva for "recreating the simple, straightforward pleasures of a pre-World War II B-movie."

ROBERT DALVA moved to San Francisco in response to a call from Francis Ford Coppola, inviting him up to be a part of Zoetrope. Dalva, who was working on government sponsored documentaries at the time, and who hated Los Angeles, agreed enthusiastically, and spent his first nights in the Bay Area sleeping on Coppola's floor. While working on the documentaries, he also directed hundreds of commercials, as part of Zoetrope's commercial division, and it was while directing commercials that he developed his skills as a cameraman—because he disliked the advertising executives so much that he escaped them by going off to shoot.

Like many of his generation of film school graduates, especially from USC, Dalva can direct (*The Black Stallion Returns*), edit (*The Black Stallion*, *Hidalgo*, and *October Sky*) and shoot (*Nash Bridges*). A native east-coaster who never felt comfortable in Los Angeles, he still classifies the migration up North as less of a move to San Francisco than an "escape from L.A."

Robert Dalva and Walter Murch at the Coppola's Easter party in Rutherford, California, Spring 2000.

"The thing about the Bay Area is its variety of looks as a location: You can go up to Napa and find not just the wineries, you go to places in Sonoma and you can find an Irish hill in the winter when everything is green... Oakland looks like the Midwest, San Jose is like L.A."

Darryl (Patrick Swayze) fights one of the SOCS.

THE OUTSIDERS

THE CAST

Ponyboy Curtis	**C. Thomas Howell**
Dallas "Dally" Winston	**Matt Dillon**
Johnny Cade	**Ralph Macchio**
Darryl "Darry" Curtis	**Patrick Swayze**
Sodapop Curtis	**Rob Lowe**
Sherri "Cherry" Valance	**Diane Lane**
Keith "Two-Bit" Mathews	**Emilio Estevez**
Steve Randle	**Tom Cruise**
Bob Sheldon	**Leif Garrett**

"You guys know what greasers are?
White trash with long, greasy hair.
You know what a soc is?
...White trash with mustangs and madras."

— Ponyboy

TRIVIA

Over a half hour of the film was cut prior to release, due to movie executives fearing that it was too long, resulting in a running time of a mere ninety-one minutes.

O N MARCH 21, 1980, A LIBRARIAN FROM THE LONE STAR School in Fresno County wrote Paramount Pictures a short letter on behalf of her students. Her request: that the runaway S.E. Hinton bestseller *The Outsiders*, which had been written when the author herself was only 15, be made into a movie. Furthermore, the students at Lone Star School had already chosen the director who would do the best job with the book: Francis Ford Coppola. The librarian wrote that she believed that her students were "representative of the youth of America." This endorsement was enough for Coppola to ask his producer, Fred Roos, to take a look at the book. Even in the midst of the financial crises rocking

Sodapop (Rob Lowe) and Steve (Tom Cruise).

Zoetrope in the wake of the *One From The Heart* and *Hammett*, Coppola managed to raise the money to get it made. He returned to the studio-on-location dream that he had originated with *The Rain People*, and brought his production studio with him to Tulsa, Oklahoma.

Coppola assembled a cast of mostly unknowns for the film, a *West Side Story*–style melodrama about the conflicts between rich and poor teenagers. C. Thomas Howell, Tom Cruise, Ralph Macchio, Patrick Swayze, Rob Lowe, and Emilio Estevez all played members of the "Greasers," the gang which was in a state of perpetual war with the town's elite, also known as the "SOCS." The film also starred Diane Lane, whose performance in *A Little Romance* a few years earlier had brought the teenager instant acclaim, as a rich girl, and Matt Dillon, who had made a stir as the townie love interest in the recent teen sexual-awakening film *Little Darlings*, as the hero of the Greasers. Coppola was so impressed with the latter two (Dillon especially was an actor whom he considered one of the finest young actors of his generation), that he cast them in his next film, another S.E. Hinton adaptation called *Rumble Fish*.

Decades ahead of the "Lindsay Lohanization" of American cinema, even before the John Hughes wave of eighties teen comedies, Coppola had assembled a dream teen cast of photogenic young actors, and he wove their performances into a fable of innocence and tenderness for alienated youth that many critics found unbearably maudlin but that teenagers themselves responded to—and still do: Ponyboy (C. Thomas

Howell) is a "Greaser" who along with his best friend Johnny (Ralph Macchio), his hero Dallas (Dillon), and a crew of going-nowhere misfits, make trouble in town because they don't know what else to do. When one of their gang clashes turns deadly, Ponyboy and Johnny find themselves on the run from the law. They escape to the country, where they share a brief idyll away from the violence of their neighborhood and read to each other from *Gone with the Wind* and the timeless Robert Frost poem, "Nothing Gold Can Stay." They return to their homes, changed, and face their fates as best they can.

In adult eyes, the plot itself is as hackneyed, simplistic, and mawkish as an adolescent daydream—which is exactly the point. By taking teen angst and idealism as seriously as teenagers take themselves, Coppola created a resonant mythic movie, drenched in the gold of Frost's poem. For the most part, critics were underwhelmed, but American teens adored the film, and its revenues almost single-handedly saved Zoetrope from its creditors.

Some teen movies transcend their audiences; *The Outsiders* never tried to. Instead it gave teenagers a film that they desperately needed, and proved the Fresno County librarian right—her students did represent young America.

Dallas (Matt Dillon) flirts with Sherri (Diane Lane).

RUMBLE FISH

"If you're going to lead people, you have to have somewhere to go...."

— The Motorcycle Boy

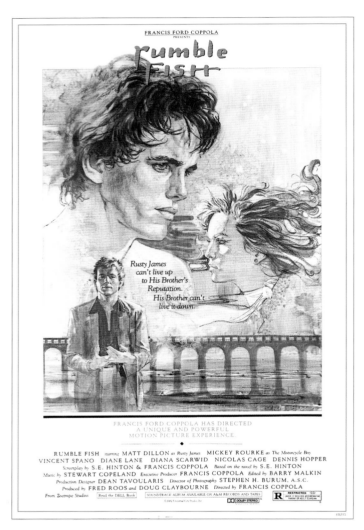

The movie poster with Matt Dillon, Diane Lane, and Mickey Rourke.

THE CAST

Rusty James	**Matt Dillon**
The Motorcycle Boy	**Mickey Rourke**
Patty	**Diane Lane**
Cassandra	**Diana Scarwid**
Smokey	**Nicolas Cage**
Father	**Dennis Hopper**

THE *OUTSIDERS* MAY HAVE BEEN THE FILM THAT SAVED Zoetrope from its third flirtation with bankruptcy, but it was *Rumble Fish* which took the bolder creative risks, and came closer to satisfying Coppola's dream of being an auteur in the tradition of Wells, Fellini, or Godard. Coppola used the same Tulsa landscape and many of the same cast and crew as in *The Outsiders*, including Matt Dillon, Diane Lane and cinematographer (and fellow UCLA graduate) Stephen H. Burum, with another delightful and all too short appearance by the legendary musician Tom Waits. The film, shot in German Expressionist black and white with gorgeous

time lapse photography, made generous use of three of the finest sets of cheekbones to grace the wide screen since James Dean found Sal Mineo and Natalie Wood in *Rebel Without a Cause*. Dillon, a bit too pretty and boyish to endow his role in *The Outsiders* with any real menace, proved perfect for Rusty James, the sweet and slightly dim-witted teenaged hoodlum desperate to follow in the footsteps of his older brother, a legendary local outlaw named, appropriately, The Motorcycle Boy.

Hinton based the character of The Motorcycle Boy on a photo she found in a magazine, and as played by Mickey Rourke, he emerges as not only a troubled hero, as elusive and lost in his own way as his younger brother, but as an amalgam of almost every American myth of the romantic, doomed loner. Part cowboy, part philosopher, part easy rider, The Motorcycle Boy was once a mythical gang leader—now, at 21, he seems old beyond his years. American critics were not kind to the film, but they may have been unable to appreciate its age-targeted power. Loaded with gorgeous images, portents of doom, and the photogenic dream team of Dillon, Lane, and Rourke, *Rumble Fish* not only taught its small but fanatical teenage audience how to strut, how to hold a pool cue, and how to smoke a cigarette (with the hand close to the lips, four fingers swinging across the chin like a hinge), but also tapped into a secret of surviving adolescence: It's OK to feel bad, especially if you look good. Coppola has called it one of the most personal of all his films, second only to *The Conversation*. European critics found more to appreciate in the film than

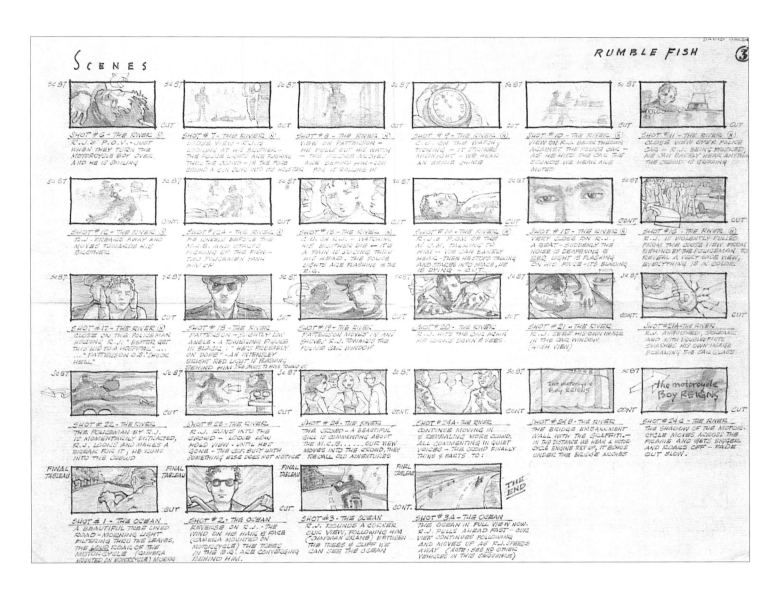

ABOVE: A storyboard depicting the final scenes.

BELOW: Rusty James's (Matt Dillon) desire to be like his older brother, The Motorcycle Boy, leads to an explosive chain of events.

AWARDS

GOLDEN GLOBES
1 Nomination

TRIVIA

Author S.E. Hinton has a cameo as a prostitute.

Americans did—in the undeniable charisma of its lead actors, especially the tragic-cool Mickey Rourke, and in its moody, thick atmosphere and spellbinding soundtrack by former Police drummer Stewart Copeland. The film remains a cult classic, a *Rebel Without a Cause* for the first generation of MTV discontents. The culture critic Cintra Wilson summed up its appeal best, writing in *Salon.com*, "It's an art film for teenagers, and it works."

"Peggy, you know what a penis is? Stay away from it!"

— Sex Education, fifties style

Charlie (Nicholas Cage) loves Peggy Sue (Kathleen Turner).

PEGGY SUE GOT MARRIED

AWARDS

ACADEMY AWARDS
3 Nominations

GOLDEN GLOBES
2 Nominations

COPPOLA'S FIRST FEATURE FILM, THE ONE HE MADE WHILE still a student at UCLA, was *You're a Big Boy Now*, an absurdist coming-of-age story. Since then, however, he had shied away from comedy in favor of the epics for which he would become most famous. With *The Outsiders*, Coppola had reminded Hollywood that he could still be a commercial director. With *Peggy Sue Got Married*, he reminded Hollywood that he could also still be a funny one.

The film, taken from the Buddy Holly song of the same name and shot in Santa Rosa just a few miles from Coppola's Napa estate, gives us a more adult, more wistful take on the Robert Zemeckis monster hit *Back to the Future*. Just like *Back to the Future*, it owes much of its humor to period jokes ("I'm an adult," announces a drunk Peggy Sue, a forty-two-year-old in a teenage body, storming out of her parents' living room, "I'm gonna go to Liverpool and discover the Beatles.").

Peggy Sue reliving high school in 1960.

But Coppola doesn't concern himself with metaphysical questions of the "kill your grandfather" strain; instead he explores the poignancy of Peggy Sue's predicament: she has lived through the sexual revolution, the Vietnam War, she has a grown daughter of her own, and her own marriage to her high school sweetheart—unevenly played by a still-inexperienced Nicolas Cage—has fallen apart. Coppola uses her trip back to the past to ask a simple question: If the person you loved most in the world had betrayed you and broken your heart, what would you do if you suddenly found yourself 'trapped' back in the sweetest days of your love? The question is funny, but there's sadness beneath it, and even something sinister. As Roger Ebert wrote in his rave review of the film, "It's like visiting a cemetery where all the people are still alive."

As Peggy Sue, Kathleen Turner navigates gracefully between fish-out-of water gags and the bittersweet encounters, as the heroine discovers that you can never go home again, even when you can. Turner, herself a beauty queen who was just beginning to be a bit too old and heavy for the breathless sexpot roles that had made her famous (*Body Heat*, *Prizzi's Honor*) is perfect as the former Homecoming Queen. And in what had become a hallmark of a Coppola film, even the actors with the smallest amount of screen time turned in fine performances (especially a very young but already elastic and rubber-faced Jim Carrey, not surprisingly playing a class clown). The film was a much-needed triumph for Coppola and served as further proof that he was still an impeccably skilled craftsman. Even his slightest work was always grazed with the light touch of his genius. Roger Ebert, praising Coppola's willingness to go back to basics and "just tell a story," called *Peggy Sue Got Married* one of the best movies of 1986.

THE CAST

Peggy Sue	**Kathleen Turner**
Charlie Bodell	**Nicolas Cage**
Richard Norvik	**Barry Miller**
Carol Heath	**Catherine Hicks**

Peggy Sue spends the night with Michael (Kevin J. O'Connor) after traveling back in time.

TRIVIA

Jim Carrey appears in an early role as Walter Getz, Sofia Coppola plays Peggy Sue's younger sister, and Helen Hunt plays Peggy Sue's daughter.

THE GODFATHER III

"I swear on the lives of my children, give me one last chance to redeem myself, and I will sin no more."

—Don Michael Corleone

AWARDS
ACADEMY AWARDS
7 Nominations
GOLDEN GLOBES
7 Nominations

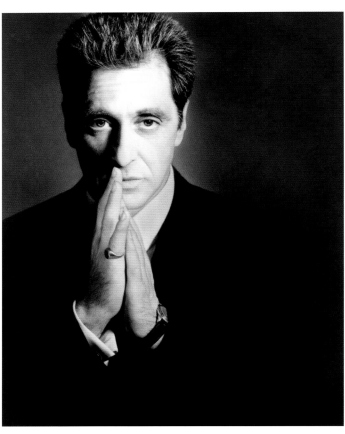

Al Pacino as The Godfather.

TRIVIA

When Al Pacino was first offered the chance to reprise the role of Michael Corleone, he demanded seven million dollars plus a share in the profits. Coppola stuck to his initial offer of five million, and when Pacino refused to budge, the director announced he could do without Pacino, and would simply start the film off with his funeral. Whether it was a bluff or not will never be known: Pacino accepted the original offer which, apparently, he couldn't refuse.

For ALMOST A DECADE, FRANCIS FORD COPPOLA HAD insisted that he would never do a third *Godfather* film. Michael Corleone seemed doomed forever—alone and unredeemable behind the glass prison of his Tahoe fortress. The idea of being forced to do another sequel in the service of a studio's desire to repeat a winning financial formula seemed to him a certain kind of artist's hell. But Coppola needed the money, and perhaps more importantly, Michael Corleone's story had never really been finished.

Continuing his tendency to focus on themes which resonated with him personally, Coppola envisioned the film as a chance to offer the now aged Michael Corleone a possible redemption—in the form of his love for his children. "What is important in a man's life," asks Coppola, "beyond fame and wealth? Those things don't really fulfill."

So what does fulfill? Family—the one thing that Michael Corleone always claimed he was fighting for. To bring the Corleone tragedy to its conclusion, Coppola brought back many of the actors from the first two chapters of the saga: Al Pacino returns as a broken, ravaged, but still wealthy and all-powerful Michael Corleone, now graying and stooped; Diane Keaton returns as a now independent and strong-willed Kay; Talia Shire, delivering one of the film's best performances, has grown into her role as a Mafiosi, lurking in the shadows like a Lady Macbeth. But Coppola couldn't afford one pivotal actor: Robert Duvall would not be playing Tom Hagen. It was, in the director's own words "a terrible loss."

The film's newest and most explosive character would be Vincent Mancini, Sonny Corleone's illegitimate son. Actors competing for the role included Alec Baldwin, Matt Dillon, Vincent Spano, Charlie Sheen, Billy Zane, and Nicolas Cage. The final choice, the smoldering Cuban-American actor Andy Garcia, offered the perfect mix of Sonny's hot temper and young Pacino's shrewd calculated intelligence. Winona Ryder was slated to play the Juliet to Garcia's Romeo, as Michael's lovely daughter Mary. But the actress became ill and pulled out at the last minute, and Coppola, desperate for an innocent, fresh, non-actorly stage presence, cast his 18-year-old daughter Sofia in the pivotal role.

Today, Coppola insists that just as Michael Corleone's enemies targeted his daughter in fiction, the critics who

Director Francis Ford Coppola with Joe Mantegna.

skewered his daughter's performance in the film were doing so as a way of coming after him. Either way, even the film's most positive reviews singled out her performance as amateurish. The third *Godfather* was a financial success, but at the time of its release, reviewers considered it less of an artistic achievement than its two predecessors. Seen now, however, as the third chapter of the saga, *Godfather III* more than holds its own: The return of Dean Tavoularis as set designer and Gordon Willis as cinematographer do much to sustain the saga's epic mood, and Pacino's masterful performance of the wrecked Michael Corleone is even more stark and gratifying in immediate juxtaposition with his performance thirty years earlier. Taking note of all of the members of his own dynasty in the film, Francis Ford Coppola has frequently described the saga as "the biggest family home video ever made."

THE CAST

Don Michael Corleone	**Al Pacino**
Kay Adam Mitchelson	**Diane Keaton**
Connie Corleone-Rizzi	**Talia Shire**
Don Vincent "Vinnie" Mancini Corleone	**Andy Garcia**
Don Altobello	**Eli Wallach**
Joey Zasa	**Joe Mantegna**
Grace Hamilton	**Bridget Fonda**
B.J. Harrison	**George Hamilton**
Mary Corleone	**Sofia Coppola**

Connie (Talia Shire) and Mary (Sofia Coppola).

Dickon (Andrew Knott) and Colin (Heydon Prowse) in the secret garden.

THE SECRET GARDEN

Mary Lennox's Uncle Craven, lost in the past.

IN THE EARLY 1990s, THE POLISH-BORN, CZECH-EDUCATED director Agniezka Holland was best known to American audiences for her Academy Award–nominated film, *Europa Europa*, the true story of a young Jewish boy who survived the holocaust by pretending to be German. Holland had studied in Czechoslovakia under Milos Forman and moved to Paris after martial law was declared in Poland. *The Secret Garden* was her first "mainstream" American film, though its serious and unsentimental reading of Frances Hodgson Burnett's beloved children's classic could hardly be thought of as mainstream.

THE CAST

Mary Lennox	**Kate Maberly**
Colin Craven	**Heydon Prowse**
Dickon	**Andrew Knott**
Mrs. Medlock	**Maggie Smith**

The film centers around Mary Lennox, a spoiled English girl raised in wealth and isolation in India. When her neglectful parents die in an earthquake, the young girl, sour, silent, and as imperious as the young rajah she believed herself to be, is sent to live with her Uncle Craven in the British Countryside. Misselthwaite Manor is a bleak, foreboding castle straight out of *Rebecca*, shot in the somber tones children understand perfectly and adults never think of as appropriate for children. As the camera zooms through the dark hallways, one can feel the chilly dampness of their corners.

On the grounds of Misselthwaite Manor, however, Mary meets up with her maid's brother Dickon, a healthy, freckled boy whose love of her uncle's grounds is matched only by his cheerful disregard for Mary's imperious ways. Together they discover a locked and abandoned garden, and they set about tending it. Mary also meets the estate's heir, her cousin Colin. He is truly spoiled, well-waited on but bed-ridden and all but abandoned by his grieving father. Young Master Craven almost deserves his name: if anything, he is even more brambly and unpleasant than Mary herself, but the three children soon forge an unlikely friendship, based on the time they spend in the garden, teasing it back to life as springtime approaches.

The beauty of the garden itself deserves special mention. Stuart Craig, the film's award-winning production designer, also responsible for *Gandhi*, *Dangerous Liaisons*, and *The English Patient*, built the garden from scratch. It becomes a character in its own right, and as it blooms to life, the film explodes into a riot of joy and color, without any of the cloying overkill one might fear from a film whose dramatic tension literally hinges on birds and flowers.

What sets this film apart, not only from the majority of movies for children, but from the majority of films about children, is the respect with which it treats the traumas of its young characters. Children, according to Holland, are neither pitiable nor adorable, but are frequently much hardier and more resilient than adults. Given the chance to come to life, to help something grow, they will. Roger Ebert praised *The*

Mary Lennox (Kate Maberly) with her sickly cousin Colin.

Secret Garden's intelligence and sensitivity: "The summer of 1993 will be remembered as the time when every child in the world wanted to see *Jurassic Park*. The lucky ones will see this one, too."

"A garden. I've stolen a garden…"
— Mary Lennox

The difficult housekeeper Mrs. Medlock (Maggie Smith).

FRANCIS HODGSON BURNETT, the author of *The Secret Garden*, won an early battle in the war between writers and show business at the turn of the century. When a theater company in London tried to put on a play based on her popular 1886 novel, *Little Lord Fauntleroy*, she took them to court, and won a precedent-setting case granting her control of the dramatic right to the novel. In gratitude for championing their cause, a group of British writers gave her an expensive diamond bracelet.

MY FAMILY

IF *THE GODFATHER* CHRONICLED THE DESTRUCTION THAT CAN befall generations of an immigrant American family as its members succumb to the dark side of the American dream, Latino director's Gregory Nava's sprawling saga about three generations of Mexican-Americans does the opposite: It affirms and celebrates the way family can be the sustaining force that keeps its members afloat. *Mi Familia* chronicles three generations of the Sanchez family, beginning with their arrival in Los Angeles in the 1920s from a small village in Mexico, and ending in the seventies, as Jimmy Sanchez, now a grown man, tries to find it in himself to be a father to his young son. Nava's explicit aim in the film is to provide an entertaining, enlightening vision of the Mexican-American experience, and due in no small part to this commitment, as well as to extraordinary performances from his cast, he largely succeeds.

The cast includes: a very young and fresh Jennifer Lopez, who would soon star in a breakthrough role as slain Tejano singer Selena Quintanilla in Navas's next film, *Selena*, as the young mother who heroically treks back to her home and husband in Los Angeles after being shipped back to Mexico during one of the mass deportations of the thirties; Esai Morales, as the young *pachuco*, whose assimilation into a country that does not accept him leads him

Jimmy (Jimmy Smits) and Isabel (Elpidia Carrillo) husband and wife and unexpected lovers.

THE CAST

Jimmy Sanchez	**Jimmy Smits**
Chucho	**Esai Morales**
Jose Sanchez (1950–80)	**Eduardo López Rojas**
Maria Sanchez (1950–80)	**Jenny Gago**
Isabel	**Elpidia Carrillo**
Toni Sanchez	**Constance Marie**
Paco	**Edward James Olmos**

TRIVIA

The final scene of My Family *is an adapted shot-for-shot reproduction of the final scene of the great Satyajit Ray film,* Apur Sansar.

The director, Gregory Nava, on the set of *My Family/Mi Familia*.

The power of family.

down a fatal path; Edward James Olmos, as the son and writer who becomes the de facto family historian; and most impressively Jimmy Smits, whose stunning performance as the Sanchez family's youngest son finally becomes the grounding force that lends emotional power to the film.

Smits plays Jimmy as a hollow-eyed stone-faced young man, a driftless ex-con whose aimless rage always seems to be burning below the surface of a half-smile. He appears at first to be the black sheep of his siblings, who include a successful lawyer, a sensitive writer, a social worker, and a happy housewife. But as the narrator suggests, Jimmy

"We have had a good life."

—Jose Sanchez

is also almost a Christ-like figure, who bears the rage and sorrow of the whole Sanchez family on his broad shoulders.

In the end, as Nava wished, the Sanchez family itself emerges as the film's central and most lasting character. The storytelling is straightforward, and sometimes clumsy, but informed with consistent love and gentle humor throughout—love for film, love for the American dream, and finally, love for family.

1995

Rudy Baylor (Matt Damon) working a case.

JOHN GRISHAM'S THE RAINMAKER

COPPOLA HAS SAID THAT IN MANY WAYS, HE HAD MORE FUN on the sets of big Hollywood productions than on his personal films, which so frequently vacillated between genius and catastrophe—sometimes combining both in one film. *The Rainmaker* was a film in which Coppola remembered "laughing, having a good time, joking around with the actors." And the film itself has a polish and ease to it that makes it look like a film in which all involved had a good time. Based on the John Grisham novel of the same name, *The Rainmaker* tells

the familiar shaggy dog story of a first time lawyer Rudy Baylor (astonishingly well-acted by a young Matt Damon, in a performance that would most likely have made him a star even without the same year's release of *Good Will Hunting*), who is hired to bring down a corrupt insurance company.

The story, with its ups and downs and ultimate triumph of the "good guys," is predictable and comfortable, but Coppola's light touch and characteristically brilliant work with actors elevated the clichéd plot to something much more

"Sworn in by a fool and vouched for by a scoundrel. I'm a lawyer at last."

—Rudy Baylor

nuanced. The "victims," the poor family being cheated by a shady insurance company, play as fully rounded characters: the teenaged boy, mortally ill with leukemia, who just wants to get drunk like a normal teenager; his tender but stalwart mother; and especially the drunk father, a Vietnam vet who spends most of the film nursing his private pain in a junked station wagon full of cats in the family's backyard.

Coppola assembled an astonishing cast around Damon: Danny DeVito, as an ambulance chasing "paralawyer," whose amoral, trench-warfare tactics in the courtroom all but win their case; Mickey Rourke, who like Coppola had seen his career flame, and then flame out, since his first successes, as shyster/lawyer Bruiser Stone; Danny Glover as a fair-minded judge; and John Voight and Roy Scheider as gluttonously reptilian villains. The film edges tantalizingly close to greatness, but is weighed down by an indecisive ending that seemed to try for grim and uplifting at the same time.

Baylor wins the case and topples the shady insurance company, but they go bankrupt and so neither he nor the bereaved family will see a penny of the $100 million awarded by the court. His first case has made him a star, but the young idealist has seen enough of the law and quits while he's ahead, knowing that he will never be able to live up to this first triumph. He might well have been speaking for his beleaguered director, the former Hollywood wonder boy who had complained just before the film's release, "There's so little to choose from for a person in my position." *The Rainmaker* proved once again that Coppola still had greatness in him, and *The New York Times* called it his "best and sharpest film in years."

THE CAST

Rudy Baylor	**Matt Damon**
Kelly Riker	**Claire Danes**
Leo F. Drummond	**Jon Voight**
Dot Black	**Mary Kay Place**
J. Lyman "Bruiser" Stone	**Mickey Rourke**
Deck Shifflet	**Danny DeVito**

Rudy and Deck (Danny DeVito).

THE VIRGIN SUICIDES

"Boys who don't understand girls grow up to be men who don't understand women."

—Sofia Coppola

IT TOOK SOFIA COPPOLA ALMOST A DECADE TO LIVE DOWN her critically panned performance as Mary Corleone, but as she later insisted, she had never really wanted to be an actor. The youngest Coppola truly was her father's daughter, as was borne out by the subtle skill she demonstrated in her first full-length feature film, *The Virgin Suicides*. Young Sofia was not an actor, but a director.

Based on Jeffrey Eugenides's haunting novel of the same name, *The Virgin Suicides* is a film driven by mood, not by plot, with its dreamlike reminiscence of young desire. The film is most notable for the light touch with which it tells the story of the blonde Lisbon sisters, five impossibly beautiful girls, all

doomed as the films title suggests, still floating in the memories of the neighborhood boys who loved them. *The Virgin Suicides* is a paean to the bubblegum taste of first love and its ties to first lust, to the gauze through which we look back on our first heartbreak and also to the irresistible beauty and mischief incarnate in its star, Kirsten Dunst, as Lux, the loveliest and most seductive of the Lisbon sisters.

The film was shot in hazy pastels by Edward Lachman, a gifted cameraman who had also worked with Gregory Nava and Wim Wenders, and its soundtrack, by the French techno-pop group Air, added a dreamlike quality to the narrative. Some reviewers found the film too vague and evocative. *The*

Sofia Coppola directing her first full-length feature film.

The Lisbon sisters, lovely and doomed.

New York Times' A.O. Scott, called the film "a hothouse flower perishing for want of sunshine and fresh air." But *Salon's* Stephanie Zacharek, a frequently scathing reviewer whose idiosyncratic tastes and passionate opinions often recall both the genius and prejudice of Pauline Kael, saw the languor as endemic to the original novel, and Sofia Coppola as the director who managed to breathe life and heart into the ephemeral beauty of the Lisbon girls and the longings they inspired: "Leave it to a woman to boil all the excess, leaden moisture out of Eugenides's book and leave just the bare-bones poetry." In Zacharek's mind, Coppola managed to unearth the true tragedy beneath what the girls had longed for, dreamed of, but never known. "They were just young girls in bad dresses, waiting to be understood. Instead, they were simply loved."

TRIVIA

Voiceovers often take away from a film as much as they add, but in this case, Giovanni Ribisi's narration, speaking for all of the boys who hopelessly loved the girls, holds the film together. As Sofia Coppola explains, "Sometimes narration can be annoying. I wanted it to feel personal, sort of remembering—a fever dream. There's something romantic about him. He was kind of lovesick. He wasn't actory. He just got it."

THE CAST

Mr. Lisbon	**James Woods**
Mrs. Lisbon	**Kathleen Turner**
Lux Lisbon	**Kirsten Dunst**
Trip Fontaine	**Josh Hartnett**
Father Moody	**Scott Glenn**
Adult Trip Fontaine	**Michael Pare**
Dr. Horniker	**Danny DeVito**
Narrator (voice)	**Giovanni Ribisi**

CQ

Valentine (Angela Lindvall) plays a sex-kitten secret agent.

"I went to NYU for a couple years and I was in the Cinema Studies program, as opposed to the Film program, so we watched a lot of movies. I took a class on French New Wave, which definitely made an impression—a lot of the images that I borrowed (or stole, whatever you want to call it) came from scenes in those films."

—Roman Coppola

ROMAN COPPOLA DIRECTED HIS FIRST FEATURE FILM AT the age of 37. By then he had already made a name for himself as a Clio-award winning director of commercials and a Grammy-nominated director of music videos. He had also steeped himself in the family business, working as Second Unit Director for his father on *Dracula*, *The Rainmaker*, and *Jack*, and with Sofia on *The Virgin Suicides*. It comes as no surprise then, that for his directorial debut, he aimed high: choosing to do not just one film-within-a-film, but three.

Set in 1969 Paris, *CQ* stars Jeremy Davies (*Spanking the Monkey*, *Saving Private Ryan*), as an aspiring auteur, now slumming as an editor on a *Barbarella*-style B movie about a sexy secret agent named Dragonfly, whose chief assignment seems to be running across artificial moonscapes in skintight

Paul	**Jeremy Davies**
Dragonfly/Valentine	**Angela Lindvall**
Marlene	**Elodie Bouchez**
Andrezej	**Gerard Depardieu**
Fabrizio	**Massimo Ghini**
Enzo	**Giancarlo Giannini**
Chairman	**John Phillip Law**
Felix DeMarco	**Jason Schwartzman**
Dr. Ballard	**Dean Stockwell**
Mr. E	**Billy Zane**

The director Roman with his father Francis Ford Coppola.

jumpsuits. Young Paul alternates between mooning over the gorgeous ingénue who plays Dragonfly (real-life supermodel Angela Lindvall), and working on his own personal film, which is so personal that it consists largely of himself sitting in his bathroom, talking to a camera. All the while he ignores his lovely and perceptive girlfriend (Elodie Bouchez) who warns him repeatedly that he's looking in the wrong places, and that while he loses himself in fantasies, his life is passing him by.

The plot, such as it is, centers around the on-set chaos of the filming, and the theme is Paul's inability to get a grip on reality. But while Sofia Coppola replaces traditional plot with mood and evocation, her brother seems to replace plot with high style—and a passionate, wide-ranging love of movies. *CQ* pays loving homage to a different variety of filmmaker: the dictatorial bon-vivant (Giancarlo Giannini), obsessive and passionate (Gerard Depardieu), swinging and modern (Jason Schwartzman—in a giddy send up of his father's old boss, Roger Corman) and finally, Paul: removed, tentative, and seeking, always seeking....

ROMAN COPPOLA's film is so dedicated to directing and directors, it should serve as no surprise that he would nod to his father: In one scene, an outraged Andrezej punches a whole through the screening room door. Later, the editors are given a framed section of the broken wall. This was not a prop but a souvenir from Roman's personal collection—a piece of a wall his father had actually broken in a temper when he was a young director.

CQ is something of a movie geek's dream, a "Where's Waldo" of nods, gestures, and visual inside references to Fellini, Antonioni, Goddard, De Laurentis, Mario Bava, Coppola Sr., as well as to some of great pulp sixties sci-fi films, like *Barbarella* and *Danger*, *Diabolik* and *Modesty Blaise*. With breathtaking sets by the always brilliant Dean Tavoularis—Roman shows a promising love for and facility with the medium itself. In interviews he said that Paul is based on himself. We know Paul is trying to learn something, but like him, we are too dazzled by the chaos and confusion around us to know what that is. By the end of *CQ*, we are led to believe that Paul has learned a valuable lesson about the relationship between creativity and desire, fantasy and reality, and he has become not an observer but a filmmaker in his own right.

Dragonfly, the film within a film.

Bob Harris (Bill Murray), lonely in a crowd, in Tokyo, Japan.

"I wrote the movie with him in mind—in that part—so a lot of when I was writing, I was saying, 'What would Bill Murray do?'"

—Sofia Coppola

LOST IN TRANSLATION

THE CAST

Bob Harris	**Bill Murray**
Charlotte	**Scarlett Johansson**
John	**Giovanni Ribisi**
Kelly	**Anna Faris**
Charlie	**Fumihiro Hayashi**

Harris doing a Suntory whiskey commercial.

THE VIRGIN SUICIDES GAVE SOFIA COPPOLA A CHANCE TO dance out from under the shadow of her family name. *Lost in Translation*, making almost every critical "Best of" list for 2003 and grossing twenty-five times what it cost to make, did much more. In the words of the film's star, Bill Murray, a gifted comedian who gave what many consider to be his finest performance thus far, "She has been able to reinvent what her last name represents."

Lost in Translation built on the sensitivity to mood and visual detail that Sofia Coppola had shown in *The Virgin*

Suicides, and added to it the ability to build a convincing love story around the chemistry between two gifted and subtle actors. Bill Murray plays Bob, an American film star who has seen better days, both in his career and in his marriage, He is staying at the Tokyo Hyatt while filming a Suntory commercial (the hysterical scenes in the Japanese director's words of advice are indeed, lost in translation, read like a toned down version of one of Murray's own *Saturday Night Live* skits). While ruefully nursing drink after drink at the hotel bar, he meets Charlotte (Scarlett Johansson) a recent Yale graduate and newlywed whose hotshot filmmaker husband—played by an appropriately repellent Giovanni Ribisi—is gone all day, "working" with his hip, rock-star clients. Like Bob, she now finds herself adrift in the luxurious but lonely hotel, unsure who she is or where she's going.

The film makes subtle use of the impenetrability of Tokyo in the eyes of two Americans who don't speak Japanese. Never

Director Sofia Coppola with costar Bill Murray.

mind that the two are separated by almost three decades. Both Charlotte and Bob have woken up in a strange place, and have no idea how they got there, and it is in this realm of disenchantment that each discovers a way of reconnecting with the tenderness and self they have lost. At times the film story is a long set piece of moods—dislocation, wistfulness, regret, but unlike *Virgin Suicides*, it is centered and grounded in a central believable connection, and its concrete vision of a world in which everything, marriage, past, and uncertainty is lost in translation, except for the temporary solace these two drifters find in each other. Coppola's sweep of the Academy Awards nominations made Oscar history: she was the first woman in history to have been nominated for both Best Picture and Best Director. And her win—for Best Screenplay—helped make the Coppola family the second family in history to boast three generations of Oscar winners (the other family was Anjelica, John, and Walter Huston).

TRIVIA

Francis Ford Coppola is an enthusiastic devotee of Digital Filmmaking, but when he tried to convince his daughter to shoot in digital, she demurred, preferring the impact of film's ability to maintain a dreamlike distance from its subject matter, because this film was like "a memory and a love story."

AWARDS

ACADEMY AWARDS
4 Nominations / 1 Awards
GOLDEN GLOBES
5 Nominations / 3 Awards

Bob Harris whispering in Charlotte's (Scarlett Johansson) ear.

"I put money up for the film. Before I produced, people said don't put your money in the picture. I thought it was weird, yet money is what has given my company control. We always had final cut."

— Saul Zaentz

THE SAUL ZAENTZ COMPANY

financing to get the movie made. That film was *The English Patient*. It garnered nine Academy Awards, one more than *Amadeus*.

What has consistently set Zaentz apart from other producers is his insistence on creative control for the artist. "We have our own say on script, casting, and marketing," he declares. And like Francis Ford Coppola, George Lucas, and many of the other Bay Area iconoclasts who choose to work far away from the centers of power, he refuses to cede control even when, as in the case of Miramax, for example, studios are backing the film.

Saul Zaentz, with all his talents and wiles and machinations directed

towards the quality of the art itself, is a throwback to the great studio heads of Hollywood's golden age. In today's system, he has explained, the first four questions a studio head asks are all delivered in the wrong order. First

and editing suites for picture and sound editing to independent filmmakers. Zaentz subsidizes officespace to local filmmakers who occupy at under market rental rates. Over the years, many major films and documentaries are edited and mixed there. In addition to Zaentz's films, they include: *The Right Stuff*, *Never Cry Wolf*, *Kiss of the Spiderwoman*, *Blue Velvet*, *Dead Poet's Society*, *Ed Wood*, *To Die For*, *Seven*, *Fly Away Home*, *The Talented Mr. Ripley*, *Finding Forrester*, *Ghost World*, remixes of *The Godfather I*, *II*, and *III*, *Boogie Nights*, *The Deep End*, *The Singing Detective*, and *Duma*.

1984

The film *Amadeus* is released—winning eight Oscars at the Academy Awards ceremony in 1985, including Best Picture, Best Director, and Best Actor. Zaentz's interest in the film began years earlier when director Milos Forman suggested they see the New York stage production.

1986

The Mosquito Coast—executive produced by Zaentz, directed by Peter Weir, and starring Harrison Ford—is released.

1988

The Unbearable Lightness of Being, produced

TOP: **Saul Zaentz, Hector Babenco, and John Lithgow during the 1991 filming of** *At Play in the Fields of the Lord*.
ABOVE: **Almásy (Ralph Fiennes) and Katharine Clifton (Kristin Scott Thomas) in** *The English Patient*.

question: What star is attached? Second question: What's the budget? Third: Who's directing? And fourth: What's the script? The ultimate genius of Saul Zaentz is that as a producer, he has always put the question of the script first.

When Zaentz bought Fantasy Records in 1967, he moved it from San Francisco to Oakland and then to Tenth Street in Berkeley, where it has remained one of the most respected labels in the industry—not only signing and promoting great jazz and rock-and-roll artists but also releasing recordings by comedians like Lenny Bruce and Mort Sahl and great San Francisco poets, such as Allen Ginsberg. Fantasy Records included Fantasy Studios, where local artists from Carlos Santana to Bobbie McFerrin, Bill Evans, and even the raunchy Oakland hip hop icon, Too $hort, have recorded. The Saul Zaentz Film Center, a seven-story building, rented out its production and postproduction facilities to both independent and national filmmakers. Its facilities lured directors to the Bay Area time and again and hosted well-known talents like Paul Thomas Anderson, Carroll Ballard, Tim Burton, David Fincher, David Lynch, Anthony Minghella, Gus Van Sant, John Waters,

The Saul Zaentz Film Center Fantasy Building.

Anthony Minghella and Saul Zaentz.

and Terry Zwigoff, among others. Along with Skywalker Sound in Marin, The Saul Zaentz Film Center helped make San Francisco one of the preeminent postproduction centers of the world.

In 2004, Fantasy Records was bought by Concord Records Inc. and the Film Center began retrenching, signaling the end of an era. As for Zaentz's own personal legacy, it is perhaps best summed up in his own words, in a letter he wrote to *Variety* in 2003. The industry paper had published an article bemoaning Hollywood's dependence on formulaic happy endings. From his vantage point more than 400 miles away from the "Center of the Universe," Zaentz reminded the paper with not unjustifiable pride that his studio had produced only nine films, but those nine films had won a total of twenty-two Oscars and thirty-four nominations. "Not one of these films," he wrote "had a screenplay and/or ending that was changed by anyone but the filmmakers." He went on to remind the readers that in seven of these films, the heroes were killed at the end, or sometimes even in the beginning. His career has been characterized by a healthy distaste for profit projections, focus groups, and decision-by-executive-committee. Zaentz's postscript to his letter serves as a perfect coda to his astonishing career:

PS Any ending that works for us is not to be construed as a legal recommendation or financial guarantee.

by Zaentz and directed by Philip Kaufman, is released.

1991
At Play in the Fields of the Lord, directed by Hector Babenco, is released.

1996
The English Patient, based on the novel by Michael Ondaatje and directed by Anthony Minghella, is released. At the Academy Awards ceremony in March 1997, it sweeps nine Oscars, including Best Picture and Best Director. At the Oscar ceremony Saul Zaentz received the prestigious Irving G. Thalberg Memorial Award "for a consistently high quality of motion-picture production."

2002
Amadeus: The Director's Cut is in limited U.S. theatrical release as a lead up to the DVD release.

2004
Fantasy Records is sold to Concord Records for $83 million. At the time of the sale, Fantasy's extensive catalog includes Miles Davis, Thelonious Monk, John Coltrane, Sarah Vaughan, and other jazz greats, in addition to soul musicians, such as Isaac Hayes and Albert King. The Saul Zaentz Company retains ownership of the Fantasy building at Tenth and Parker Streets in Berkeley.

"You pass through life once,
and it may as well be in a Cadillac."

— Maury Dann

PAYDAY

After discovering that *One Flew Over the Cuckoo's Nest* and *At Play in the Fields of the Lord* had already been optioned, Zaentz became intrigued with another story: The tragic-comic tale of a second-rate country singer. Zaentz's years working for Norman Granz had afforded him a first-hand view of the touring life, and the project struck him immediately as authentic. Zaentz financed the picture with profits from Fantasy Records, although at the time he wasn't taking nearly the financial risk one would expect: The whole film was shot for $767,000.

Payday's plot was as lean as its budget: a loose, episodic account of two days in the life of the pill-popping, womanizing, not-quite-famous country-western singer named Maury Dann. Dann has the Cadillac, the driver, his own groupies, and the means to indulge his vices, but so far genuine stardom has eluded him. The endlessly self-serving performer, now careening through Alabama on the way to Nashville, where he's got a guest shot on the Buck Owens show and even a chance at the Johnny Cash show, faces one mishap after another on the way to his Promised Land: troublesome pickups, a disastrous attempt to play father, a payola-tainted meeting with a local DJ, and finally, the inevitable catastrophe that his life seems to have been barreling towards. What makes the film special is not the plot, which is common for a road movie, but its loose-

OPPOSITE: **Maury Dann (Rip Torn) on the road.**
ABOVE: **Rosamond (Elayne Heilveil), Maury Dann, and Mayleen (Ahna Capri).**

ness and mood. In the spirit of the seventies cinematic inventiveness, the film moves easily from laughter to something far less comfortable driven by Rip Torn's excellent performance as Maury Dann, and Don Carpenter's clever, witty script.

At the time, *Payday* was dismissed by most critics, but not by Pauline Kael, then the most powerful movie reviewer in the nation. Kael recognized that the film was part of a new movement in American cinema, and singled out Torn's performance with high praises, noting also that the movie's finale was crafted, as opposed to blueprinted from formula: "Even halfway through, we're not quite sure of where it's heading.... The editing seems to carry us along on the undercurrents; when from time to time the plot surfaces, we receive small hair-trigger shocks."

Universal, Warner Brothers, Twentieth Century Fox, and Columbia all turned it down for distribution before it was picked up by Cinerama Releasing Corp. Today, *Payday* stands as a cineaste's favorite—if not a date movie, at least the kind of movie that will impress your date with your iconoclastic and refined taste.

THE CAST

Maury Dann	**Rip Torn**
Mayleen Travis	**Ahna Capri**
Clarence McGinty	**Michael C. Gwynne**
Bob Tally	**Jeff Morris**
Chicago	**Cliff Emmich**
Rosamond McClintock	**Elayne Heilveil**

TRIVIA
The music for the exceedingly adult film was written by none other than Shel Silverstein, author of the beloved children's poetry collections Where the Sidewalk Ends, *and* A Light in the Attic.

R.P. McMurphy (Jack Nicholson) and Chief Bromden (Will Sampson).

ONE FLEW OVER THE CUCKOO'S NEST

THE CAST

Randall Partick McMurphy	**Jack Nicholson**
Nurse Mildred Ratched	**Louise Fletcher**
Harding	**William Redfield**
Martini	**Danny DeVito**
Chief Bromden	**Will Sampson**
Taber	**Christopher Lloyd**

"Our whole budget might have covered the cost of catering Terminator 2. *"*

— Milos Forman

WHEN DIRECTOR MILOS FORMAN FIRST MET WITH PRO-ducer Saul Zaentz in 1973 to discuss filming Ken Kesey's novel, Forman was a recently emigrated Czech director, still living hand to mouth at New York's Chelsea Hotel. Forman saw Zaentz as a "grizzled veteran" when, in fact, at that point, Zaentz had made exactly one movie. Zaentz was unsure whether or not Forman would be able to grasp the specifically American countercultural nature of Kesey's book, but Forman, a political refugee from communist Czechoslovakia, understood the struggle for freedom better than most Americans, and quickly proved that he had firm command of the novel's subject matter: the power struggle between a profane, rebellious, free-spirited inmate in a mental institution, and the controlling, rules-obsessed Nurse Ratched, who runs her unit with absolute authority.

Kirk Douglas had owned the rights to the book for years, and even played the role of McMurphy on Broadway. He had tried to shop the book around Hollywood, but since no film made inside an insane asylum had ever shown a profit, he received rejection after rejection, and eventually passed the rights on to his son Michael, who teamed up with Zaentz. They began to calculate how they could make the movie for less than $2 million, by casting unknowns—as well as hiring the relatively obscure Forman to direct. Forman had been a highly respected filmmaker in his native Czechoslovakia, but his only American film, *Taking Off*, had not done well. He was talented, strong-willed, and—much to Zaentz's delight—cheap. In the end, Forman's lack of a specific American context made him an ideal candidate for seizing the elemental universal truths behind the mental-ward drama, truths he knew intimately from his time fighting the censors in Czechoslovakia: the battle between the individual and the institution.

Jack Nicholson was already a bankable star, and hiring him doubled Zaentz's projected budget from $2 million to $4 million. Still unable to interest studios in the film, Zaentz ended up underwriting the project through Fantasy Records. They shot *Cuckoo's Nest* in the Oregon State Hospital in Salem, and except for Nicholson, cast unknown actors: Christopher Lloyd, Danny DeVito, and for the sinister Nurse Ratched, a pretty, soft-spoken actress named Louise Fletcher. For the role of Chief, the huge Indian inmate who inherits McMurphy's legacy at the end of the film, he cast Will Sampson, an ex-rodeo rider from Yakoma, Washington.

One Flew Over the Cuckoo's Nest launched the careers of Forman and many of the actors in the film, including DeVito, Lloyd, and Brad Dourif (who now plays a troubled alcoholic doctor in HBO's brilliant western drama, *Deadwood*). It also took home five Academy Awards, including Best Picture, Best Director, Best Actor, and Best Actress, and many consider Randall P. McMurphy to be Jack Nicholson's greatest role.

AWARDS
ACADEMY AWARDS
9 Nominations / 5 Awards
GOLDEN GLOBES
6 Nominations / 6 Awards

TRIVIA
Many extras and crewmen were actual mental patients from the Oregon State Hospital where the film was shot.

KIRK DOUGLAS, then owner of the rights to a popular counterculture novel, was traveling through Eastern Europe in the mid-sixties as a Goodwill ambassador. At a party in Prague, he met Milos Forman, and the two men hit it off immediately. Douglas asked the Czech director to take a look at a novel he was hoping to film, and promised to send him the book in the mail. Forman never received the package, Douglas never heard from Forman, and both men spent a good few years thinking the other had simply dropped the ball. The culprit: Czech government censors. The novel: *One Flew Over the Cuckoo's Nest*.

TRIVIA
One Flew Over the Cuckoo's Nest *became the first film in forty-one years to sweep the major categories of Best Picture, Best Director, Best Actor, Best Actress, and Best Screenplay.*

"*I must be crazy to be in a loony bin like this.*" — Randall P. McMurphy

R.P. McMurphy.

AMADEUS

"Too many notes!"

— Emperor to Mozart after hearing
Mozart's opera *Abduction from the Seraglio*

TRIVIA

The filming of Amadeus *was a homecoming for director Milos Forman. His first trip to his home city of Prague in seventeen years was not sentimental but financial, as he scouted affordable locations. As his collaborator Saul Zaentz explains, "We also had a communist government that you could negotiate with." The lavish onsite production cost only $18 million, according to Zaentz. "People don't believe that, but we are known for being very cheap."*

M ILOS FORMAN HAS SAID THAT FOR HIM THE CASTING IS the most important part of directing a film, and this is particularly evident in the casting of *Amadeus*. When F. Murray Abraham, a New York character actor who was reading for a minor part, showed up for his audition, Forman decided to cast him as Salieri, the embittered, second-rate composer who is cursed with the ability to recognize the genius of Mozart's music, but not the ability to match it. Forman loved Abraham immediately not because he thought that Abraham could *do* Salieri, but because he *was* Salieri. Tom Hulce, another relatively unknown actor, he cast as Mozart. And as the diplomatic, musically incompetent Emperor, he chose the wonderful Jeffrey Jones, soon to be known to wider audiences as the hapless principal in *Ferris Bueller's Day Off*. Meg Tilly was to play Constanze, Mozart's commoner wife, but when she tore a ligament playing soccer in Prague the role went to newcomer Elizabeth Berridge. Throughout filming, communist agents milled about posing as crew, and several of the actors found their rooms bugged. Still, Prague was the

Wolfgang Amadeus Mozart (Tom Hulce).

perfect place to film: They needed a European city, and as Forman explains, "Thanks to Communist inefficiency, in Prague the eighteenth century had never been touched." One of the scenes was actually shot in the Tyl Theater, where the real Mozart conducted the first performance of *Don Giovanni*.

Amadeus was another example of a Saul Zaentz gamble: This was the era of *Flashdance*, *Risky Business*, and *E.T.*, and Zaentz was personally funding a three-hour-long period drama about classical music, with no major stars and a climactic scene that would involve two men reading notes of music to each other in a dimly lit room. On top of that, the film asked the viewer to feel compassion for a rather pathetic villain, to recognize his evil and then forgive him. But *Amadeus*, rich with tragedy, the comic vulgarity of Hulce's Mozart, lush costuming, bawdy humor, and an obviously unbeatable soundtrack, was a smashing success. The film won eight Academy Awards, including Best Director, Best Actor, and Best Picture. Roger Ebert called it a "magnificent film, full and tender and funny and charming."

Antonio Salieri (F. Murray Abraham).

THE CAST

Antonio Salieri	**F. Murray Abraham**
Wolfgang Amadeus Mozart	**Tom Hulce**
Constanze Mozart	**Elizabeth Berridge**
Emanuel Schikaneder	**Simon Callow**
Leopold Mozart	**Roy Dotrice**
Katerina Cavalieri	**Christine Ebersole**
Emperor Joseph II	**Jeffrey Jones**
Count Orsini-Rosenberg	**Charles Kay**

**Wolfgang Amadeus Mozart and
Constanze Mozart (Elizabeth Berridge).**

AWARDS

ACADEMY AWARDS
11 Nominations / 8 Awards
GOLDEN GLOBES
6 Nominations / 4 Awards

TRIVIA

The entire film was shot with natural light. In order to get the proper diffusion of light for some scenes, the Director of Photography, Miroslav Ondricek, covered windows from the outside with tracing paper.

WALTER MURCH, the legendary film editor, sound designer, writer, director, and innovator, has lived and worked in the San Francisco Bay Area for over thirty years since moving north in 1969 to join Francis Coppola and George Lucas in the formation of American Zoetrope. In addition to collaborating with Coppola and Lucas, he has worked with the regions most important filmmakers, including Carroll Ballard, Philip Kaufman, Terry Zwigoff, and, of course, Saul Zaentz. When asked how it happened that Murch, perhaps more than any other local figure, connected so many of the area's players, Zaentz said simply: "Well, he's the best." While Murch has both edited film and mixed sound in the best post-production facilities in the Bay Area, it is the Fantasy Building, where he worked on *The English Patient*, that has a suite named after him.

As a freshman at Johns Hopkins University in the sixties, however, Murch had no intention of going into film. He wanted to be an oceanographer. Fortunately, a desultory science class combined with a stimulating lecture from an art history professor drew Murch, the son of an accomplished painter, to the humanities, and like several of his classmates (who included Matthew Robbins and Caleb Deschanel), he became enamored of European film. He returned to a childhood fascination with the magic of the tape recorder, and soon after graduation, applied to graduate film school out West. Murch became one of the brightest stars at school, second perhaps only to one other student. When he and his collaborator and rival were both named finalists for a prestigious internship at Warner Brothers, the two young men made a deal: Whichever of them won the internship would turn around and help the other as soon as the chance arose.

Pacts like this have been made by aspiring artists the world over, to no avail. But in this case, the film school was USC, and the other contestant was George Lucas. Lucas won the prize, and true to his word, when Coppola was looking for someone to do sound on *The Rain People*, Lucas, who was shooting the "making of" documentary, mentioned Murch. The three of them, Coppola, Lucas and Murch, plus their wives and families, loaded up a truck with equipment and moved from Los Angeles to San Francisco.

Today Murch remembers the hectic early days at

In 1965, immediately following their wedding, Walter and Aggie Murch rode across America for a six-week honeymoon to begin married life in Los Angeles, CA.

American Zoetrope as "a student's dream come true." He finished *The Rain People* in an unbelievable four days, to meet a deadline for entry into the San Sebastian Film Festival and the film won first place.

Since then, Murch's career has been characterized by excellence and invention—from the "worldizing" technique he developed working on *THX-1138*, to his late-night stomps in the San Francisco Natural History Museum to approximate the footfalls of robots. Even the term *sound design* can be attributed to Murch, who, along with his cohorts, invented it for *Apocalypse Now*. In addition to directing *Return to Oz*, he has edited or done the sound, or both, on some of the best films of the past three decades, including *THX 1138*, *The Godfather I, II, and III*, *American Graffiti*, *The Conversation*, *The Black Stallion*, *Apocalypse Now*, *The Right Stuff*, *The Unbearable Lightness of Being*, and, of course, *The English Patient*, for which he won Academy Awards for both Best Film Editing and Best Sound.

ABOVE: Walter Murch, in his lucky sweater, which has put out truck fires and been worn on every film Murch has mixed.
OPPOSITE: Katharine Clifton (Kristin Scott Thomas) and Almásy (Ralph Fiennes) in *The English Patient*.

"The resonance you find about San Francisco filmmakers is that it's personal, it's a kind of off-the-wall vision of things or a personal idea that doesn't go through any kind of corporate reality or marketing testing or 'will this be popular?'"

— George Lucas

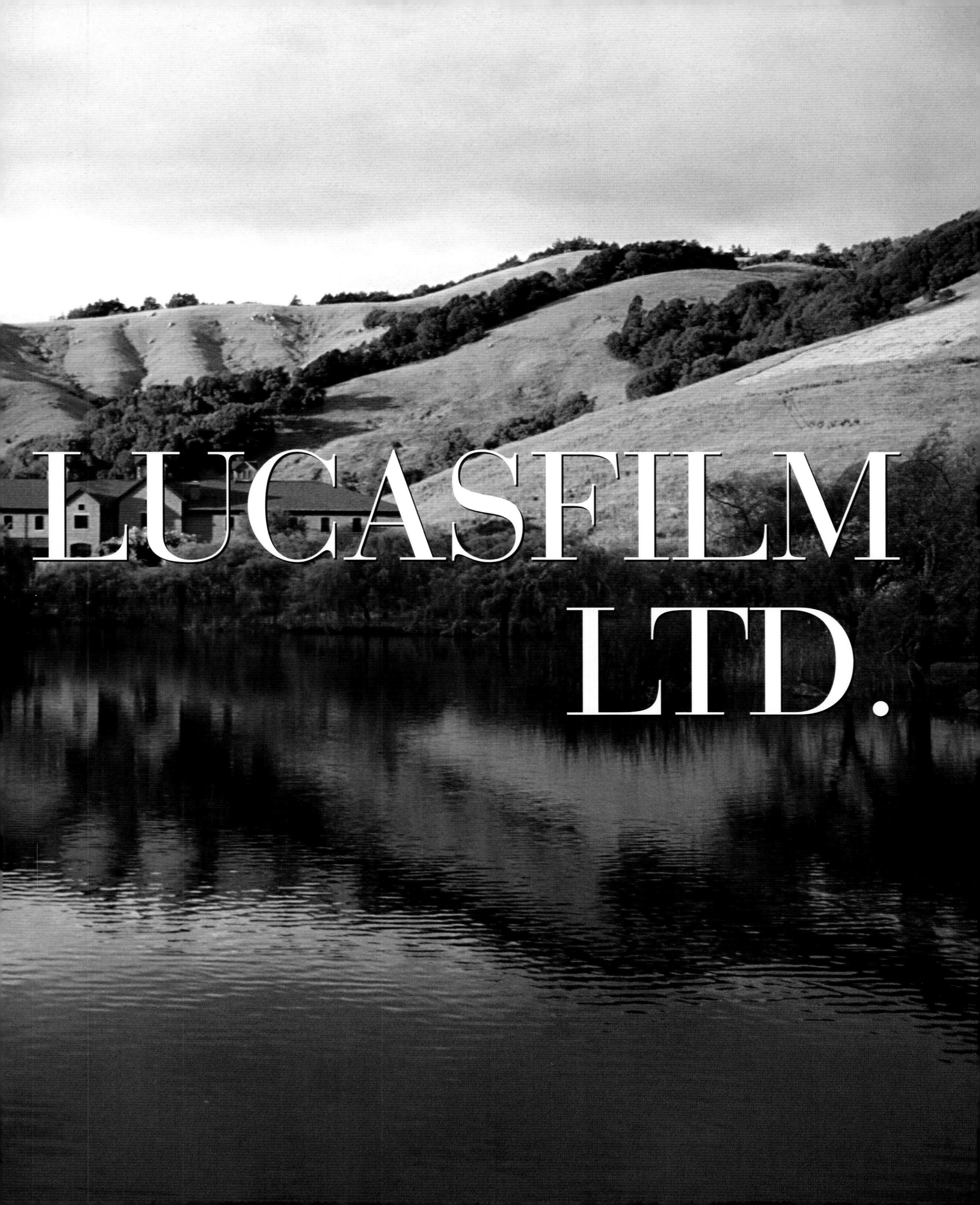

LUCASFILM LTD.

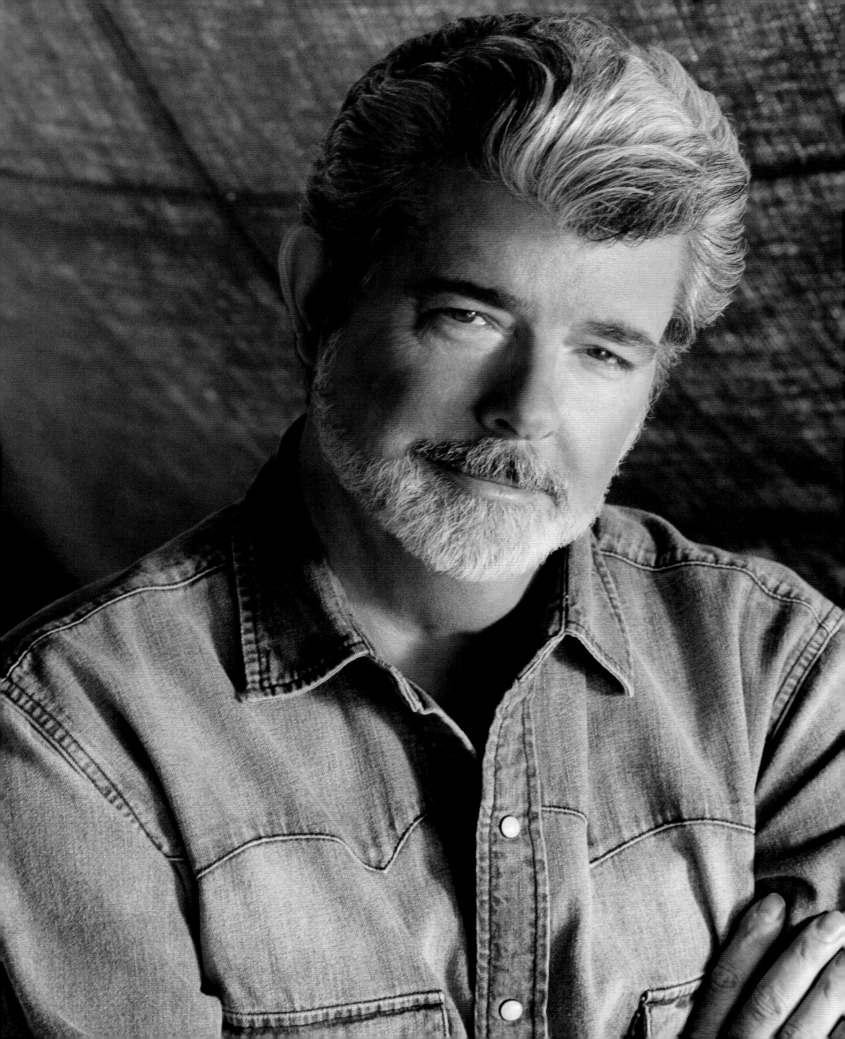

M uch like the history of Bay Area cinema, the history of Lucasfilm—from the release of *THX 1138* and *American Graffiti* to the seismic impact of *Star Wars* and *Raiders of the Lost Ark*—can be read as one long series of innovations, all of which have had an enormous influence both on what kinds of movies get made and on how movies get made. Innovations like advances in special effects, developments in animated film, and the 2005 digital Letterman facilities in San Francisco's Presidio are due to George Lucas's combination of vision, willingness to reinvest profits, and accountability in every aspect of his work: the storytelling, the production, the effects, and the editing. As he says, "You can like my films or not, but they're my films."

The emphasis on the word "my" suits a child of the James Dean generation and of the American West. George Lucas was born in 1944 in Modesto, California, less than one month before D-day. His father owned a stationery store and his mother was a homemaker. A middle child with two sisters, Lucas had an idyllic fifties childhood, building soapbox race cars, enjoying Saturday-afternoon adventure serials, reading comic books, and listening to the radio. Though he liked reading he was an indifferent student, and as a teenager, he was mainly interested in girls and auto racing— that is, until he crashed his beloved Fiat Bianchina into a tree, destroying both the car and the tree. Lucas almost died and spent the next two days in a coma and the next two months in intensive care.

The wreck gave Lucas an early taste of mortality and convinced him to pursue other interests besides auto racing, but to his father's dismay, those interests still didn't include the family business. They did, however, include frequent trips to sixties-era San Francisco, then known not only for its buzzing North Beach scene but also for the experimental filmmakers of the Canyon Cinema Group. The child who had loved Saturday matinees was a young adult now. Although he was taking classes at a junior college in psychology and anthropology, his new idols were filmmakers like Stan Brakhage, James Broughton, Jordan Belson, Bruce Conner, and Norman McLaren, the Canadian animator who had first inspired John Korty.

Lucas applied to the University of Southern California on a whim and began taking classes in the fall of 1964. He suffered through his film-writ-

PORTFOLIO

GEORGE LUCAS

Academy Award Nominations	**40**
Academy Awards	**17**
Golden Globe Nominations	**7**
Golden Globe Awards	**1**
Academy Award Nominations for non-Lucasfilm movies (ILM and Sprocket Systems)	**47**
Academy Awards for non-Lucasfilm movies (ILM and Sprocket Systems)	**20**
Academy Sci-Tech Awards	**20**
Films Listed on the AFI Top 100	**2**

JOINT PRODUCTIONS FRANCIS FORD COPPOLA AND GEORGE LUCAS

Academy Award Nominations	**10**
Golden Globe Nominations	**6**
Golden Globe Awards	**3**
Cannes Film Festival Awards	**2**
Films Listed on the AFI Top 100	**1**

MILESTONES

1969
Production is begun on *THX 1138* with Lucas working out of his office at American Zoetrope's 327 Folsom facility.

1970
Lucas edits *THX 1138* out of his home in Mill Valley.

1971
THX 1138 is accepted for the prestigious Directors' Fortnight program at the Cannes Film Festival. At the festival, Lucas makes a deal with David Picker of United Artists for $10,000 to develop a script for *American Graffiti*. *THX 1138* is released theatrically. Lucasfilm Ltd. is incorporated.

1972
American Graffiti goes into production in Marin and Sonoma counties.

1973

American Graffiti is released. Made for under $1 million it brings in over $115 million at the Box Office and is nominated for five Academy Awards and one BAFTA award. Lucas begins writing *Star Wars*.

1974

Parkway is established as Lucasfilm's Northern California headquarters in Marin County. The company is made up of four people. Other offices are occupied by writer/director team Matthew Robbins and Hal Barwood and by director Michael Ritchie.

1975

Industrial Light and Magic is established in a warehouse in Van Nuys, California to handle special effects for the new *Star Wars* film. Sprocket Systems, Inc. is incorporated to handle sound and post-production.

ing and drama classes. "I was not into storytelling," he remembers. "I was trying to create emotions through pure cinematic techniques." But he discovered he had a knack for shooting and editing, and soon began making a name for himself at school with several stand-out student films, including a montage of images from *Life* magazine, a satirical teen beach movie, a seven-and-a-half-minute-long film of a race-car driver, and, finally, his award-winning student film, *THX-1138: 4EB*.

In addition to making movies, the 20-year-old also made many life-long friends, including John Milius, Willard Huyck, Matthew Robbins, Hal Barwood, Caleb Deschanel, Robert Dalva, and Walter Murch, the film school's other "star" and the man who would design the sound for Lucas's first two feature films. Lucas would later become known, along with UCLA's Francis Ford Coppola, NYU's Martin Scorsese, Steven Spielberg,

"We [USC film students] were all helping each other and getting involved and appreciating film no matter what it was, no matter where it came from."

—George Lucas

Caleb Deschanel (Director of Photography), Howard Kazanjian (Producer), and George Lucas (Executive Producer) on the set of *More American Graffiti*.

George Lucas and Francis Ford Coppola on location during the shooting of *The Rain People.*

and Brian De Palma, as the "Film School Brats," but in the late sixties, neither he nor any of his peers had any idea that their careers would actually amount to anything.

Still, if anyone at USC then might hope for a future in film, it was Lucas. In 1967 he won the Sam Warner Scholarship, which would pay a small stipend and give him a chance to observe the films being made at Warner Brothers—that is, if there were any. Warner Brothers had just been sold to Seven Arts, so when the 24-year-old Lucas showed up at the Warner's building on the first day of his internship, the whole place was shutting down. He found his way to where Francis Ford Coppola was directing his production of *Finian's Rainbow* on the old *Camelot* lot. Lucas had already spent time observing a big Hollywood production, J. Lee Thompson's Western *MacKenna's Gold*, and he found the production to be bloated and inefficient. "It takes a week of watching to get bored," he said. "Watching does not do anything." Sure enough, Lucas got bored watching Coppola as well, and so the (slightly) older director recruited him to help out on set. Coppola, just 28 at the time, was discovering firsthand the meaning of "decision by committee" and finding it impossible to direct his movie the way he wanted to. The two men became friends, and when Lucas finished his internship he joined Coppola on the road, taking a production crew and editing equipment in a makeshift caravan across America to film Coppola's *The Rain People.* By day Lucas made a documentary about the production, by night he worked on a draft for a full-length feature version of *THX.* In between takes and rest stops, he and Coppola built their studio in the sky: a free collective of filmmakers pursuing their own personal projects away

1976
Star Wars begins principal photography on location around the world.

1977
Lucasfilm's licensing group operates out of a converted warehouse purchased across the street from Universal Studios called the Egg Company. Within two weeks of the *Star Wars* theatrical release on May 25th, 20th Century Fox's stock doubles. The movie garners eleven Academy Award nominations and seven wins.

1978
Lucas, Larry Kasdan, and Steven Spielberg have the first story conference for *Raiders of the Lost Ark* from a story Lucas developed in 1975. ILM moves to San Rafael. Lucas purchases the 1,700 acre Bull Tail Ranch on Lucas Valley road.

1979
Filming begins on *The Empire Strikes Back.* A new Computer Research and Development Division is established to bring high technology into three areas—video editing, digital audio and computer graphics. Lucasfilm is granted a re-zoning permit to develop a "think tank for filmmakers" and renames "The Bull Tail Ranch" Skywalker Ranch. *More American Graffiti* is released.

1980
The Empire Strikes Back is released and sets a new industry record for the highest single day per theatre gross. Construction begins on Skywalker Ranch. *Kagemusha (The Shadow Warrior)* is released.

1981
The balance of Lucasfilm's corporate group moves north from Universal City and rents office space in San Rafael. Larry Kasdan's *Body Heat* is released with Lucas as uncredited executive producer. *Raiders of the Lost Ark* is released.

1982
Production begins on *Return of the Jedi. Star Wars* is released on video and quickly becomes the best-selling video of its time. John Korty's animated feature *Twice Upon a Time* is released. Sprocket System's THX Sound System is introduced to the film industry and the Theatre Alignment Program (TAP) is created to ensure quality of the 70mm release of *Return of the Jedi.* ILM begins to expand their effects work on third-party films winning the Best Visual Effects Academy Award for their work on Steven Spielberg's *E.T.: The Extra-Terrestrial.*

1983
The Computer Division moves to new offices in San Rafael and forms three new groups: Pixar, EditDroid, and Games. The Pixar group generates seven elements for *Return of the Jedi* which releases in May, breaking the record for the largest single day gross in history: $6.2 million. Cumulative *Star Wars* licensing retail

John Milner (Paul Le Mat) being questioned by a cop in his souped-up yellow roadster in _American Graffiti_.

sales exceed $2 billion. _Indiana Jones and the Temple of Doom_ begins principal photography in Sri Lanka. _Return of the Jedi_ is nominated for five Academy Awards.

1984
Indiana Jones and the Temple of Doom opens in May and has the largest one-week gross in history: $45.8 million. Production begins on _Mishima_ and _Latino_. The Pixar group's short _Andre and Wally B._ is introduced at SIGGRAPH. The new Computer Games division releases their first two games to market: "Ballblazer" and "Rescue on Frattalus". Ground is broken at Skywalker Ranch for a state of the art post-production Technical Building. _The Ewok Adventure_ a made-for-TV movie directed by John Korty, airs, winning an Emmy for Outstanding Visual Effects. Production begins on two separate _Star Wars_ television-animation series: _Ewoks_ and _Droids_. George Lucas and Steven Spielberg place their footprints in cement at Mann's Chinese Theatre in Hollywood and Lucasfilm donates R2-D2 and C-3PO to the Smithsonian. The Editdroid disk-based editing system designed to emulate film-style editing is shown at NAB in Las Vegas.

1985
Mishima is released. Principal photography begins on the Lucasfilm/Henson co-production _Labyrinth_ starring David Bowie. Production begins on _Howard the Duck_ with George Lucas as executive producer. EditDroid and

from the grip of the Hollywood system. They were both attracted to San Francisco; Lucas because it was the city of his youth, Coppola because of it was "happening." Lucas and Coppola celebrated their decision to establish American Zoetrope in John Korty's Stinson Beach barn on July 4, 1968, but their declaration of independence really began to mean something after Coppola struck a seven-picture deal with Seven Arts. Lucas rented a house in Mill Valley and spent the next year making _THX_, inviting Murch up to help out. Warner Brothers hated the film and ended up cutting five minutes out of it, an experience that led Lucas to seek more distance and control on his next films. In 1971, Lucas formed his own company, Lucasfilm Ltd., but continued to work with Coppola on the joint Lucasfilm/Coppola Company production _American Graffiti_.

Where Lucas's first American Zoetrope feature _THX 1138_ had showcased his technical wizardry and visual imagination, _American Graffiti_ was a sweet rock-and-roll story about a small group of teenagers cruising the streets on the night of their high school graduation. Filmed primarily in Marin County, it was based on his own memories of growing up in Modesto, California. As he did with _THX_, Lucas had to fight to realize his vision—this time with nervous studio executives who thought the nonlinear narrative style and four

George Lucas directing the first of six _Star Wars_ serials.

**Luke Skywalker (Mark Hamill), Princess Leia (Carrie Fisher)
and Han Solo (Harrison Ford) in the original *Star Wars*.**

intertwined stories set against a pop-music soundtrack was "too confusing." As Lucas says, "After the script was turned down by every studio at least twice," it was a commercial and critical smash, earning the 29-year-old director five Academy Award nominations.

For more than a year, Lucas had been planning a fantasy film about robots, heroes, and some kind of mysterious force, which he started out calling *The Star Wars*. Needless to say, it was a hard sell, but Lucas found a backer for the new film in Alan Ladd, Jr., at 20th Century Fox and began casting and choosing locations in London and Tunisia. In 1975, in order to meet his production needs, he established Industrial Light and Magic to handle special effects and Sprocket Systems to manage sound and post-production. Anyone young, creative, or foolish enough to take on the task was welcome. "I think the average age at ILM at that point," says Lucas, "was 23."

Those kids are now the legends and elders of the F/X and postproduction industry, and the talents at ILM and Sprocket Systems (now Skywalker Sound) have become masters of their craft. But when ILM started, it was just a converted warehouse full of puppets, blue screens, cameras, and young men scratching their heads over each film frame, trying to come up with ways of rendering their boss's vision on-screen.

Star Wars opened on May 25, 1977, and transformed the industry and the imaginations of the people lucky enough to see it when they were still young. The audience experienced a dazzling world unlike any they'd ever seen before—a whole universe with its own mythology, battles, life forms, planets, and weapons. No sooner had *Star Wars* hit theaters than Lucas, who could

SoundDroid are spun off into a separate joint venture between Lucasfilm and Convergence Corp. Lucas doubles his land holdings on Lucas Valley Road to 4,759 acres by purchasing three neighboring ranches including Big Rock Ranch. Lucasfilm moves its corporate headquarters from San Rafael to The Skywalker Ranch.

1986
Latino, directed by Haskell Wexler, is released. Pixar is sold to Steve Jobs. With no more *Star Wars* movies planned, approximately fifty of Lucasfilm's 450 employees are let go. *Labyrinth* and *Howard the Duck* are released. "Captain EO" opens at Disneyland. The park stays open for sixty straight hours to accommodate the ground breaking attendance.

1987
"Star Tours" is created as a joint project between the Walt Disney Company, Lucasfilm, ILM, and Sprocket Systems. Principal photography begins on *Willow* and *Tucker*. The Lucasfilm Research Library acquires Paramount Picture's Research library and triples the size of the total collection.

1988
The films *Willow, Tucker, Powaqqatsi*, and *Land Before Time* are released. Filming begins on *Indiana Jones and the Last Crusade*.

1989
ILM wins the Academy Award for Best Visual Effects on *The Abyss*, their tenth such win since *Star Wars* in 1977. Lucasfilm Commercial Productions is established. *Indiana Jones and the Last Crusade* is released both as a feature film and computer game, marking the first time the games group interpreted a Lucasfilm movie for interactive entertainment.

1990
The company consolidates its nine business subsidiaries, excluding film production, under the title LucasArts Entertainment. The post-production facility at Skywalker Ranch is now Skywalker Sound rather than Sprocket Systems.

1991
Skywalker Sound handles post-production on eight non-Lucas films, winning two Academy Awards for *Backdraft* and two for *Terminator 2: Judgment Day*. This makes six Oscars to date since their first Special Achievement Award for *Star Wars* in 1977. The George Lucas Education Foundation (GLEF) is established. The television series *The Young Indiana Jones Chronicles* begins principal photography in eleven countries.

1992
The Young Indiana Jones Chronicles TV series has its initial broadcast on ABC. George Lucas receives the Irving G. Thalberg Life Achievement Award from the Academy of Motion Picture Arts and Sciences for helping to establish standards of technical perfection in the motion picture industry.

1993
Avid Technology acquires the EditDroid and SoundDroid technologies. A wine tasting is held for the first Chardonnay wine bottled from the Skywalker Ranch vineyard.

1994
Radioland Murders is released. The new THX digitally mastered *Star Wars* Trilogy VHS ships more than thirteen million units.

1995
LucasArts Games finishes the year with the number two market share for PC entertainment. Research is begun on the *Star Wars* prequel trilogy. The Library of Congress honors *American Graffiti* as one of the twenty-five films named to the National Film Registry.

1996
Lucasfilm forms Lucas On-Line to develop Internet entertainment with starwars.com. ILM wins three Academy Sci-Tech awards bringing their total Sci-Tech awards to twelve.

1997
Production begins on *Star Wars: Episode I The Phantom Menace*. Carrie Fisher presents Chewbacca with an MTV Lifetime Achievement Award.

now start financing his own movies, was making plans to realize the rest of the trilogy while at the same time convincing Spielberg to join him on another film: an old-school adventure story based on Saturday adventure serials, about a world-wandering archeologist named Indiana Jones.

For the next twenty years, Lucas would focus on producing films and on building Skywalker Ranch, his dream campus for filmmakers. He also continued to push the technical barriers to filmmaking by starting up a three-purpose computer division in 1979 to change the way editing, sound, and digital effects are created and bring filmmaking technologies out of the old analog world into the modern digital world. Lucasfilm would shatter one barrier after another: The company developed the software that would become RenderMan; introduced the EditDroid (the world's first digital, nonlinear editing system); created SoundDroid (which transformed the art of sound design); established the Computer Graphics Division (which would eventually become Pixar); and advanced ever more ambitious special effects—including those in some of the most memorable scenes in films like *The Abyss*, *Terminator 2*, and *Jurassic Park*.

The Main House at Skywalker Ranch.

ABOVE: **Big Rock Ranch viewed from across the lake.**
BELOW: **Interior of the research library at Skywalker Ranch.**

1998
Lucas On-Line generates the biggest Internet event in history with 1.1 million downloads of the *Star Wars: Episode I The Phantom Menace* trailer exclusively using Apple Computer's QuickTime technology.

1999
The Phantom Menace has the biggest opening day and opening week in box-office history. Trustees of the Presidio National Park in San Francisco select Lucasfilm as the preferred developer of twenty-three acres for its proposed Letterman Digital Center pending an environmental review.

2000
The all-digital production of *Star Wars: Episode II* goes into production. The Lucasfilm research library acquires Universal Studio's research library. *Star Wars: Episode I The Phantom Menace* is the number one VHS release for 2000. After more than fourteen years and three separate plan submissions, the Marin Planning Commission gives approval for Lucasfilm to build an office complex at Big Rock Ranch.

2001
Star Wars: Episode I is released on DVD with six hours of extra material and makes $45 million the first week of sales. Lucasfilm signs an agreement with the Presidio Trust to build a new studio campus in San Francisco.

2002
Skywalker Ranch is the host for its first digital conference. *Star Wars: Episode II Attack of the Clones* is released and is shown theatrically on sixty-three digital screens out of close to 7,000 total screens in North America. Later it debuts on approximately fifty IMAX screens in the US and Canada. The Lucasfilm company moves to Big Rock Ranch leaving the production company, JAK Films, at Skywalker Ranch.

2003
Star Wars: Episode III goes into production. Lucasfilm establishes a new animation unit. LucasArts launches the first ever *Star Wars* online game, "Star Wars Galaxies", which has 50,000 people playing within one month of launch. Digital Yoda is nominated for best virtual performance at the MTV Movie Awards for *Star Wars Episode II*.

2004
Viandante del Cielo ("sky walker" in Italian) Chardonnay and Merlot wine from grapes grown at Skywalker Ranch has its first initial commercial release through Francis Ford Coppola's Niebaum-Coppola Estate Vineyards and Winery.

2005
The final and sixth *Star Wars* film *Star Wars: Episode III The Revenge of the Sith* is released. Lucasfilm moves to the Presidio.

A scene from the short *The Adventures of André and Wally B.* done for SIGGRAPH partly to illustrate
a breakthrough innovation in motion blur (a process that in 1984 could take a Cray supercomputer hours).

THE ADVENTURES
OF ANDRÉ AND WALLY B. (1984)

ANDRÉ AND WALLY B. IS THE VERY FIRST FILM THAT JOHN Lasseter animated in 3-D. Director Alvy Ray Smith came up with the concept and title for the short after seeing the film *My Dinner With Andre*, in which the main characters were named Wally and Andre. The Lucasfilm Graphics Group made a big showing at SIGGRAPH, with seven technical papers, four tutorials, two panels, the presentation of the Pixar Graphics Computer, and the film. The savvy audience knew they were seeing the cutting-edge result of new technology (Bill Reeves's breakthrough design and rendering) married to a high level of artistic talent (John

Lasseter's character design and animation). By today's standards, the animation is simple. But the two-minute story was a quantum leap forward in motion blur and 3-D animation and paved the way for the glories of CGI animation as we know them now. The positive reception to the short opened the door for Edwin Catmull and Alvy Ray Smith to co-found the animation studio when Lucasfilm Ltd. sold Pixar Technology to Steven Jobs in 1986.

Trying to make a distinction between the "creative" and the "technical" aspect of Lucasfilm's thirty-plus-year endeavor isn't possible. All of Lucas's work—from self-financing his films

The Computer Graphics Group in front of C Building in the early eighties.
Left to right: Loren Carpenter, William Reeves, Ed Catmull, Alvy Ray Smith (clicking the shutter), Rob Cook, John Lasseter, Eben Ostby, David Salesin, Craig Good, and Sam Leffler.

Howard, and Jim Henson, were joyful experiences, as was the Emmy award–winning television show *The Indiana Jones Chronicles*.

All the films, including those that were not mega-successes, like *Willow* and *Labyrinth*, gave the wizards at ILM opportunities to develop and experiment with their new technologies, and by the early nineties, both ILM and Skywalker Sound were turning profits as highly respected post-production facilities for outside films. By 1997 when Lucas began production on the eagerly anticipated prequel to the original *Star Wars* trilogy, *The Phantom Menace*, ILM had won fourteen Academy Awards and Skywalker Sound seventeen.

Lucas's return to the director's chair gave him a chance to realize much of

to pouring money into research and improving the filmmakers' tools to building a production facility nestled in the dreamlike splendor of the Marin countryside—accords with his firmly held belief in the need to free up the hands of filmmakers so that financial and technical limitations don't interfere with the realization of their on-screen vision.

It was not easy. Even with all the blockbusters, the eighties was a period of constant challenge and a complicated juggling act: Lucas was a single father with children who needed his time and a business that was expanding very quickly. "There was a point," he remembers, "when I think we had twelve companies." Still, several of the films he produced, all fruitful collaborations with friends like John Korty, Ron

what he'd been unable to get on-screen with the first three movies in the *Star Wars* saga. *The Phantom Menace* and *Attack of the Clones* both made use of extraordinary innovations in digital filmmaking, but it was with *Revenge of the Sith*, the sixth and final installment, that the digital effects had become so profound they were invisible.

In 2005 Lucasfilm opened its Letterman campus in San Francisco, the city where Lucas was first turned on to the glories of cinema. The Presidio location is devoted to the newest form of cinema, the one Lucas helped create—digital.

LEFT AND ABOVE: **Letterman Digital Arts Center.**

Luke Skywalker (Mark Hamill) stunned by the death of his adoptive parents on Tatooine.

STAR WARS: EPISODE IV A NEW HOPE

"The Force is strong with this one."

— Darth Vader

THE CAST

Luke Skywalker	**Mark Hamill**
Han Solo	**Harrison Ford**
Princess Leia Organa	**Carrie Fisher**
Grand Moff Tarkin	**Peter Cushing**
Ben Obi-Wan Kenobi	**Alec Guinness**

1977

I N HINDSIGHT, IT'S EASY TO SCOFF AT THE EXECUTIVES WHO turned their backs on what would prove to be one of the most successful and, arguably, most influential movies of the seventies. But as screenwriter Walter Goldman points out in his own memoir of a life lived in the Hollywood trenches, studio executives are usually smart, film-loving women and men who know that they are always just inches away from being fired. Even after Lucas had proven he knew how to connect with audiences in *American Graffiti*, no one knew what to make of his new project, a sprawling space saga. His 200-page script called for robots and special effects that had never been seen before and, as Lucas chuckles today, a major character that was "basically a large dog." The studio executive who agreed to take a chance and finance the script was Alan Ladd, Jr.

The problems ranged from a mundane janitorial issue (as in *THX*, the director was aiming for a "used future," a dented and dusty landscape, and had to restrain overeager production assistants from constant mopping and scrubbing) to a

Rebel X-wing starfighters fly past the planet Yavin on their way to battle the Death Star.

brief hospitalization for Lucas when he came back from a harrowing shoot in England to find that his whiz kids at ILM had burned through half their budget and only gotten one useable shot. In between there were disdainful British crewmen, a freak storm in the Tunisian desert that blew all the sets away, and always the fear that the studio would pull the plug. At one point the director lost his voice and had to deliver his verbal cues in a hoarse whisper. On Lucas's side, however, were the talents of his crew: Ben Burtt, a newly discovered sound guru; John Dykstra and Richard Edlund, who did wonders with their new motion-control camera; and recommended by Spielberg, John Williams, whose now-classic score added so much to the film. Also on his side was the cast of near unknowns who brought Luke Skywalker, Leia Organa, and Han Solo to life, as well the gravitas of Sir Alec Guinness. Finally, there was the material itself: a refreshingly exuberant adventure story which combined several of Lucas's long-standing interests from montage to racing to the writings of Joseph Campbell on mythology.

Nobody—not Lucas, not the studio, not the crew, and not his friends—was prepared for the phenomenon *Star Wars* became. Twentieth Century Fox didn't even have all their posters ready by the release date. But May 25, 1977, turned out to be one of the biggest openings in cinema history, with lines stretching around the blocks and theaters full of stomping feet and spontaneous cheers from the moment the audience first saw the opening shot of an endless spaceship flying over their heads. *Star Wars* would go on to break almost every record there was, making it the top-grossing film of all time for almost twenty years (it was finally unseated by James Cameron's *Titanic*).

In perhaps the most moving of all the thunderstruck rave reviews, Vincent Canby described it as "the movie that the teenagers in *American Graffiti* would have broken their necks to see." One can't help but wonder if Canby is right: If those kids had had a *Star Wars* to light their imaginations on fire, maybe they'd have all dared to seek out a bigger future than the one that awaited them in their hometown.

ABOVE: **Darth Vader and Obi-Wan Kenobi (Alec Guinness) in a lightsaber duel on the Death Star battle station.**
OVERLEAF: **Luke, Chewbacca, and Han Solo (Harrison Ford) are decorated for their heroic efforts.**

STAR WARS: EPISODE V THE EMPIRE STRIKES BACK

"Laugh it up, fuzz ball!"

—Han Solo

PERHAPS NAIVELY, AN EXHAUSTED LUCAS THOUGHT THAT stepping into a producer's role and hiring a director might ease his workload, and so he offered the directing job to Irvin Kershner, a former visiting professor at his old alma mater, and also a director who had studied under Slavko Vorkapich, the Yugoslav-born montagist whom Lucas and his peers had so admired in film school. Kershner approached the project with trepidation. "How do you make a picture better than *Star Wars*?"

Kershner wasn't the only one who had the shakes. *Star Wars* had made a great deal of money, but this was the first time Lucas would try to finance a film himself. In order for him to recoup his investment, he said, "it would have to be the biggest grossing sequel of all time."

AWARDS

ACADEMY AWARDS
4 Nominations / 2 Awards

GOLDEN GLOBES
1 Nomination

There were new technical hurdles as well: The movie's opening shot required white objects on white matting, and shooting in the frigid temperatures in Norway made Tunisia look like a picnic.

Working with mostly the same team who had done wonders with the first movie and with additional help from visual-effect wizard Dennis Muren, and screenwriters Leigh Brackett and Lawrence Kasdan (who was also writing another screenplay for Lucas about an adventuring archaeologist), Kershner and Lucas drew out the Tracy-Hepburn chemistry between Ford and Fisher to turn Han Solo and Princess Leia into a glorious romantic sparring

AT-ATs advance toward the defending Alliance troops during the Battle of Hoth.

Princess Leia (Carrie Fisher) and Han Solo (Harrison Ford) kiss.

match. The film also revealed more of Vader's history, who's secret only Lucas knew. This Vader emerged as a disturbing combination of villain and victim, with the revelation he was Luke's father so top secret that not even the actors knew what they were shooting. It also introduced one of the single darkest scenes in the series: Lando Calryssian's betrayal of his friend to the Empire.

The Empire Strikes Back followed Mark Hamill's Luke through his Jedi training and the others through a desperate chase through the galaxies. It was lively, warm, and funny, but it was also in many ways a much darker movie, with some terrifying moments that included a bloody swordfight, a grisly animal death on Planet Hoth, a torture sequence, and then finally, Han Solo's own uncertain fate at the hands of Boba Fett. Lucas had some concerns. "This one doesn't get resolved until the next movie," he recalls. "It wasn't an ending, it was the bad guys win, the good guys went home wounded ... and if a kid saw it when he was nine, he wouldn't see the next one until he was twelve." Lucas even consulted psychiatrists to ensure

that it wasn't too disturbing for kids. The film broke box-office records and received rave reviews, as its predecessor had, although at The New York Times, Maslin did question the violence of some of the scenes. Still fairy tales started out with the Brothers Grimm, who knew that kids are a lot tougher than adults like to think they are, and the film became the second classic of the series. As Charles Champlin wrote: "What can you say about The Empire Strikes Back that has not already been said about the Acropolis, the cotton gin, Ella Fitzgerald's voice, and Star Wars?"

George Lucas, Darth Vader, and Director Irvin Kershner
in Vader's chamber

"The whole process is a guessing game. You guess the script will be good, that the actors will be right, that you'll have enough money to finish the picture and after every scene you guess that this is the scene that will work. It's a helluva way to spend millions of dollars."

— Irvin Kershner

Stuart Freeborn (Makeup and Special Creature Design) working on Yoda, who he modeled after his own face married with Einstein's.

RAIDERS OF THE LOST ARK

Indiana Jones (Harrison Ford) with Marion Ravenwood (Karen Allen).

adventure serials he'd grown up on—an adventuring playboy-archeologist named Indiana Smith.

Spielberg was wise enough not to protest the name Indiana, which was the name of Lucas's malamute. But he put his foot down on Smith, and Lucas agreed to a name change.

Though it's now difficult to imagine anyone but Harrison Ford in what most consider to be the star's most appealing role, the original choice to play Indiana Jones was Tom Selick, who ultimately couldn't sign on because he was locked into the television show *Magnum, P.I.* But Ford had proven his stuff in *The Empire Strikes Back.* As Champlin wrote, "He was the perfect antihero as reluctant hero." For Marion, they hired Karen Allen, a stage actress from New York who made a splash in Philip Kaufman's *The Wanderers*, and whose combination of freckled beauty and spunk was the right fit for a girl whose first scene would require her to drink a 400-pound Nepali under the table and then sock her first love in the jaw. The stellar supporting cast included Alfred Molina as an untrustworthy guide, the Peter Lorre–like Ronald Lacey as the evil Toht, and finally, Jonathan Rhys-Davies as Indy's comrade Sallah. Rhys-Davies was the kind of actor who could deliver a

"Snakes. Why did it have to be snakes?"

— Indiana Jones

STEVEN SPIELBERG HAD ADMIRED GEORGE LUCAS SINCE first seeing *THX 1138* as a student, but by the time *Star Wars* opened, the two men had been close friends for several years. *Raiders of the Lost Ark* was born on a beach: After the *Star Wars* opening, Lucas and Spielberg had escaped for a vacation in Hawaii. As Spielberg tells it, he confided to Lucas that he'd always wanted to make a James Bond picture. "I've got something better," said Lucas, and introduced him to a hero he'd been dreaming of based on the old

"Actually, that's one of the reasons Steven directed the movie and I didn't. Because I didn't want to sit on a sound stage with 1,000 snakes for a week, trying to get that sequence shot."

— George Lucas

George Lucas and Steven Spielberg on the *Raiders* set.

TRIVIA

Phil Kaufman had been an early choice to direct Raiders, *and it was he who suggested that the main character should be seeking the Ark of the Covenant, but when Kaufman got hired to direct* The Outlaw Josey Wales, *Lucas was forced to shelve the project for several years.*

line like "Oh, my friends, I'm so pleased you're not dead!" in a way that felt as if the words were popping up, comic-book style, in bubbles on-screen. The entire film was shot in less than two months, and its heart-thumping verve was driven much less by special effects than by expert stunt work and action footage.

The production process was almost as fast paced as the adventures in the movie. Lucas encouraged the meticulous Spielberg to base his style on old-fashioned moviemaking, like the old Republic series and Bronco Billy films that had years earlier been made at the pace of more than one per week. In response, Spielberg moved quickly, took fewer takes, planned less, and worked more from the hip.

Working with a director he trusted implicitly gave Lucas a chance to avoid spending too much time on set. Instead he could focus on what he loved best, the conceptualizing and editing. "He knows the secret of what an editor can do to a movie," says Spielberg "I would trust George with any movie I ever direct to re-edit in any way he sees fit."

The film was a hit with both audiences and critics. "To get to the point immediately," wrote *New York Times* critic Vincent Canby, "*Raiders of the Lost Ark* is one of the most deliriously funny, ingenious, and stylish American adventure movies ever

made. It is an homage to old-time movie serials and back-lot cheapies that transcends its inspirations to become, in effect, the movie we saw in our imaginations as we watched, say, Buster Crabbe in *Flash Gordon's Trip to Mars* or Sam Katzmans's *Jungle Jim* movies."

Not surprisingly, *Raiders of the Lost Ark* was 1981's highest-grossing film, as well as the best thing to happen to leather jackets since Marlon Brando first rode into town in *The Wild Ones*.

Indiana Jones on a treasure hunt with Satipo (Alfred Molina), his less-than-reliable guide.

STAR WARS: EPISODE VI RETURN OF THE JEDI

AWARDS

ACADEMY AWARDS
5 Nominations / 1 Award

Harrison Ford, Richard Marquand, George Lucas, Howard Kazanjian, and Robert Watts observe the action.

TRIVIA

Blue Harvest was the code name for the film on location, both to avoid getting fleeced by suppliers who saw the Lucas production as a cash cow and as a way of staying incognito to discourage snooping. Even today, hitting the Web site www.blueharvest.com, will bring you directly to the official Star Wars site.

BY THE TIME THEY BEGAN WORKING ON *RETURN OF THE Jedi*, the final chapter of the original *Star Wars* trilogy, the crew at ILM had learned a great deal about how to make special-effects movies, or as the producer said, "We'd learned to build the scale up."

Lucas hired Richard Marquand, the Cambridge-educated director of *Eye of the Needle*, who had to contend with his producer's watchful eye. Marquand joked that the experience was like "trying to direct *King Lear* with Shakespeare in the next room," (and perhaps even more specifically, *King Lear*'s conclusive third act). As Lucas said "one of the advantages of being in the third act is that you get to tie up all the loose ends. But one of the *problems* of the third act is that you have to tie up all those loose ends." The sense of closure for the now world-famous trilogy added an entirely new series of narrative and logistical dilemmas, including a need for absolute secrecy on set, and new hurdles for the F/X crew (especially the final chase scene and the challenge of bringing a magnificently repugnant Jabba the Hutt to life), but the big constraint was the need to build a satisfying conclusion. As Lucas said, the story was now "dictated by everything that came before." The children who had been left hanging on the edge of their seats since Han Solo was frozen in 1980 were now to be given the answers to their questions: Would Solo be saved? What was the connection between Luke and Leia? And, finally, who would win the final confrontation between Darth Vader and Luke Skywalker?

Return of the Jedi opened on May 25, 1983, six years to the day after the premier of *Star Wars*. As Janet Maslin wrote in her extremely positive review in *The New York Times*, "It was a film of endings: an ending for Yoda, for Leia and Han, whose rapid-fire courtship would give way to dewy-eyed love vows, and of course, a conclusion to the ongoing question of how far gone the evil Darth Vader really was, and whether he could ever be redeemed." The final climax had two layers: Luke's confrontation with his father, Anakin Skywalker, and Anakin's confrontation with his "father" the evil Lord Sidious. "The Jedi return to us, at last, older, wiser, and frankly irresistible," wrote Maslin. "In this last of the central cycle, there is a sense of the

ABOVE: Princess Leia (Carrie Fisher) in her slave costume with C-3PO (Anthony Daniels), Jabba the Hutt and Bib Fortuna.
BELOW: Darth Vader (David Prowse) and Luke Skywalker (Mark Hamill) duel with lightsabers in the throne room on the Death Star.

THE CAST

Luke Skywalker	**Mark Hamill**
Han Solo	**Harrison Ford**
Princess Leia Organa	**Carrie Fisher**
Lando Calrissian	**Billy Dee Williams**
C-3PO	**Anthony Daniels**
Darth Vader	**David Prowse**
R2-D2	**Kenny Baker**
Chewbacca	**Peter Mayhew**
Yoda (voice)	**Frank Oz**

closing of the circle, of leaving behind real friends. With 'Jedi' George Lucas may have pulled off the first triple crown of motion pictures."

At the *Los Angeles Times*, Sheila Benson called the final film "fully satisfying." "It gives honest value to all the hopes of its believers," she said. But the series also brought home the understanding that the story belonged to Darth Vader. As Lucas reminds us in *Episode III*, where Vader is first introduced as a loathsome villain, the great demon of the *Star Wars* films was really just a man who made the wrong choices.

Darth Vader: *A small rebel force has penetrated the shield and landed on Endor.*

The Emperor: *Yes, I know.*

Darth Vader: *My son is with them.*

The Emperor: *Are you sure?*

Darth Vader: *I have felt him, my master.*

— from *Return of the Jedi*

The Goblin King Jareth (David Bowie) and Sarah (Jennifer Connelly).

"Jim and I both wanted to work with each other. Labyrinth was a movie nobody wanted—we had to do a real song-and-dance to get people behind it. Everything we've done has been a little bit offbeat."

— George Lucas

LABYRINTH

George Lucas, David Bowie, and Jim Henson.

LABYRINTH WAS DIRECTED BY THE GREAT PUPPET MASTER Jim Henson, and scripted by Monty Python's Terry Jones. The movie starred a very young but already disturbingly beautiful Jennifer Connelly as a novice adventuress, and a just plain disturbing David Bowie as a reluctant villain named The Goblin King.

Connelly plays a girl who is sick of taking care of her baby brother and makes the mistake of wishing—just a little too vehemently—that goblins would come and get him. When the goblins do indeed come to take him away, she is forced to seek him out in the Labyrinth, a sort of Alice in Escherland, full of mazes within mazes, upside-down hallways, and doorways that lead nowhere. She is joined by a gruff sidekick named Hoggle, one of the films most endearing characters and perhaps the most difficult to construct. Hoggle was played by a little person named Shari Weiser, who had to coordinate her performance with the four puppeteers controlling all nineteen motors of Hoggle's face.

The other, only slightly less-loveable labyrinth dweller was David Bowie, a legendary performer whose stylized approach to performance rendered him a perfect counterpoint to the puppets. The Goblin King falls in love with young Connelly and his attempt to win her heart, in a dream within a dream, is one of the films best-realized scenes, when the Labyrinth becomes not just physical place but a surreal state of mind. Another of Bowie's great sequences, showed an extraordinary balance between its live-action characters and its puppeteers. In one dance scene, there were twenty puppets all being operated by several puppeteers, as well as eight to twelve little people in costumes, jumping up and down in harnesses. The scene was chaotic, but fresh, full of a live-action energy that would take more than a decade to approximate in digital film.

Always surprising, if uneven, *Labyrinth* served as a show-case for an art form that today runs the risk of being over-shadowed by digital animation, even though so many contemporary directors of both live-action and animated films (including Lucas), have singled Henson out as a major source of inspiration. As Nina Darnton wrote in *The New York Times*, "It removes storyboard creations from the flat celluloid-cartoon image and makes them three-dimensional, so that they actually come alive and interact with living people. Mr. Henson's creations have put him in the forefront of a development that expands the possibilities of imaginative fantasy that can be transferred onto the screen."

THE CAST

Jareth the Goblin King **David Bowie**
Sarah **Jennifer Connelly**

TRIVIA

Cheryl McFadden (better known as Gates McFadden, the actress who played Dr. Beverly Crusher in Star Trek: The Next Generation*) was one of the choreographers on the film.*

David Bowie as the Goblin King in the Labyrinth.

WILLOW

"Magic is the bloodstream of the universe."

— High Aldwin

THE CAST

Madmartigan	**Val Kilmer**
Sorsha	**Joanne Whalley**
Willow Ufgood	**Warwick Davis**
Queen Bavmorda	**Jean Marsh**
High Aldwin	**Billy Barty**

General Kael rides to Tir Asleen.

RON HOWARD, FORMERLY KNOWN AS OPIE AND RICHIE Cunningham, now known as one of the top directors in Hollywood, had already made several successful movies by the mid-eighties, including *Splash* and *Cocoon*. Lucas considers Howard a kindred spirit and says of their relationship, "We can finish each other's sentences." Howard was Lucas's first choice to bring to life the story of Willow Ufgood, an apparently unremarkable Nelwyn in a mythological land out of a Middle Ages fable.

The story itself owed bits and pieces to the Moses story in the Bible, with an endangered royal child in a river, and to

The Hobbit, with salvation coming from a humble man. As with *Star Wars*, it also drew on a rich pool of mythology. The hero was classic Lucas: an everyman who longs to be a great magician but hasn't yet found his confidence. Ufgood was played by Warwick Davis, a little person who first caught Lucas's eye five years earlier as an ewok in *Return of the Jedi*. "I thought it would be great to use a little person," says Lucas. A lot of my movies are about a little guy against the system, and this was just a more-literal interpretation of that idea."

When Ufgood finds a baby in a stream, he becomes a reluctant hero and sets off to deliver her to safety, with "help" from two tiny and temperamental brownies, Rick Overton and a very young and nearly unrecognizable Kevin Pollak.

Ron Howard's people skills have made him famous for being one of the only directors to work with Russell Crowe without making a permanent enemy. It may well have been Howard's legendary struggles with Val Kilmer on the set of *Willow* that honed his skill. Kilmer played a roguish soldier, half–Han Solo, half-Chewbacca, a gruff and unromantic mercenary who accidentally drinks a love potion which makes him fall desperately, lyrically in love with the daughter of the evil queen Bavmorda. Most reviewers singled him out espe-

Willow (Warwick Davis) seeking the great sorceress Fin Raziel.

ABOVE: **Madmartigan (Val Kilmer) and Sorsha (Joanne Whalley).**
BELOW: **Ron Howard directing** *Willow*.

cially for praise, including Rita Kempley at the *Washington Post*, who called Kilmer "one of America's great screen secrets." But with hindsight, the most important character in the film was probably Fin Raziel, on whom Ufgood cuts his magician's teeth, turning her first into a goat, then an ostrich, then a tortoise, and, finally, a tiger before restoring her to her right human shape. The morphing sequence that resulted was a milestone in digital imaging, and it was Dennis Muren, a key figure at ILM since *The Empire Strikes Back*, along with David Allen and computer programmer Douglas Smythe who developed the digital techniques for the effect. *Willow*, like other Lucasfilm productions, not only told a good story, it advanced the technology of filmmaking and won the Smythe and the Computer Graphics Department at ILM a Technical Achievement Award in 1992 for the "Morf" system—their sixth Sci/Tech Award (out of eighteen awards they would garner by 2003).

AWARDS
ACADEMY AWARDS
2 Nominations

TRIVIA

For the more dangerous scenes, Elora Danan was played by a thirteen-pound animatronics baby with a remote-controlled moveable head and opening mouth.

TUCKER: THE MAN AND HIS DREAM

"I see a number of similarities between Francis and Tucker. I mean they're both very flamboyant and creative. I think Francis's style speaks for itself. He likes innovation, he likes new ideas, he likes interesting cinematic techniques."

— George Lucas

Preston Thomas Tucker (Jeff Bridges).

CONSIDERING LUCAS'S LOVE OF CARS, COPPOLA'S IDENTIfication with larger-than-life personalities, and the appreciation both men share for the idea of the "little man" struggling against corporate America, it's almost a wonder they didn't begin collaborating on the Tucker story earlier. Coppola had been fascinated with both the Tucker car and the story behind it ever since he was 9 years old, attending car shows with his father, and he had even written a play about Tucker while at Hofstra University. He had envisioned several ways of telling Preston Tucker's story: first as a dark *Citizen Kane*–style drama, then as a musical , but it almost didn't get made at all. Pre-production was announced as early as 1976, but it wasn't until 1986, when Lucas agreed to executive produce, that pre-production actually began. Coppola had backed Lucas's 1973 feature *American Graffiti*, and Lucas could now return the favor.

Coppola transformed an essentially tragic story (the real Preston Tucker never did fulfill his promise—he was undone by the coordinated machinations of Ford, Chrysler, and General Motors, who cut off his supply of steel), into a sunny paean to innovation and progress. Working with his old regulars, production designer Dean Tavoularis and cinematographer Vittorio Storaro, Coppola opened the movie with a promotional video which would set the tone for the whole film: bright, sunny, with a big-band soundtrack and the sheen of optimism that we like to associate with an America on the eve of winning the Second World War. As Maslin points out, there is a darkness beneath the optimism—as Coppola knows a future that the relentlessly optimistic Tucker is constitutionally unable to see: even as it is foreshadowed in a meeting with an already ruined and reclusive Howard Hughes. "Just beneath that sunny, stylized exterior...." writes Maslin, "lies a story of disappointment and failure. And the film's compulsive

Tucker shows off a new design concept.

THE CAST

Preston Thomas Tucker	**Jeff Bridges**
Vera Tucker	**Joan Allen**
Abe Karatz/	**Martin Landau**
Voice of Walter Winchell in radio	
Eddie Dean	**Frederic Forrest**
Jimmy Sakuyama	**Mako**
Howard Hughes	**Dean Stockwell**

New cars parade through town.

jauntiness, instead of generating easy irony, gives the film a wistful, bittersweet edge."

Even as the walls close in on the hero (played to the hilt by Jeff Bridges, teeth perfect, dimples in place), Tucker doesn't believe that anything can happen to stop the dream.

Despite several positive reviews, including Maslin's assertion that Tucker was the best film Coppola had made in years, the film did not fare well at the box office, perhaps because beneath its relentlessly optimistic surface lay the glum truth. Tucker lost, and American audiences tend to not like their sweet and their bitter in the same movie.

"If Benjamin Franklin were alive today, he'd be arrested for flying a kite without a license!"

— Preston Tucker

1988

Dr. Elsa Schneider (Alison Doody) kisses Indy (Harrison Ford) while his father (Sean Connery) grimaces.

INDIANA JONES AND THE LAST CRUSADE

AWARDS
ACADEMY AWARDS
3 Nominations / 1 Award
GOLDEN GLOBES
1 Nomination

Prof. Henry Jones: *They're trying to kill us!*

Indiana Jones: *I know, Dad.*

Prof. Henry Jones: *This is a new experience for me.*

Indiana Jones: *It happens to me all the time.*

— from *Indiana Jones and the Last Crusade*

Indy cracks his famous whip while Elsa waits to be saved.

ORIGINALLY, LUCAS WAS INTERESTED IN A HAUNTED-house theme, but Spielberg had had enough of ghosts with his 1982 film *Poltergeist*. Lucas was looking for something deeper, more emotionally rich, and also wanted to bring the series "back to the light" after its dark turn in the second sequel, both in terms of moving the film story forward, and giving some insight into how Indiana Jones became who he was. Instead of introducing a love interest, he brought in a familiar Spielberg theme: the relationship between son and father.

To play young Indy, Harrison Ford suggested River Phoenix, who had played his son in *The Mosquito Coast* and who he thought looked most like him at that age. (The fact that Ford saw a resemblance in Phoenix's delicate, elfin features and his own may be due more to the young actor's talent than any real physical resemblance. Phoenix later said

Steven Spielberg, Harrison Ford, and George Lucas
on location in Venice, Italy .

TRIVIA

Describing his collaborations with Spielberg, Lucas says that the two filmmakers share such a strong common vision that they see exactly eye to eye at least ninety percent of the time, and the other ten percent of the time they defer to each other. Lucas initially opposed the idea of hiring Sean Connery to play Indy's father because he was afraid that the former James Bond would overpower the film, but deferred to Spielberg. Spielberg on the other hand, fresh off Empire of the Sun, wanted to avoid working with children, but Lucas insisted that this time the film's opening action sequence should take place in the past, as an early adventure of Indy as a boy. Spielberg disagreed, but deferred. Two better creative submissions were rarely made.

that he had based his performance on observing Ford on the set of *The Mosquito Coast*, rather than trying to imagine a young Indy). It is a wholly convincing performance, a highlight in the actor's much too short career, and it clears up many of the mysteries of the older Indy, including the story behind the future adventurer's hat, his fear of snakes, his affection for a bullwhip, and even the real-life scar on Jones (and Ford's) chin.

The opening sequence also sets up Indiana's troubled relationship with his distant father, a remote scholar more interested in studying the Holy Grail than in his own son. When Jones, Jr. (we find out in this film that his name really is Henry) whines to his father that he left home early for want of attention, his father snaps, "You left just when you were about to get interesting!"

This time, Indy is hired to find both the Grail and his father. The story balances well the chemistry between the two men, as they battle Nazis on blimps, Nazis in the desert, Nazis in tanks, and one particularly attractive Nazi in a slim wool skirt. The unethical Elsa Schneider (a 23-year-old Irish actress named Alison Doody) provides both an appropriately lovely leading lady for the playboy hero and one of the film's best gags, but by the film's end, even Elsa becomes a sympathetic figure. The choices she and Indiana are forced to make as they decide whether or not to continue pursuing the Holy Grail takes a turn towards tragedy and adds a dimension of regret. With the final episode, Lucas and Spielberg restored the lightness to the series and also added to the depth of its characterizations. This is perhaps what led Caryn James to praise the movie so highly, writing that of the three it would be this last that might "become the sentimental favorite," the *Indiana* to end them all.

THE CAST

Indiana Jones	**Harrison Ford**
Professor Henry Jones	**Sean Connery**
Dr. Marcus Brody	**Denholm Elliott**
Dr. Elsa Schneider	**Alison Doody**
Sallah	**John Rhys-Davies**
Walter Donovan	**Julian Glover**

Indiana Jones meets the grail knight and takes the final test.

STAR WARS: EPISODE I THE PHANTOM MENACE

"Always two there are, no more, no less: a master and an apprentice."

— Yoda

George Lucas directing young Anakin Skywalker (Jake Lloyd).

AWARDS
ACADEMY AWARDS
3 Nominations

"Your imagination is sort of limited by the technology whenever you're telling a story in the cinematic medium."

— George Lucas

WHILE MAKING THE FIRST TWO *STAR WARS* SEQUELS, Lucas had undertaken the formidable task of competing with himself. That was nothing, however, compared with the task of competing with his legend. The children who had grown up on *Star Wars* were now husbands, wives, parents—and film critics, and the prequel was, as Janet Maslin wrote, "pathologically anticipated."

For the long-awaited prequels, Lucas returned to directing. By waiting fourteen years from the release of *Return of the Jedi* in 1983 until the start of production on *The Phantom Menace* in 1997, ILM had pushed technology to the point where Lucas would be able to come much closer to realizing his vision. The new film, the first chapter of Darth Vader's story, would be shot in London, Tunisia, and Italy, but with 1900 of the film's 2200 shots requiring digital effects, it would be "made" in Marin. Ben Burtt was the sound designer and now also co-editor, and John Knoll, Dennis Muren, and Scott Squires headed three separate teams handling the visual effects. It would be the longest post-production period of any Lucas movie to date.

Lucas focused on Anakin Skywalker's early years in slavery and his first encounter with the Jedi Knights. Twenty years earlier, he had flouted convention by viewing the world through the eyes of two droids : C-3PO and R2D2 (in a nod to *The Hidden Fortress*). This time, even though he intended the prequels to be more somber than *Episodes IV*, *V*, and *VI*, he

Queen Amidala's decoy (Kiera Knightley) with her royal handmaidens, including Amidala (Natalie Portman) in disguise.

Qui-Gon Jinn (Liam Neeson) and Obi-Wan Kenobi (Ewan McGregor) in the underwater city Otoh Gunga.

told the story from the point of view of a boy. Lucas recalls feeling grateful that there was no one left to be accountable to but himself. "I remember saying "Boy, am I glad I'm not making this for a studio, because they'd never let me make this film, never.... You'd never take your lead character in a film like *Star Wars* and make him a 10-year-old boy. That's death."

It was the "Portrait of The Villain as a Young Boy." 10-year-old Jake Lloyd, with his stoic face and round, chubby cheeks, was not a likely candidate for the future symbol of evil he was to become, but then children never are. The whole film had the sense of something bright and clean that was about to undergo a fall. The Republic, not yet the bleak rundown world of the first trilogy, which had been made decrepit and ramshackle by twenty-two years of war, was still lush and prosperous, and the movie's most thrilling chase scene was not a fight to the death but a competitive pod race. Scottish actor Ewan McGregor played a young, impetuous Obi-Wan Kenobi. He was joined by Liam Neeson as Obi-Wan's master, Natalie Portman as Princess Amidala, and martial-arts expert Ray Park as the evil Darth Maul. Anthony Daniels and Frank Oz reprised their roles as C-3PO and Yoda.

The Phantom Menace did more than any film before it to integrate digital and live-action filmmaking, introducing the all-digital character Jar Jar Binks, and opening the door for movies like *Lord of the Rings* and *Harry Potter*. The magic had returned. Roger Ebert called it "an astonishing achievement in imaginative filmmaking" and Maslin wrote in *The New York Times*: "Whether dreaming up blow-dryer-headed soldiers who move in lifelike formation or a planet made entirely of skyscrapers, Mr. Lucas still champions wondrous visions over bleak ones and sustains his love of escapist fun. There's no better tour guide for a trip to other worlds."

Obi-Wan Kenobi, Darth Maul (Ray Park), and Qui-Gon Jinn engage in a lightsaber battle in Theed's central hangar.

THE CAST

Qui-Gon Jinn	**Liam Neeson**
Obi-Wan Kenobi	**Ewan McGregor**
Queen Padmé Naberrie Amidala	**Natalie Portman**
Anakin Skywalker	**Jake Lloyd**
Sen. Palpatine/Darth Sidious	**Ian McDiarmid**
C-3PO	**Anthony Daniels**
R2-D2	**Kenny Baker**
Shmi Skywalker	**Pernilla August**
Yoda (voice)	**Frank Oz**

Ben Burtt with the Jedi Kit Fisto on the set of
Star Wars: Episode II – Attack of the Clones.

BEN BURTT was a graduate student at USC when Lucas recruited him to do sound for his new space Western. It was Burtt who imagined and then concocted R2-D2's endearing chirps, the roaring of the Millennium Falcon, the ripping of guns in the vacuum of space, and of course Darth Vader's ominous breathing. Since then the kid from USC worked on and off for Lucasfilm for thirty years. On *Star Wars: A New Hope* he is credited as "Creator of Robot and Creature Voices" but he has also given us the buzz of the lightsaber, the rolling boulder in *Raiders of the Lost Ark*—and even the voice of ET. Burtt has directed two feature IMAX films, edited pictures at Lucasfilm since 1992, and written

The Neimoidians cower before Darth Sidious's hologram.

TV scripts. He has been nominated for eight Academy Awards and won four.

Here are some of the greatest Ben Burtt trademark sounds, and where they started:

Chewbacca: Chewbacca's voice is a mix of whimpers, barks, and growls from several animals, including lions, walruses, and one particularly significant bear from a zoo in Tehachapi, California. The bear's name was Pooh.

The boulder at the beginning of *Raiders of the Lost Ark*: The sound was produced by the tires of a Honda Civic crunching gravel as it coasted down a road at Skywalker Ranch.

Jabba the Hutt: Jabba-speak is based on an imitation of the sounds that make up a real Peruvian dialect called Quechua. The rubbing of wet towels inside a mud-filled garbage can was used to enhance Jabba's movement. Additional sound produced by squishing macaroni and cheese in a bowl were used for Jabba's movement as he spoke.

The closing of Ark of the Covenant: The sound of a toilet lid being dropped into place.

STAR WARS: EPISODE II ATTACK OF THE CLONES

Anakin Skywalker: *You're the closest thing I have to a father.*
Obi-Wan Kenobi: *Then why don't you listen to me?*

— from *Attack of the Clones*

Jedi Yoda (Frank Oz) with lightsaber in hand in the Secret Hangar on Geonosis readies for battle.

A*TTACK OF THE CLONES* INTRODUCED THE CANADIAN actor Hayden Christensen, as the teenaged Anakin Skywalker, a combination of fierce fighter, rebellious teen and conflicted Jedi whose passions, both for the beautiful Princess Amidala and for revenge and glory, would one day lead him to the dark side of the Force. It boasted grand, new special effects, a more comfortable and more Obi-wan–like

Ewan McGregor, and the forbidden love between Luke and Leia's doomed future parents. For the most part it won kudos even from critics who had had problems with *The Phantom Menace*, and introduced ever more glorious and well-executed background sets. Anakin Skywalker moved further toward his doom, partly though the error of his ways but also largely by the machinations of the film's real villain, the power hungry Senator Palpatine.

But for the loyal fans who had grown up on the saga, the film's triumph could be summed up in one glorious, exhilarating, breathtaking, foot-pumping, spine-tingling, adjective-spawning scene: The Ascension of Yoda.

It had always bothered Lucas that Yoda, the great master fighter, the teacher of all teachers, couldn't move from the waist down. His prowess as a warrior had always been alluded to, but with CGI not yet advanced enough to render him as well or as effectively as Frank Oz's puppetry, audiences had

Jedi fight for their lives and the future of the galaxy in the Execution Arena on Geonosis.

Obi-Wan Kenobi (Ewan McGregor) inspects the clone hatchery on Kamino.

never had a chance to see it, and as Lucas put it bluntly, Yoda basically ambled through the series "with a hand up his ass."

Whether he could ever be free from that hand was still open to question. While making *Phantom Menace*, Lucas had declared the first all-CGI Yoda "unready." Ron Coleman and his team had spent three years back in the shop, and this time they presented Lucas with a revamped scene from *The Empire Strikes Back* in which a CG Yoda explains the meaning of the Force to Luke. This time around, the director was impressed.

"In the script," explains Lucas, "it just says, two-and-a-half-foot-high green frog fights six-foot-high, uh, vampire." But on-screen, thanks to the F/X crew who took to heart Yoda's own dictum, "Do or do not. There is no try." The vampire doesn't stand a chance. Yoda whirls, leaps, dives, and ducks like a demon. And for the audiences, *Attack of the Clones* not only struck at the heart of the excitement of the *Star Wars* phenomenon, but also gave the so-called grown-ups in the audience a chance to reconnect with what had always made the films so loveable in the first place. "When the now-computerized Yoda reveals his martial artistry," wrote *Time* magazine's Roger Corliss, "the film ascends to a kinetic life so teeming that even cranky adults may rediscover the quivering kid inside. That child doesn't think about the labor that went into all those cyber saber dances. He doesn't think at all. He just stares up in innocent awe, at one with movie magic."

THE CAST

Obi-Wan Kenobi	**Ewan McGregor**
Senator Padmé Amidala	**Natalie Portman**
Anakin Skywalker	**Hayden Christensen**
Sen. Palpatine/Darth Sidious	**Ian McDiarmid**
Mace Windu	**Samuel L. Jackson**
Count Dooku/Darth Tyranus	**Christopher Lee**
C-3PO	**Anthony Daniels**
R2-D2	**Kenny Baker**
Yoda (voice)	**Frank Oz**

C-3PO (Anthony Daniels) and R2-D2 (Kenny Baker)
witness the wedding of Anakin Skywalker (Hayden Christensen)
and Padmé Amidala (Natalie Portman).

Darth Vader (Hayden Christensen) on the bridge of the Death Star.

"Henceforth, you shall be known as...Darth Vader."

— Darth Sidious

STAR WARS: EPISODE III REVENGE OF THE SITH

George Lucas, Director (center) with cast Hayden Christensen (Anakin Skywalker), Natalie Portman (Senator Padmé Amidala), and Ewan McGregor (Obi-Wan Kenobi) and crew Rick McCallum (Producer) on Stage 2 during the filming of the final *Star Wars* movie, *Revenge of the Sith*.

GEORGE LUCAS HAS VOWED THAT *REVENGE OF THE Sith*, the story of Anakin's fall, will be the last full-length feature in the *Star Wars* saga. Though it takes place midway through the series chronologically, it still carries the weight and heft of a conclusion—not only because the children who grew up on *Star Wars* are, indeed, now a bit long in the tooth, but also because the story feels less like adventure now than fate. And if the story had new added dimension, ILM had never been so ready to tell it.

Excellent special effects are like excellent service in a French restaurant: Their job is to not be noticed. With *Revenge of the Sith*, George Lucas and his team at ILM have achieved that level of excellence. If some of the joy of the first trilogy was watching the story be told in ever wilder and more visually exhilarating ways, much of the suspense of the first two prequels can be attributed to American filmgoers' troubled relationship with the viability of digital cinema. Audiences anticipated the final movie with the question: Will he pull it off? With *Revenge of the Sith* we see American digital cinema nearing full transparency, and the suspense goes back where it belongs: in the story. Even Lucas has admitted there isn't much left to invent: "We have fire and a few little things to sort out, but with this one, in terms of the technology and everything it's just a matter of using it to tell a story, and we don't actually have to invest too much."

Also working to the film's advantage were actors who now had much more experience acting to a blue screen. This time Hayden Christensen brought a new ferocity to Anakin's inevitable journey to the dark side. An older and more relaxed Ewan McGregor was uncannily believable as a younger Alec Guinness. Ian McDiarmid, who played the Emperor Palpatine with a delicious sneer lurking in his eye, never actually licked his lips, but we felt as if he's just about to. As for the story, it ascended to pure tragedy, as A.O. Scott wrote in a review in which he declared the film "nothing short of breathtaking. We are witnessing a flawed hero devolving into a cruel and terrifying villain. It is a measure of the film's accomplishment that this process is genuinely upsetting."

Scott went on to place the film in its complete saga: "But of course the rise of the Empire and the perdition of Anakin Skywalker are not the end of the story, and the inverted chronology turns out to be the most profound thing about the *Star Wars* epic. Taken together, and watched in the order they were made, the films reveal the cyclical nature of history, which seems to repeat itself even as it moves forward. Democracies swell into empires, empires are toppled by revolutions, fathers abandon their sons, and sons find their fathers. Movies end. Life goes on."

As of this writing, on a constant-dollar basis all six of the *Star Wars* films rank in the top fifty films of all time, having brought in a combined $3.5 billion at the domestic box office. The curtains close on the film with a sigh of bittersweet relief. The story is told. We can all grow up now.

THE CAST

Obi-Wan / Ben Kenobi	**Ewan McGregor**
Senator Amidala / Padmé Naberrie-Skywalker	**Natalie Portman**
Anakin Skywalker / Lord Darth Vader	**Hayden Christensen**
Supreme Chancellor / Emperor Palpatine / Darth Sidious	**Ian McDiarmid**
Mace Windu	**Samuel L. Jackson**
Count Dooku / Darth Tyranus	**Christopher Lee**
C-3PO	**Anthony Daniels**
R2-D2	**Kenny Baker**
Yoda (voice)	**Frank Oz**

ABOVE: **Obi-Wan Kenobi (Ewan McGregor) battles General Grievous on Utapau.** OVERLEAF: **The nightscape on Coruscant.**

"There are heroes on both sides. Evil is everywhere."

— from Opening Prologue

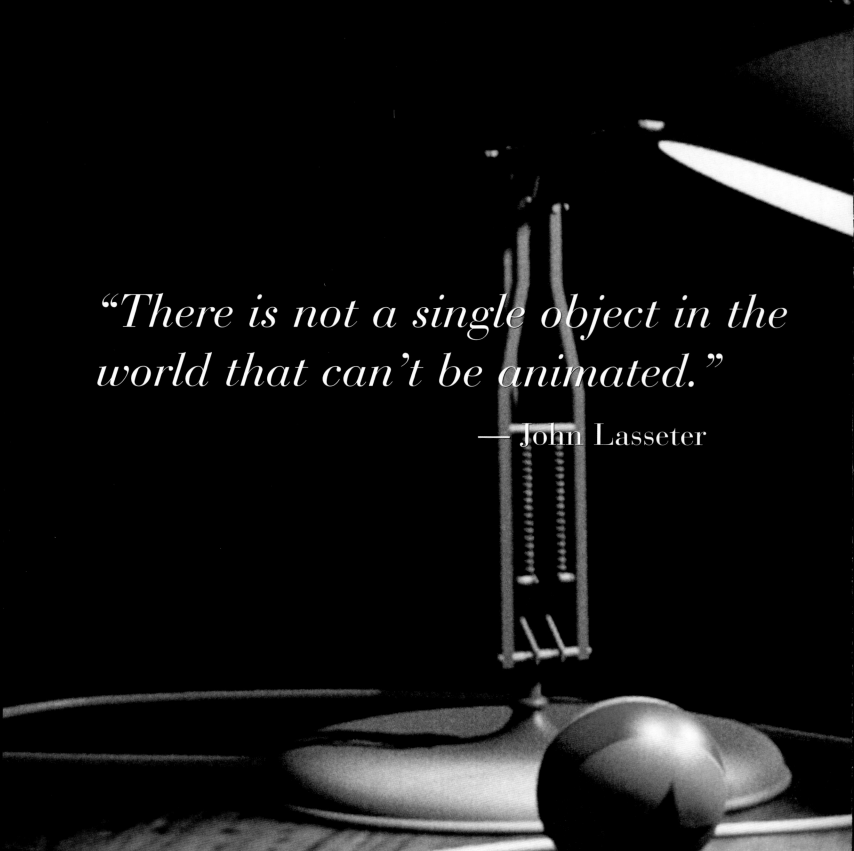

"There is not a single object in the world that can't be animated."

— John Lasseter

PIXAR
ANIMATION
STUDIOS

In 1995, Steve Jobs, the charismatic co-founder of Apple computer, extolled the virtues of his first full-length feature, which was being made by a small company he'd bought from George Lucas a decade earlier: He announced that his movie company, the "first digital studio," sported "far and away the best animation and artistic talent in the whole world." In the case of this particular studio, and this particular movie, Job's statement held true: The movie was *Toy Story*, in its own way as significant for the Bay Area's place in film history as *The Godfather* and *Star Wars* were in the seventies. The world's first fully digital animated feature film, *Toy Story* was also one of the warmest, wittiest, and most sophisticated movies in years, animated or otherwise, and also had the biggest cumulative domestic box office of all 1995 film releases, beating out both Jim Carrey's *Ace Ventura* sequel and the latest movie of the *Batman* franchise. Its heroes, an old-fashioned cowboy doll named Woody and a tricked-out space ranger named Buzz Lightyear, begin as rivals and end up buddies, and their reconciliation is a perfect metaphor for the company's philosophy that technology never trumps heart.

The mantra at Pixar has always been "Story is king." In almost every public interview they have given since revolutionizing the field in the eighties, its directors and animators have insisted that, despite their many technical innovations (as of 2005 Pixar had forty-two patents to its name), their priority has always been creating plots and characters that amuse and entertain audiences. But this mantra is something so often glibly repeated by studio heads that even Ed Catmull, Pixar's president, recognizes it as an empty cliché: "It's what you do that matters."

In the doing, Pixar is on firm ground. Over the past ten years, they have produced a steady stream of technologically innovative and emotionally satisfying movies. Rather than follow Disney's lead and adapt existing fairy tales and world folklore into their films, Pixar creates original stories: toys that spring to life the moment their owners leave the room; monsters that live not in our closets but in a world beyond them; superheroes with homework and chores; an ant colony as intricate and varied as the daydreams of any amateur entomologist who ever lost hours watching an anthill on a spring day; and fish that are as bewildered by the ocean's depths as we are.

PORTFOLIO

Academy Award Nominations	**23**
Academy Awards	**8**
Academy Scientific and Technical Achievement Awards	**10**
Golden Globe Nominations	**6**
Golden Globe Awards	**1**

MILESTONES

1986
Steve Jobs purchases the Computer Graphics Division from Lucasfilm Ltd. for $5 million, investing an additional $5 million in his new company. *Luxo Jr.* premieres at SIGGRAPH.

1987
Luxo Jr. receives an Academy Award nomination for Best Animated Short Film. The short film *Red's Dream* premieres at SIGGRAPH.

1988
The short film *Tin Toy* premieres at SIGGRAPH.

1989
Pixar makes its first commercial, *Wake Up*, for Tropicana. *Tin Toy* wins an Academy Award for Best Animated Short Film. The short film *Knick Knack* premieres at SIGGRAPH.

1990
Pixar moves to their new Point Richmond offices and creates five new commercials: California Lottery's *Dancing Cards*, Trident's *Quite a Package*, Lifesavers' *Babies*, Volkswagen's *La Nouvelle Polo*, and Pillsbury's *Plump*.

1991
Steve Jobs makes a deal with the Walt Disney Studios to develop and produce three feature-length animated films. *Toy Story* will be their first feature film. They win the first of many Academy of Motion Picture Arts & Sciences Scientific and Technical Awards.

1992
Pixar makes nine commercials. They win a second Scientific and Technical Award, this time for the development of RenderMan software.

Ed Catmull, Steve Jobs, and John Lasseter, the men whose shared vision propelled Pixar to a string of successes starting with 1995's *Toy Story*.

In doing so, they have humanized digital filmmaking and reinvigorated the art form of animation.

This is what they've done. As for how they did it, the roots go back twenty years when three men—Steve Jobs, Ed Catmull, and John Lasseter—came together with a shared vision to build a world-class animation studio.

John Lasseter was born in Whittier, California, in 1957, the son of a high school art teacher and a parts manager for a car dealership. He first began dreaming of a career in animation after stumbling upon Bob Thomas's classic *The Art of Animation* in his school library. He started writing letters to Disney, and by lucky coincidence, the year he graduated high school was also the year that Disney started its animation program at the California Institute for the Arts in Valencia, California—known for short as CalArts. Lasseter was only the second student admitted to the nascent program, but just as UCLA and USC had been breeding grounds for a new generation of filmmakers in the late sixties and early seventies, CalArts was destined to do the same for a new crop of innovators: That first year included Lasseter's classmates Henry

Selick, Brad Bird, and Tim Burton, and succeeding classes would later send dozens of top animators to Disney, Pixar, and PDI. After graduation Lasseter was hired by Disney, where he spent five years working on traditional hand-drawn animation for films, such as *The Fox and the Hound* (1981) and *Mickey's Christmas Carol* (1983). CGI (computer-generated imagery) was already being used in background shots for hand-drawn films, but it was 1982's *Tron*, which had fifteen minutes and 235 scenes of computer-generated images, that first thrilled the young Lasseter. "I thought, this is incredible—this is amazing," says Lasseter. "And it wasn't what I was [literally] seeing. It was the potential of what I was seeing."

Meanwhile, at Lucasfilm, George Lucas had started a computer division in 1979, hiring Ed Catmull away from his position as director of the computer graphics lab at the New York Institute of Technology to bring more computer expertise into the film industry. Catmull put together a stellar team, which produced the seminal computer animation for *Star Trek II: The Wrath of Khan* (1982). In 1983, Lasseter joined the team at the request of Alvy Ray Smith, Director of Computer Graphics Research at Lucasfilm and worked on *Young Sherlock Holmes* (1985). In order to show their stuff at SIG-GRAPH 84, the graphics industry's biggest annual convention, the decision was made to create what would prove a landmark in digital animation—a little film called *The Adventures of André and Wally B.* The short, just two minutes long, revolutionized the medium.

Lucas sold Catmull's division to Steve Jobs in 1986, and the group took the Pixar name with them. To this day, the two companies have a close relationship, one which Lasseter sees as a prime example of the general "we're in it together" spirit of the Bay Area film community: "George is so proud of Pixar. We're very close; we're separate companies, but we're very close, and he's always been really proud and really supportive of us—I've really admired that. And we always use their post-production facility because they're the best in the world. In fact, our theater here at Pixar uses THX because we wanted the best theater on the planet."

But in 1986 the fledgling company could barely afford office space, much less a theater. Fortunately, Steve Jobs invested millions more into the company, and perhaps more importantly, he

1993
Pixar makes nine commercials and an IBM logo.

1994
Pixar makes eleven commercials and a Paramount logo.

1995
Toy Story is released on Thanksgiving weekend, becoming the highest grossing film of that year. Pixar goes public with an initial offering of 6.9 million shares at $22 per share.

1996
Pixar makes nine commercials. John Lasseter is given the Special Achievement Award at the Oscars "for his inspired leadership of the Pixar Toy Story team..." Buzz and Woody make an appearance at the awards show.

1997
Pixar and Disney revise their agreement to jointly produce five movies. They dissolve their commercials and interactive-software units to focus entirely on narrative filmmaking and expand to a second building in Point Richmond with a staff of 375.

1998
Geri's Game wins an Academy Award for Best Animated Short Film. *A Bug's Life* is released and breaks all previous Thanksgiving weekend box-office records in the U.S.

1999
Production begins on *Monsters Inc. Toy Story 2* is released.

2000
Pixar moves to its new offices at 1200 Park Avenue, Emeryville, the old headquarters of the Del Monte Company. *For the Birds* premieres at

The landmark short film, *The Adventures of André and Wally B.*

Pixar Animation Studios in Emeryville, CA.

Like the shorts before them, these films were enormously expensive to produce, and Pixar's deal with Disney gave the upstart production company the financial backing it needed. But as Pixar became more successful Jobs, Catmull, and Lasseter, avoided the pitfalls of quick growth and tried to keep creativity and collaboration as much a driving force in the company as they could. "As I see it," Lasseter is fond of saying, "if I'm having fun, then it gives the rest of the crew permission to have fun too." In 2000, they abandoned the Point Richmond offices and built a new home for the company in Emeryville, just outside San Francisco, which looks like a high-tech fantasy loft for 10-year-old boys—with scooters, foosball tables, tiki lounges, a swimming pool, and even "secret" rooms—but their commitment to a spirit of creative collaboration extends beyond interior design and furniture.

Perhaps one of the significant examples of that commitment is the company's in-house education program, Pixar University, where everyone from Catmull on down takes classes outside their specialization, in everything from improvisation and sculpture to computer design. The challenge, explains Randy Nelson, Dean of Pixar University, is to "do art as a team sport." The classes are designed to encourage creative growth, and also to help people overcome their fears of failing in front of peers and superiors. As Nelson puts it, "You have to honor failure, because failure is just the negative space around success."

A SELECTION OF PIXAR SHORT FILMS

FOR THE BIRDS (2000)

For the Birds tells the amusing story of a flock of small birds perched upon a telephone wire and what happens when an unwelcome larger bird attempts to join them.

LUXO JR. (1986)

Luxo Jr. is the story of a lamp and its offspring, who is always getting into trouble.

MIKE'S NEW CAR (2002)

In *Mike's New Car*, all Mike wants is to give his pal Sulley a ride to show off his brand-new car. But everything works against Mike as his beautiful new car turns into his worst enemy.

RED'S DREAM (1987)

Red's Dream reveals what philosophers and poets have long wondered: What do unicycles dream about on rainy nights?

BOUNDIN' (2003)

When a lamb's lustrous coat—along with his pride—is sheared for the first time, it takes a wise jackalope to teach him that it's what's inside that will help him rebound from life's troubles.

TIN TOY (1988)

Looking at the world through the perspective of toys, *Tin Toy* tells the humorous story of a windup toy's first encounter with a playful baby. This concept served as the inspiration for Pixar's first feature film, *Toy Story*.

KNICK KNACK (1989)

Knick Knack follows the adventures of a hapless snowman enticed to escape his glass snow globe by partying vacation souvenirs.

JACK-JACK ATTACK (2005)

Kari the babysitter spends a harrowing night with the littlest Incredible, baby Jack-Jack, as he discovers his superpowered talents for the first time.

GERI'S GAME (1997)

Geri's Game tells the tale of an old gentleman who loves to play chess in the park—usually against himself. He manages to win every time, even if it means cheating.

ONE MAN BAND (2005)

With one coin to make a wish at a piazza fountain, *One Man Band* tells the tale of a peasant girl who encounters two competing street performers who'd prefer the coin find its way into their tip jars.

Buzz (Tim Allen) is confronted by Woody (Tom Hanks) about his delusions of being a real space ranger.

"That wasn't flying, that was falling with style."

— Woody

TOY STORY

AN AVID COLLECTOR, JOHN LASSETER HAD ALWAYS wanted to make a feature film about children's toys, and as a huge fan of live-action buddy movies like *Midnight Run* and *The Odd Couple*, he wanted to tell one of his own, and make something entirely new. "The great Disney classics were remakes of fairy tales," he explains. "One of the things we didn't want to do was a fairy tale with a main character, a lot of side characters, and eight songs. We wanted to do something different."

Pixar's first pitch to Disney was a short scene with Woody playing a rather nasty trick on gullible Buzz. The characters were already well realized visually, but as people, they still had a long way to go. (Today the filmmakers credit actors Tom Hanks and Tim Allen with fleshing out the characters and bringing in the warmth we now associate with them). Disney greenlighted the film, but Lasseter remembers a Hollywood executive asking, "OK, so where are we going to put the eight songs?"—another reference to the old Disney template. For *Toy Story* the filmmakers went a different route, choosing

instead a soundtrack similar to the coherent background soundtracks of Cat Stevens in *Harold and Maude*, or the Simon and Garfunkel songs in *The Graduate*. The ensuing collaboration with respected songwriter and composer Randy Newman proved magical, extending over four films and producing a steady stream of awards and nominations.

Still, much of the drama and glamour in live-action filmmaking lore comes from the happy accidents and near disasters of working in real time, with brilliant and neurotic actors, fading afternoon light, and inclement weather. One thinks of

Buzz greeting what he believes to be aliens.

Howard Hughes spending $18,000 a day waiting for clouds to film the fight scenes for *Hell's Angels*, or Marlon Brando's inspired use of the orange peels to engage his 3-year-old costar in what became one of the most famous death scenes in film history in *The Godfather*. Because in animation it can take days to produce just a single frame, the creative process follows a different trajectory, one which begins with wild story brainstorms and then moves to a meticulously plotted and convincing demo reel, in which the movie is pre-visualized before the animation even starts. The core writing team, Lasseter, Andrew Stanton, Pete Docter, and Joe Ranft, spent two years plotting out the story for their first feature, and then more than another two years working with their animation team to push the art form far enough to match the story, one which most Americans now know by heart: Woody, a talking cowboy rag doll, who has been the favored plaything of his beloved owner, is now in danger of being upstaged by newcomer Buzz Lightyear, an ultramodern space action figure complete with lights, stun gun, hinged helmet, and the backing of his own television show. The twist: Buzz himself doesn't know he's a toy, and he thinks he's been waylaid in the middle of a space mission. As the rivals battle each other, a naughty next-door neighbor, and their own internal demons, their struggles resonate with both adults and children. Woody's fear of losing the love of Andy, his owner, is as recognizable to a 5-year-old with a new baby brother as it is to a salesman fearing obsolescence at work, and Buzz's agony when he discovers the truth of his identity is a dark existential moment that would rock Sartre back on his heels: How many of us have believed we were here

Woody and Buzz in a dramatic chase scene.

on an important mission that might change the shape of human history and then woke with a shock to discover that our only real mission to was to learn to love and be loved in return? And how many of us ever really recovered?

From start to finish, the film took five years to make, but the final product, released in 1995, took even the filmmakers by surprise. *Toy Story* was the highest grossing feature of the 1995 releases with almost $200 million in cumulative domestic box office, and immediately established Pixar as a revolutionary force. Critics fell over themselves to praise the film's style, humor, and heart. Roger Ebert called it "a visionary roller-coaster ride." Janet Maslin wrote in *The New York Times*, "Thanks to exultant wit and so many distinctive voices, *Toy Story* is both an aural and visual delight." Lasseter was awarded a 1996 Special Achievement Oscar for the film.

THE CAST

Woody	**Tom Hanks**
Buzz Lightyear	**Tim Allen**
Mr. Potato Head	**Don Rickles**
Slinky Dog	**Jim Varney**
Rex the Green Dinosaur	**Wallace Shawn**
Hamm the Piggy Bank	**John Ratzenberger**
Bo Peep	**Annie Potts**
Andy Davis	**John Morris**
Sid	**Erik von Detten**
Andy's Mom	**Laurie Metcalf**
Sergeant	**R. Lee Ermey**
Hannah	**Sarah Freeman**

TRIVIA

The books on the shelves depicted in Toy Story *all bear the titles of the short films that preceded them—Red's Dream, Knick Knack, Tin Toy— as an homage to all those short films that helped the team at Pixar develop the chops for their first feature film.*

THE CAST

James P. "Sulley" Sullivan	**John Goodman**
Mike Wazowski	**Billy Crystal**
Boo/Mary	**Mary Gibbs**
Randall Boggs	**Steve Buscemi**
Henry J. Waternoose III	**James Coburn**
Celia	**Jennifer Tilly**
Roz	**Bob Peterson**
Yeti	**John Ratzenberger**
Fungus	**Frank Oz**
Needleman/Smitty	**Daniel Gerson**
Floor Manager	**Steve Susskind**
Flint	**Bonnie Hunt**

TRIVIA

One of animation's great advantages over live action is the spontaneity and naturalness of the youngest voice actors, who perform without the self-consciousness of having a camera in their faces. Mary Gibbs, the toddler who played Boo, wouldn't even sit still for her sessions in the recording studio, so the filmmakers just followed her around with a microphone and spliced her "performance" together later in the editing room.

MONSTERS, INC.

"We Scare Because We Care"

—Waternoose

PIXAR'S FOURTH FEATURE WAS SPEARHEADED BY PETE Docter, one the youngest members of their creative team, and co-directed by Lee Unkrich and Simpsons alumnus David Silverman. Its plot sprung from a simple question: Why do the monsters in our closet need to scare us? In this case, the answer lies somewhere between *Where the Wild Things Are* and *The Chronicles of Narnia*...on the other side of the closet door, in the city of Monstropolis.

Monstropolis runs on children's screams, and those screams are collected by the professional scarers who work the closet doors manufactured by Monsters, Inc.—popping into our world to do their jobs and popping back in to make

James P. "Sulley" Sullivan (John Goodman) is horrified to find Boo (Mary Gibbs) in Monstropolis.

A production sketch of Monstropolis.

their daily quotas. The top scarers at Monsters, Inc. are city heroes, and perhaps the most revered of them all is a big purple-and-aqua fur ball named James P. Sullivan, or Sulley, whose daily scream count is the highest in the business. Into his world, complete with enigmatic boss, slimy coworker, and trusty sidekick, comes the most dreaded contagion in all Monstropolis: a 2-year-old girl from the other side of the closet door, whom Sulley appropriately nicknames Boo.

The relationship between Sulley and Boo develops as one would expect, adorably, which contrasts with the sharp and snappy dialogue between John Goodman as Sulley and Billy Crystal as his best friend, Mike Wazowski. But from the point of view of story, what differentiated Monsters, Inc. from even Pixar's most sophisticated prior films were the thrills of the action sequences, especially a dazzling climax in the door vault, which was so complex that it had to be storyboarded thirty-six times.

That scene was child's play compared to the problems of character design. Hair and fur are among the most difficult things to animate, and Sulley had been designed with over

2 million strands of it. The solution: The animators worked with a bald Sulley, and the hair was added later with a proprietary software tool the team developed especially for Monsters, Inc. "The technical artists may grumble a little bit," says Lasseter, "but they love being challenged."

The effort was handsomely rewarded, with Monsters, Inc. topping once again Pixar's own box-office records, and further crumbling the distinctions between "adult" and "family" entertainment. Polls showed that more than forty percent of the opening-weekend ticket buyers were adults without children. "Pixar has created a genre that others merely imitate," wrote Elvis Mitchell in The New York Times, and added, "What makes Monsters, Inc. so wonderful is that it's about scream deficit, yet all great cartoons are powered by screams. It's a tribute to noise, so how can you not fall in love with it?"

Pals Mike (Billy Crystal) and Sulley on a typical work day.

TRIVIA

With "If I Didn't Have You," a song he wrote for Monsters, Inc., *Randy Newman finally broke his record-making streak of sixteen Academy Award nominations without wins.*

"If witnesses are to be believed, there has been a child-security breach for the first time in monster history!"

—Newscaster

AWARDS

ACADEMY AWARDS
4 Nominations / 1 Award

2001

FINDING NEMO

"You know, for a clown fish, he really isn't that funny."

—Tad's father

Nathan Stanton's storyboards based on character studies of the diver.

As part of the research for *Finding Nemo*, Director Andrew Stanton sent his crew to the Great Barrier Reef and required them to get certified in scuba diving. That was the fun part. There were also countless hours spent with oceanography professors, filming underwater at the Pixar pool, and even scanning dead fish into computers for study. One major challenge was rendering the water, which had not yet been animated convincingly in a CGI feature film. "Our first test," said Oren Jacob, the film's supervising technical director, "looked like a chlorinated swimming pool, or a foggy day on a heath somewhere in Scotland." Their next tests, however, were perfect reproductions of underwater camera work, but moved too far in the other direction, towards photo-realism. "We want you to believe that it exists," said Stanton, but "we also want you to believe that you are in a make-believe world."

The next hurdle was mastering the new physics of swimming. From action figures to toys to monsters and bugs, Pixar animators had proven they could handle anything that walked, but to depict swimming was one of the new, unexpected challenges, like designing expressive characteristics for a species that has no eyebrows. There was also the tricky parallel structure of the plot: A timid clownfish named Marlin races across the ocean to find his young son, Nemo, while Nemo and his captive friends plot their own escape from a fish tank in Sydney, Australia. The filmmakers had to be sure to make both narratives equally compelling to keep the audience invested in both, as father and son fought to come back together, both

AWARDS
ACADEMY AWARDS
4 Nominations / 1 Award
GOLDEN GLOBES
1 Nomination

Gill (Willem Dafoe) and Nemo (Alexander Gould) in the fish tank.

TRIVIA

Dory, the absent-minded blue fish, may be the most true-to-life character in the movie, because she's based on scientists' assumption that fish really do work with just a thirty-second memory-span. Over the course of the film, Dory manages to call young Nemo by almost every name except his own, including Fabio, Elmo, Bingo, Chico, and Harpo.

Dory (Ellen DeGeneres) and Nemo's father, Marlin (Albert Brooks), in the Big Blue.

literally and metaphorically. Stanton and Co-director Unkrich took to driving down to L.A. for recording sessions rather than flying, and would use their hours in the car to work through thorny moments balancing the two stories.

The result is perhaps the most visually enthralling Pixar movie to date, as well as a moving and thoughtful tale of love, fear, and letting go, all framed by an opening nightmare, the likes of which hadn't been seen in an animated film since Bambi lost his mother to a hunter in 1942. Marlin's fears are not imaginary or exaggerated—the ocean is exactly as dangerous as Marlin thinks it is, and as a father, he has to learn to let his son explore it anyway. Much like the sadness in *Toy Story*, there is a sadness at the film's core: the weight of love. That weight is of course lightened by stellar performances from Albert Brooks as Marlin, Willem Dafoe as Gill, a Papillion-styled tank inmate intent on escape at all costs, and finally Ellen DeGeneres's showstopping turn as Dory, the warm-hearted sidekick with short-term memory loss. The film's best vocal performance, however, may have been Stanton himself, as a sage surfer-dude seaturtle named Crush.

The film broke box-office records and sparked critical adulation. Perhaps the most enthusiastic fan of the film was *Slate.com's* Dave Edelstein. "You can sense that every frame,"

he wrote, "contains hundreds of decisions about light and color and movement—and, more to the point, they're all inspired decisions!" But he also lavished praise on the humor and wisdom of the story: "You could trawl the seven seas and not net a funnier, more beautiful, and more original work of art and comedy than *Finding Nemo*."

THE CAST

Marlin	**Albert Brooks**
Dory	**Ellen DeGeneres**
Nemo	**Alexander Gould**
Gill	**Willem Dafoe**
Bloat	**Brad Garret**
Peach	**Allison Janney**
Gurgle	**Austin Pendleton**
Bubbles	**Stephen Root**
Deb/Flo	**Vicki Lewis**
Jacques	**Joe Ranft**
Nigel	**Geoffrey Rush**
Crush	**Andrew Stanton**
Coral	**Elizabeth Perkins**

The Parr family at their Incredible best.

THE INCREDIBLES

"Normal? What do you know about normal? What does anyone in this family know about normal?"

— Violet Parr

THE CAST

Bob Parr/Mr. Incredible	**Craig T. Nelson**
Helen Parr/Elastigirl	**Holly Hunter**
Lucius Best/Frozone	**Samuel L. Jackson**
Buddy Pine/Syndrome	**Jason Lee**
Bomb Voyage	**Dominique Louis**
Newsreel Narrator	**Teddy Newton**
Mrs. Hogenson	**Jean Sincere**
Gilbert Huph	**Wallace Shawn**
Dashiell "Dash" Parr	**Spencer Fox**
Bernie Kropp	**Lou Romano**
Principal	**Wayne Canney**
Violet Parr	**Sarah Vowell**

THERE IS A TELLING EXCHANGE IN THE "MAKING OF" FEAture on the best-selling *Incredibles* DVD: Producer John Walker and Director Brad Bird are wrangling over a scene which Bird thinks needs more work. "I'm just trying to get you over the line," says Walker, in the weary measured tones of a man used to having to repeat himself, but Bird snaps back "And I'm just trying to get over the line in first place!"

This kind of drive was exactly what Pixar needed in 2002. The company had hit upon what was veering close to a winning formula: charming and heartfelt stories, brilliantly animated, with warm chuckles and reliably funny outtakes rolling after the credits. John Lasseter thought that the company needed to grow, instead of rest on their laurels. "We were worried about becoming complacent," explained Lasseter. Brad Bird, Lasseter's brilliant classmate from CalArts, former executive consultant on *The Simpsons*, and a legend among animators, mostly on the basis of his film, the marvelous *The Iron Giant*, which he made in 1999.

Bird was known for his passion, his outspokenness, and his tendency to ruffle corporate feathers. He had struggled famously with what he now generally dismisses as "Hollywood

> *"Your identity is your most valuable possession. Protect it."*
> — Helen Parr, aka Elastigirl

idiocy" and had seen several of his projects back-burnered, rejected, or, worse, accepted and then mangled. Primarily a traditional 2-D cel-animator, Bird was lured to Pixar from L.A. not by the digital format, but by Pixar's promise that they would protect his story.

Bird had very little idea of what was and what was not then feasible in CGI, and had he known, he probably wouldn't have cared. Almost everything his script called for lurked just on the edge of feasibility: water, storms, scores of costume changes, explosions, explosions in water, explosions under water, long hair, long and wet hair, long hair with wind in it, and of course, people. Everywhere.

In addition to the special effects, there was also Bird's ambitious set design to accomplish: (*Finding Nemo* has 23 sets, *The Incredibles*, 130), as well as his overall vision. "The purpose of animation is not to reproduce reality," he once said, "but to bump it up." In this case, "bumping it up" meant establishing the believable physics of superheroism—with a palpable representation of weight. The fact that Bob Parr (Mr. Incredible) can lift a car with ease does not make that car any less heavy.

Apparently, the world embraced Bird's vision. Since its release in 2004, the movie has grossed over $630 million in worldwide box office and garnered two Academy Awards. *The Incredibles* is also a true original: part sophisticated

AWARDS

ACADEMY AWARDS
4 Nominations / 2 Awards

GOLDEN GLOBES
1 Nomination

Character development art of the scene-stealing Edna Mode, voiced by director Brad Bird.

family drama, part thoughtful meditation on greatness, and, of course, part adrenalin-infused action movie. On the DVD, which itself won accolades and set several sales records, Bird can be seen rallying his troops with an enthusiasm that history will look on as prophetic: "Do it, do it, do it, man," he says, fist pumping. "Because it's gonna be so awesome if we get it right!"

TRIVIA

The island in which fanboy-turned-nemesis Syndrome keeps his lair is called Nomanisan, as in "No Man is an Island."

In forced retirement as super heroes, Bob (Craig T. Nelson) and Helen Parr (Holly Hunter) put their powers to other uses.

"CGI is finally becoming the tool that we all said it was. It is a tool. And so, then it's a matter of finding creative filmmakers who do really great stuff with it."

— Carl Rosendahl, Co-founder of Pacific Data Images

PRECEDING SPREAD AND OPPOSITE:
**The previously zoo-bound heroes of
PDI/DreamWorks 2005 hit *Madagascar* find
themselves stranded on a wild jungle island.**

I f Carl Rosendahl were attending college today, he would be a computer-science major. But in the late seventies, even at Stanford University, the major didn't exist, so the undergrad had to settle for a degree in electrical engineering. Right after graduating in 1979, he took a job in Palo Alto working for Memorex, but spent most of his time fooling around with computers. "I'd been playing with an Apple II," he recalls, speaking in the hybrid techno-surfer vernacular of the Silicon Valley whiz kid. "Making all these wire-frame rotating cubes, and I just thought, that is sooooo cool—you can draw 3-D on computers. Awesome, that's what I want to do."

Rosendahl had grown up in L.A. sharing an equal passion for math, science, and making movies with his friends, and those three-dimensional cubes would, literally, shape his destiny. When his department at Memorex dissolved in 1980, he borrowed $50,000 from his father, bought a new computer, programmed it to do graphics, and within months had landed a gig making business slides for Hewlett Packard. There he met Richard Chuang, a satellite-transmissions specialist from Sacramento who'd had to shelve his dreams of being a painter because of an allergy to turpentine. Around the same time, he also met Glenn Entis, an artist by training, at a local get-together called Graphics Gathering (which Steve Jobs and Steve Wozniak frequented as well), and the three men decided to join forces.

In 1982, they borrowed an additional $200,000 from Rosendahl's father, rented a small office in Sunnyvale, and set about building their new company. "Wisely," remembers Rosendahl, "when they joined me we threw away everything I'd done and started from scratch." They chucked his old computer and programs, bought a refrigerator-sized PDP/11-44 computer with UNIX capability and 128k of memory, and worked together to design the architecture of their animation system. One of their first relationships was with Colossal Pictures in San Francisco, which brought them work in commercials, stand-alone graphics, and early MTV logos, and in turn led to television network clients from here to Brazil.

Rosendahl, Entis, and Chuang were barely breaking even, but they knew exactly where they were headed: full-length animated feature films. To achieve that goal they "only" needed to stay in business and build up their

PORTFOLIO

Academy Award Nominations	**4**
Academy Awards	**1**
Academy Scientific and Technical Achievement Awards	**4**
Golden Globe Nominations	**2**
Cannes Film Festival Nominations	**2**

MILESTONES

1980
Carl Rosendahl starts PDI (Pacific Data Images) doing business slides with CGI (computer-generated images).

1981
Richard Chuang and Glenn Entis join PDI in Sunnyvale, California, to build a business around 3-D CG animation.

1982
Rosendahl contracts with Rede Globo in Brazil to develop software for the network's television promotions. PDI designs show opening credits and specials. This helps finance the development of PDI's software, which includes an animation-scripting language, modeling, rendering, and motion-design programs. PDI's early CG production is for *Entertainment Tonight*, *ABC Sports*, 1984 Olympic promos, *NBC News,* the Pillsbury doughboy, Crest, and Bud Bowl.

1983
Richard Chuang develops PDI's first lighting-and-compositing tool.

1985
By this year PDI has captured over fifty percent of the computer-graphic market for network-television graphics productions. Creates first detailed production plan for an all-CG long-format project, including staffing profile and specification for the tools needed.

Founders Richard Chuang, Glenn Entis, and Carl Rosendahl with the PDP/11-44 computer that started it all in 1986.

PDI/DreamWorks, the Northern California studio of DreamWorks Animation SKG, in Redwood City.

skills and capabilities, so they could move from logos to storytelling. They had a tough-love ally in Rosendahl senior, a no-nonsense businessman who demanded monthly financial reports and kept the ambitious young men from spending more than they had. By the mid-eighties, the company had repaid Rosendahl senior and was in the black, and it was time to take the next step: a temporary move to Los Angeles.

Rosendahl headed down to L.A. in 1989 making the rounds with Tim Johnson, the co-head of his new character-animation group. They worked on conceptual art, story treatments, and screenplays, and tried their best to sell the new technologies to the notoriously slow-moving industry. "In the late eighties we went door-to-door pitching computer-animated features to anyone who would listen to us. It was pretty easy to get the meetings, because people were so curious about the technology and stuff, but it would always end with: 'Nobody's going to sit through an hour and a half of computer animation. Sorry guys, but it's just not gonna happen.'"

Hollywood skepticism notwithstanding, the eighties brought an ongoing round of lucrative commercial and special effects work, and PDI, ILM (Industrial Light and Magic), and to a lesser degree, Pixar, were among the leaders in a growing industry. In these early years there was a strong sense of community to go along with the spirit of competition amongst all these digital Orvilles and Wilburs. "It was the sense," says Rosendahl, "of being co-conspirators. You could be in a cutthroat bidding situation, but then if you lost the bid you'd hope that whoever won would do a kickass job, so they could see how good it could be and want to keep using it."

Those were heady days for PDI, as Entis, Chuang, and Rosendahl began pursuing their dream of making CGI feature films in earnest. In 1989, they made several all-CGI characters for the Jim Henson hour, and they began making plans with Henson to do a film together. Indeed, were it not for the brilliant puppeteer's untimely death in May 1990, the first all-CGI feature film may well have been a Henson/PDI co-production.

Back then relations were so amicable between PDI and a still-struggling Pixar, that the two companies had even thrown parties together at SIGGRAPH. But no amount of industry-wide goodwill could prevent a drop in PDI morale when word got out that Pixar, their biggest rival, had just landed a partnership with Disney. PDI had grown to more than one hundred people, their short films won consistent accolades, and their animated television special *The Last Halloween* had won an Emmy, but still, someone else had beat them to the first big milestone: "We knew *Toy Story* was coming out, and we were all really excited about it, but we also knew there might be a morale issue when the movie came out. We had all these people struggling to make that happen and then someone else does it, sure you're gonna get depressed about it."

The early days at PDI in 1987. Back row on the wall, left to right: Jim Ward, Graham Walters, Joe Palrang, Richard Chuang, Delle Maxwell, Scott Anderson, Dick Walsh, Glenn Entis, Nick Ilyin, Steve Goldberg. Front row, left to right: Jim Rygiel, Larry Lessler, Shari Glusker, Patty Wooton, Jamie Dixon, Bill Foss, Rich Cohen, Roger Gould, Carl Rosendahl, Thad Beier, Michelle Tsui, Adam Chin, and Howard Baker.

1989
PDI develops real-time motion capture and puppeteering for the Waldo television character for the Jim Henson Company. A real-time CG character, Waldo, aired on the Jim Henson Hour.

1990
PDI introduces the digital-film-scanning process in 1990, which they use to popularize automated rig removal and image touchup. PDI forms first CG-character-animation group with Tim Johnson and Rex Grignon.

1991
Black and White, the first Michael Jackson video with effects by PDI, helps pioneer the use of morphing computer-graphics effects. Completes the CG characters and effects for the stereoscopic 3-D Muppetvision show for Disney World Themepark, including the first CG version of the most famous Disney character. For the first time, PDI provides digital compositing for a feature film, *Terminator 2: Judgment Day* in conjunction with ILM, which handled the majority of the visual effects work on the project. PDI completes *The Last Halloween*, a primetime-TV special, integrating CG characters with live action. This show won an Emmy Award for visual effects and became the first long-format pipeline for future character-animation projects.

1992
PDI provides digital effects for *Toys* and digital compositing for *Batman Returns*.

1994
Les Dittert of PDI receives the Academy of Motion Pictures Arts & Sciences (AMPAS) Scientific and Engineering Award for his development work with film-input-scanning systems.

1995
Glenn Entis leaves PDI to start an interactive company and later joins DreamWorks Interactive (now Electronic Arts) as CEO. PDI delivers motion-captured digital stuntman for *Batman Forever*. PDI completes the first CG *Simpsons* episode for a Halloween special.

1996
PDI signs with DreamWorks SKG to fully coproduce computer-animated feature films.

1997
Richard Chuang, Glenn Entis, and Carl Rosendahl receive the AMPAS Technical Achievement Award for PDI's proprietary animation system.

1998
PDI's R&D team member, Nick Foster, is awarded an AMPAS Technical Achievement Award for his development of software tools built to simulate water and fluid. PDI's first feature, *Antz*, hits theatres on October 2. It grosses more than $170 million worldwide.

> *"Some things change and some things don't. I have software that I wrote in 1982 which we still use in our films"*
>
> —Richard Chuang,
> Co-founder of
> Pacific Data Images

RIGHT: **A frame from** *The Simpsons*'s **"Last Halloween" episode.**
BELOW: **The "Last Halloween" wrap party in October 1991. Back row: Eric Darnell, Glenn McQueen, Carl Rosendahl, Rex Grignon, Henry Anderson, Dick Walsh, Tim Johnson, Sharon Calahan, and Brad Lewis. Front row: Todd Heapy, Ken Bielenberg, Patty Wooton, Richard Chuang, Raman Hui, and Deb Giarratana.**

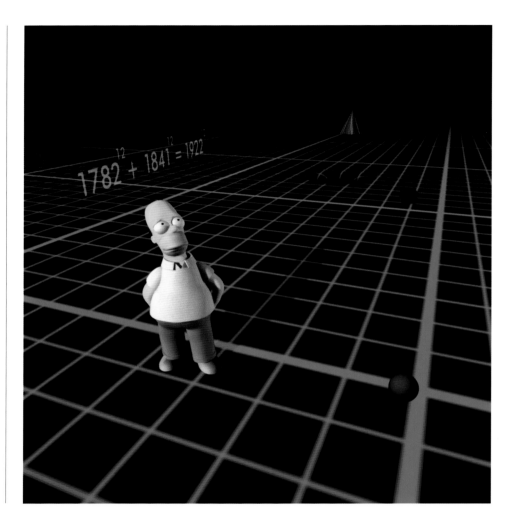

When the producers of *The Simpsons* approached them in 1994 to do 3-D work for their next Halloween special, PDI jumped at the chance. If animation has gods, surely Homer and Bart rank high in its pantheon, and the opportunity to work on the acclaimed special would be exactly the self-esteem boost the company needed. This solution to the morale problem also became one of the smartest decisions PDI ever made.

The catch? *The Simpsons*'s producers had barely any budget for digital animation.

So PDI took a gamble and did the job for free. The animation team responsible for putting the episode together worked double overtime, and since the rest of the staff had to take on extra work to make up for lost profits, it became a team-building company mission. Always his father's son—a canny businessman—Rosendahl had a strategy. The Halloween episode would showcase PDI's best work and talents less than two weeks before the Thanksgiving opening of *Toy Story*. In anticipation of what he knew would be a smashing success for Pixar and a huge window of opportunity for PDI, Rosendahl accompanied by Johnson made the rounds to the L.A. studios again, planting seeds. "We were not going in saying, 'Please, let us make a movie,'" he recalls. "Instead, we were saying, 'You'll see. And when you decide you want to do that, give us a call.'"

Sure enough, *Toy Story* made over $29 million its opening weekend, and on Monday morning, PDI's phones were ringing off the hook. After some negotiation and comparison shopping, the company struck a deal with DreamWorks, and to this day Rosendahl credits Jeffrey Katzenberg's unwavering belief in CGI as a driving force behind the partnership's success. The company tripled in size for their initial full-length feature *Antz* in 1998. Rosendahl left the company in early 2000 in the middle of the production of the first *Shrek* movie and in 2001, Patti Burke took over the reins. With *Shrek* earning the first-ever Academy Award for an animated feature film, and with *Shrek 2* as the third-highest grossing film to date, the company remains, along with Pixar and ILM, an undisputed Northern California contingent and pioneer in the bursting field of computer animation.

2000
Carl Rosendahl sells his interest in PDI and leaves to become managing director for Mobius Venture Capital and a board member of iVAST, an MPEG4 software company, and several other Bay Area technology firms. DreamWorks acquires majority interest in PDI. PDI becomes PDI/DreamWorks.

2001
Shrek is screened at the Cannes Film Festival. After its May 16th U.S. release, it goes on to earn more than $267 million in domestic box office. *Shrek* is nominated for a Golden Globe for Best Picture—Musical or Comedy.

2002
Shrek wins the first-ever Academy Award for Best Animated Feature Film. Also receives an Academy Award nomination for Best Original Screenplay. In March, Dick Walsh is awarded the AMPAS Technical Achievement Award for the development of the PDI/DreamWorks Facial-Animation System. This software is used to create and control natural, expressive, highly nuanced facial animation on a wide range of computer-generated characters.

2004
Shrek 2 released to a $108 million opening weekend in the U.S. It goes on to gross more than $920 million worldwide and becomes the third-highest grossing domestic release of all time at $441.2 million in U.S. box office receipts. Screened at Cannes in May and nominated for the Palme d'Or. DreamWorks spins off DreamWorks Animation in an initial public offering that raises $635 million to fund its own productions. The new company also acquires the remaining interest in PDI/DreamWorks. *Shrek 2* nominated for a Golden Globe for Best Original Song, "Accidentally in Love."

2005
Shrek 2 receives two Academy Award nominations—Best Animated Feature and Best Original Song, "Accidentally in Love." *Madagascar* opens with a U.S. box office of $61 million.

Shrek (Mike Myers) thinks Puss In Boots (Antonio Banderas) is just an adorable little kitty cat and decides to keep him in *Shrek 2*.

A SELECTION OF PDI SHORT FILMS

MAX'S PLACE (1984)

A simple and short experimental piece to create the CG-neon look of the early eighties. Instead of the traditional back-lit animation camera technique, this film brings the old visual style of neon on film to the digital age.

CHROMOSAURUS (1984)

Before chrome was the rage in the early days of CG animation, this piece takes the timeless icon of a dinosaur into the world of computer graphics. Primitive by today's standard, this was a significant development at the time, bringing excitement and anticipation to the industry.

OPÉRA INDUSTRIEL (1988)

A redefinition of the classic images from Charlie Chaplin's *Modern Times* using computer animation as the medium. This small tribute to a cinema classic is one of the earlier fusions of CG and traditional film techniques.

BURNING LOVE (1988)

Created as a work of art to reflect the desire of love through experimental non-photo-realistic rendering techniques. This helped to start a tradition of experimental animation in short films covering a wide scope of artistic direction.

LOCOMOTION (1990)

The story of a proud steam engine and a reluctant caboose that need to overcome a great obstacle—a broken rail on a bridge high above a ravine. The engine tries to jump over the gap but is held back by the fearful caboose and backs down in resignation. Afraid of not making his delivery on time, the engine suffers from a dreadful nightmare and the vision of his own tombstone reading: HE WAS LATE ONCE TOO OFTEN. He awakes with renewed determination and finds a way to cross the gap, cargo, and caboose in tow.

GAS PLANET (1992)

In a distant galaxy, three natives of Gas Planet carry on with their quest for nourishment. Their behavior is definitely alien, but also comically familiar to an earthling audience.

SLEEPY GUY (1994)

Seeking a state of uninterrupted slumber, Sleepy Guy attempts to meet and spend eight hours of bliss with the girl of his dreams.

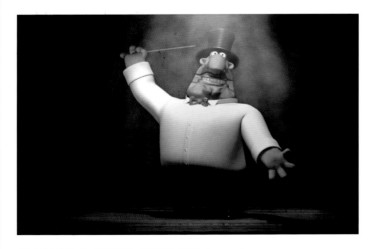

GABOLA THE GREAT (1997)

A classic story of a vaudeville magician whose tricks never seem to work as planned. Set on a dimly lit stage, a single smoky spotlight illuminates the magician as he prepares to amaze a rather sparse audience. Nervously trying to impress them, the hapless magician attempts to pull a rabbit from his top hat. The outcome is darkly humorous.

MILLENNIUM BUG (1998)

A tongue-in-cheek Surrealist peek at the future of urban sprawl. Black-and-white footage featuring squeamishly fun industrial consumer accidents is juxtaposed with handy entries from a "New Millennium Dictionary." It's as short as it is sweet–don't blink.

FAT CAT ON A DIET (1999)

Fat Cat is tired of his usual bland diet cat food and is desperate for anything with even a touch of fat. Luckily, he finds a delectable piece of pizza that he cannot resist. However, getting the pizza is much more burdensome than he anticipated.

FISHING (2000)

The story of a fisherman whose wildest daydream becomes his worst nightmare. Told in the style of an animated watercolor painting, *Fishing* utilizes the 3-D fluid simulation tools to convey the mutable experience of longing.

METROPOPULAR (2001)

Frantic about a popularity contest in which the cities of America are competing, each jockeys for top position while arguing between themselves. Highlighting their separate personalities, each city has his or her own reason why they should be "America's favorite city."

SPROUT (2002)

Sprout is a slippery, green embryo confined inside a small egg who is surprised to discover that a much larger world exists beyond his umbilical cord.

SHREK 4-D (2003)

Shrek 4-D is a multisensory, multimedia continuation of the Academy Award-winning blockbuster *Shrek*. Picking up where the movie left off, the attraction combines original 3-D animation, state-of-the-art digital cinema projection and audio systems along with unique in-theatre sensory immersion that physically expands the *Shrek* characters and their world to create a four-dimensional entertainment experience.

Z (Woody Allen) laments to his best friend Weaver (Sylvester Stallone) about his lot in life in the romantic comedy adventure, *Antz*.

ANTZ

"I've got to believe there's someplace better for me. Otherwise I'll just curl up into a larval position and weep."

— Z

TRIVIA

One of the motivational signs in the ant colony, FREE TIME IS FOR TRAINING, is an actual sign at PDI.

THE CAST

Z	**Woody Allen**
Chip	**Dan Akroyd**
Queen	**Anne Bancroft**
Muffy	**Jane Curtin**
Barbatus	**Danny Glover**
General Mandible	**Gene Hackman**
Azteca	**Jennifer Lopez**
Foreman	**Grant Shaud**
Weaver	**Sylvester Stallone**
Princess Bala	**Sharon Stone**
Colonel Cutter	**Christopher Walken**

WHEN PDI FIRST STARTED HAVING CONVERSATIONS with Jeffrey Katzenberg, they pitched him several ideas and he nixed them all, but counter-offered with a few projects being developed at DreamWorks. One was a fairy tale send-up featuring a monster, a donkey, and a princess, and another one featured the inhabitants of a troubled ant colony in the middle of an internal power struggle. After much complex deliberation amongst themselves (which according to Rosendahl finally amounted to the simple formula "bug easier than ogre"), PDI took on the project which would eventually become their first full-length animated feature: *Antz*.

In the mid-nineties even that so-called easier film came loaded with potential quagmires, such as water, light, facial expressions, and crowd scenes—all new frontiers in computer animation. The technical team and animators had to stretch to invent the software and write the code that would make the film possible. Two of their most crucial innovations were a facial-animation system to handle the actors expressions and crowd-simulation software to manage the tens of thousands of ants that would appear in the crowd scenes.

While PDI was working on *Antz*, Pixar was making *A Bug's Life*. Both companies were growing exponentially and were in a heated race to bring out their respective movies. By the time *Antz* premiered (first, by just one month) in October, 1998, the press was already buzzing with questions about which "insect" film would do better. But it turned out that besides their subject matter, and perhaps the kind of "little man against conformist system" theme that one would expect from any story about an ant colony, the two films had very little in common. Tim Johnson and Eric Darnell, who had put together award-winning and critically acclaimed shorts for PDI before *Antz*, took the enormous risk of making the movie PG, in a hyper-referential and sometimes bleak comedy, with a sensibility reminiscent of Woody Allen circa 1975, complete with jokes about Marxism, psychoanalysis, and smug philanthropic urges. The film balanced a stark political drama (there is a rather heartbreaking battle scene that contains an implicit critique of fascism) with an adventure story for children, complete with slapstick comedy and wondrous special effects. In contrast, Pixar was still working squarely within the wholesome G-rated system of its Disney distributor, one they wouldn't deviate from until the release of *The Incredibles* six years later.

Whether or not one thinks *Antz* succeeds in its attempt to exist on two different levels of sophistication depends largely on how one feels about the casting of Woody Allen. Despite the star-studded cast, which included Sharon Stone, Gene Hackman, Christopher Walken, and Sylvester Stallone, it was certainly Allen's portrayal of Z as a neurotic, whiny, pessimistic antihero that dominated the film's tone. Some critics found his character unappealing, but *USA Today* applauded the film, calling it Allen's best role in years, and Roger Ebert found the double edge more than satisfying: "It's sharp and funny—not a children's movie, but one of those hybrids that works on different levels for different ages."

Still, despite the film's critical and commercial success, Rosendahl says what he's most proud of is the fact that the company managed to grow so quickly to prepare for the production of *Antz* without becoming a corporate monolith: "We tripled in size, but kept our DNA intact."

Princess Bala (Sharon Stone) explores the world outside the ant colony in the romantic comedy adventure *Antz*.

"I was having a drink with Jeff Katzenberg, and he said I was the voice he needed for an ant. I've never seen Antz, but it made more money than my last five pictures put together. I wish it was mine. "

— Woody Allen

SHREK

WHEN IT WAS TIME TO MAKE *SHREK*, THE ORDER FROM the top was loud and clear. The animators were told to make *Shrek* "ten times as complex as *Antz*." But even if the directive hadn't come from above, the increased complexity would have been demanded by the new movie's plot, which called for princess hair, donkey fur, and—most complicated—human faces. To solve this last challenge, technical director Dick Walsh and his team built on their model for *Antz*. They developed a facial-animation system based on an understanding of the physiology of human motion. Rather than start the programs from what viewers see—the external parts of the body like skin and facial expressions—he built his characters literally, from the bare bones. The facial-animation system began with skeletons and from there built on muscle groups, fatty tissue, and so on. In some ways, that first step was the easy part. Next up was making

THE CAST

Shrek	**Mike Myers**
Donkey	**Eddie Murphy**
Princess Fiona	**Cameron Diaz**
Lord Farquaad	**John Lithgow**

the system user-friendly so the animators would not need to memorize medical charts about the muscle groups in order to be able to make their characters' movements appear natural and lifelike. The operation was incredibly complex: It took over 200 controls to animate the face. But the system worked well, in some cases, almost too well: The first versions of Fiona were

A heartbroken Shrek (Mike Myers) looks on as Princess Fiona (Cameron Diaz) considers Lord Farquaad's (John Lithgow) proposal to be his wife and queen, in the computer-animated comedy *Shrek*.

Shrek (Mike Myers) tries to convince Donkey (Eddie Murphy) that he does not need a friend.

"almost photorealistic," according to producer Aron Warner. "It was too good, we had to dial her back to make her fit the fairy tale world."

Like *Antz*, this classic ogre-saves-girl, ogre-fights-with-girl, ogre-burps-with-girl story was very much a collaboration. The co-directors were brought in from DreamWorks, the animators came from PDI, and the production itself took almost four and a half years, blocked initially by the tragic death of Chris Farley, who had been the first choice to play the not-so-jolly green giant. Fortunately Mike Myers fulfilled the role grandly, with a delightful Scottish brogue borrowed from his *Austin Powers* Fat Bastard character. But the true comic-scene stealer was Eddie Murphy's Donkey, whose alternate midstream shifts from wisecracks to sycophantism to unexpected

AWARDS

ACADEMY AWARDS
2 Nominations / 1 Award

GOLDEN GLOBES
1 Nomination

CANNES
1 Nomination (Palme d'Or)

TRIVIA

As research for the film, the effects department took real mud showers!

wisdom infused the whole film with manic energy and unpredictability. And when *Shrek* finally opened in 2001, the response was exactly that: manic. Elvis Mitchell praised its "scrappy, brash comedy" and "demolition-derby zest," *Variety* called it "an instant animated classic," and Roger Ebert pronounced it "jolly and wicked...an astonishing visual delight."

Finally, *Shrek* was the first movie to win an Oscar in the Academy's new Animated Film category, and was also the first animated film in almost fifty years to be selected for competition at Cannes.

"Okay, let me get this straight: You gonna go fight a dragon and rescue a princess just so Farquaad'll give you back your swamp, which you only don't have 'cos he filled it full of freaks in the first place. Is that about right?"

— Donkey

Princess Fiona (Cameron Diaz) nervously introduces her new husband Shrek (Mike Myers) to her parents, King Harold (John Cleese) and Queen Lillian (Julie Andrews), the rulers of Far Far Away, in the computer-animated comedy *Shrek 2*.

SHREK 2

"Oh, Shrek. Don't worry. Things just seem bad because it's dark and rainy and Fiona's father hired a sleazy hitman to whack you."

— Donkey

AWARDS

ACADEMY AWARDS
2 Nominations

GOLDEN GLOBES
1 Nomination

CANNES
1 Nomination (Palme d'Or)

TRIVIA

A few of the puns that can be found in the kingdom of Far Far Away: Burger Prince, Old Knavery, Saxxon Fifth Avenue, Romeo Drive, Versarchery, Gap Queen, Farbucks Coffee, Friar's Fat Boy, Tower of London Records, Baskin (XXXI) Robbinhood.

ON A TECHNICAL LEVEL, THE MAKERS OF *Shrek 2* wanted to capitalize on the huge advances that animation had made since 2001, but they had to be sure not to stray too far from the look audiences had come to love. They added a new character, the almost prohibitively furry Puss In Boots, threw in some dazzling fireballs, and even gave Shrek an Adam's apple. But the two chief innovations were much more subtle: first, a "bounce shader" program simulated the way light really bounces from one object to another and did wonders for lighting up the characters in a more natural way; and second, "subsurface scattering," which came much closer to approximating the natural translucence of human skin. To illustrate that translucence, Visual Effects Supervisor Ken Bielenberg uses the example of a flashlight pressed up to the palm of your hand. The differences might be virtually unrecognizable to the average theatergoer, but the added sophistication would not be lost on animation professionals.

The sequel's plot was also in many ways much more sophisticated than the original. Katzenberg described the sequel as *"Guess Who's Coming to Dinner* meets *Shrek,"* and his description was one example of truth in Hollywood sound

THE CAST

Shrek	**Mike Myers**
Donkey	**Eddie Murphy**
Princess Fiona	**Cameron Diaz**
Queen	**Julie Andrews**
Puss In Boots	**Antonio Banderas**
King	**John Cleese**
Prince Charming	**Rupert Everett**
Fairy Godmother	**Jennifer Saunders**

among other things, the unpredictability of sexual attraction.... I only wish that there were more live-action pictures written with as much careful shaping."

This is not to say that the second film sags under the burden of any undue maturity. Compared with the original, *Shrek 2* is, if anything, broader, more scatological, and more shamelessly willing to pillage pop culture (the film even rides the shoulder-pads and synthesizer nostalgia wave, with callouts to the eighties' hits *Flashdance* and *Footloose*) and with an even higher pun-per-frame ratio than the first. Furthermore, the sequel gives us two new splendid performances: Jennifer Saunders, hilarious as a fairy godmother for the upwardly mobile and spiritually null, and Antonio Banderas, who is pitch perfect as Puss In Boots—a welcome reminder that before he let his career get hijacked by America's love for Latin lovers, Banderas was one of Spain's top comic actors.

In short, *Shrek 2* was just like *Shrek*, only much more so. And, like Pixar's *The Incredibles*, *Shrek 2* is proof that CGI has come into its own at last. It's so good that we don't notice it. Or, as Bielenberg puts it: "I think a lot of challenges have reached a certain level of being tackled, if not solved. I think it's more about refining everything so that we remove further creative roadblocks. The point of technical development is to remove any constraints on the creative process."

biting. *Shrek 2*, far from repeating the fairly obvious message of the original, which finally amounted to the familiar moral that beauty only runs skin deep, sends Shrek and Fiona home to Fiona's parents in the land of Far Far Away, where the young couple must face the real life after "happily ever after": meddling, closed-mindedness, value conflicts, and the sad spectacle of parents hurting their children in the name of what they claim to think is best. Even Stephanie Zacharek, a film critic who had previously written that digital animation in general and *Shrek*, in particular, left her cold, was won over almost against her will: "This is the first animated feature about,

Shrek 2 visual development artwork depicting the grand courtyard entrance of the Far Far Away castle.

Today, Ballard still lives in the Bay Area, in the hills of St. Helena, and although he has not played nearly enough, he has carved out a special niche for himself as a superior poet of the eye. In Pauline Kael's words: "The visual imagination Ballard brings to the natural landscape is so intense that his imagery makes you feel like a pagan—as if you were touching when you're only looking." With a firm hand, Ballard forces the viewer to slow down and adjust his or her rhythm to the events at hand. The best moments in his films appeal to an adult's sense of wisdom and a child's sense of wonder.

NEVER CRY WOLF (1983)

C arroll Ballard came to *Never Cry Wolf* through his fascination with a book by Peter Matthiessen called *The Snow Leopard*. He had just finished *The Black Stallion* and, expecting the film to be a failure, had absconded with his wife to a small village in Switzerland to nurse his wounds after a considerably strife-filled production. During his stay, however, *The Black Stallion* had begun gaining momentum in the movie theaters, outlasting and outselling Disney's much more heavily advertised movie, *The Black Hole*. Disney tracked Ballard down in Switzerland and promptly signed him on to develop and direct *Never Cry Wolf*.

For much of the first half of the film, the audience is left alone in a barren snowscape with Charles Martin Smith (best known for his performances as Terry the Toad in *American Graffiti* and Agent Wallace in *The Untouchables*). Smith plays Tyler, a naturalist who has been sent to the Alaskan wilderness as part of "The Lupine Project," an attempt to observe—or, rather, condemn—the arctic wolves, known by legend, myth, and greed-induced wishful

ABOVE: **Behind the scenes with two Innuit actors (left to right) Zachary Ittimanqnaq (Ootek) and Samson Jorah (Mike) and crew member Colin Michael Kitchens.**
RIGHT: **Tyler (Charles Martin Smith) and Rosie (Brian Dennehy) confront each other.**

Charles Martin Smith goes wild in Alaska.

thinking to be vicious killers in need of extermination. Naive and unprepared for life in the wild, he tells us he has been hoping to "go out in the wilderness and test myself against all the dangers lurking there."

Dangers there are aplenty, as Tyler finds himself lost and alone in the infinite icebound landscape that is the wolves' home turf. He almost freezes to death, and several early scenes are devoted to Tyler's efforts not at research but at survival. As he did in *The Black Stallion*, Ballard relies largely on silence and the remarkable work of his cinematographer (this time, the gifted Hiro Narita, an *Apocalypse Now* alumnus) to tell the story. The landscape, huge, engulfing, and implacable, begs for more than just a high-tech IMAX screen to reveal its glory. It also requires an act of patience on the part of the viewer, a willingness to let the plot unfold at a slower pace than audiences had come to expect.

Predictably, Tyler discovers over the course of this movie that the human race is a far more dangerous enemy of the caribou than the wolves, and although there is a greedy developer on hand (lustily played by Brian Dennehy with a cavalier cruelty one rarely associates with the actor's generally tough and jolly persona), Ballard doesn't let the ongoing conflicts, between human and nature play out in simple terms. Instead, Tyler is befriended by two Native Americans, Ootek and Mike, who help guide him to an understanding of the wolves, but even they are not quite what they seem at first. The wolves are

Ballard (left) confers with cast members.

"He wants me to tell the story of when there was nothing in the world, except for a man, and a wolf."

—Mike

filmed not as doglike friends-in-training but as remote beings that belong to the landscape in a way that the humans never quite achieve.

The film is in no way a children's movie, nor is its final message particularly soothing. While he comes to love the wolves as he'd never expected, Tyler's presence in their home leads to inevitable calamity for the wolf family, and he realizes that the answers he came in search of are unattainable. "In the end," he tells us, "there were no simple answers, no heroes, no villains, only silence." This lack of easy resolution made for a nature film that is almost religious in its respect for its subject matter, but one that never quite found the audience it deserved. It should be seen again, for its grandeur, its subtlety, and its reverence for a disappearing world—and for the sadness at its core.

FLY AWAY HOME (1996)

Environmentalist Thomas Alden (Jeff Daniels) leads the geese south in his Ultra Light airplane in *Fly Away Home*.

Common filmmaker's wisdom has it that the director's two worst nightmares are animals and children. For the filming of *Fly Away Home*, one more nightmare ought to be tacked on: Canadian weather. The early days of the film shoot were plagued by apocalyptic

Ontario rains, which add to the movie's bleak, dark tone early in the film. *Fly Away Home* tells the story of a young girl named Amy who moves to the country with her eccentric inventor father after her mother's death in a car wreck. As played by Anna Paquin, already an accomplished actress at the age of 13, Amy is at first closed off, angry, and unwilling to try to get to know the man who in her mind abandoned her and her mother. What changes their relationship is her discovery of a nest of geese eggs—also abandoned in a recently bulldozed lot near her new home. Showing both tenderness and

vulnerability for the first time, she secretly adopts the eggs. By the time her father discovers what she's done, the eggs have already hatched and the goslings have bonded to Amy. Believing Amy to be their mother, the baby geese follow her everywhere she goes. This sets the scene for a well-crafted adventure and a touching story of reconciliation and love.

The film, based on a true story, received excellent reviews, even from critics who had been disappointed with Ballard's post–*Black Stallion* career, calling it a return to early form. "The tender beauty of Carroll Ballard's *Fly Away Home*," raved Janet Maslin of *The New York Times*, "falls beyond what might be expected from a movie about things that hatch. Rekindling the delicacy and invigorating naturalness he brought to *The Black Stallion* and again helped immensely by the radiant cinematography of Caleb Deschanel, Mr. Ballard turns a potentially treacly children's film into an exhilarating nineties fable."

The exhilaration comes largely from the father's and daughter's attempts at flight, and their many efforts to find a way to keep the geese with them. They do not connect as a family through arbitrary emotional catharses but rather by having to work together for a cause they believe in. Perhaps the most valuable lesson in the film is the story of a father who wins his daughter's love and respect by showing her how much he loves and respects her. In addition, the flight scenes rank, along with the moonlit cycling in the sky shots in *ET*, as some of the most satisfying moments of cinematic wish-fulfillment any adult or child could ever hope for.

"Daddy, can I keep them? Please?"

—Amy

Amy (Anna Paquin) with the geese she hatched from eggs.

TRIVIA

Most of the gadgets in the film, including its fabulous futuristic icebox, were actual inventions of Bill Lishman, the real-life inventor upon whom the story was based. To imprint the geese before star Anna Paquin's arrival on the set, Lishman played recordings of her voice for the still unhatched eggs.

JOAN CHEN

San Francisco director, actress, wife, and mother, Joan Chen was born Chong Chen in Shanghai in 1961. Her parents, both doctors, were sent to the countryside when she was 7 years old, and for almost ten years she lived with aunts and cousins who moved into the family home. At age 14, she was picked out by the Shanghai Film Studio from a high school rifle team to be in a film called *Jin Gong Shan*, a saga about the Long March, executive produced by Jiang Qing, Mao Tse-tung's wife. The film was never completed because Qing was arrested in 1976 as a member of the Gang of Four, but that same year Chen was cast as a deaf-mute girl in the film *Youth*, which, in turn, led to the title role in the film *Xiao Hua* (Little Flower) in 1977. For her performance in *Xiao Hua*, she won the Chinese equivalent of the Best Actress Oscar in 1979, as well as the nickname "the Elizabeth Taylor of China."

After her parents were invited on research fellowships to Memorial Sloan-Kettering in New York, Chen applied to follow them. It took almost a year to get her Visa, but in 1981, she moved to the U.S. to study medicine, first in New York and then at California State University in Northridge. Chen soon went back to acting and, eventually, distinguished herself in several films, most notably, Bernardo Bertolucci's *The Last Emperor* (1987), David Lynch's cult classic *Twin Peaks* (1989/1990), and Oliver Stone's *Heaven and Earth* (1993). By the mid-nineties, however, she found herself reduced to vixen roles in Sylvester Stallone and Steven Seagal vehicles, and driven in part by disgust with these movies, she set to work adapting for film a novella written by her friend Geling Yan, called *Tian Yu* (Celestial Bath). Chen would later say that she was also motivated to work on the screenplay by the bleakness of the films she saw as a juror in the 1996 Berlin Film Festival, where she encountered nothing but "urban-despair, end-of-the-millennium, *doom* films…doom without any elevation."

Yan's tragic novella—a moving story of one teenage girl's life after forced relocation during the Chinese Cultural Revolution—concludes with a kind of grace Chen could recognize and appreciate. When Chen decided to try to make the story into a film, she and Yan worked together in China to write the screenplay for what would become *Xiu Xiu: The Sent-Down Girl*. They waited several months for Chinese-government approval to film the script, and

From the film *Little Flower*, 1978. Joan Chen won the Best Actress award in China for her performance in the title role.

Joan Chen directing Richard Gere
in *Autumn in New York*.

when it didn't come, Chen finally gave up and went to Tibet to film without permits, smuggling the tapes out each day, constantly expecting to get expelled from the country.

Xiu Xiu tells the story of a young girl, who is "sent down" from the city to the country to eradicate class differences and help forge a new purely egalitarian society. Xiu Xiu is moved from her home city of Cheng Du to a lonely outpost on the Tibetan Steppes, with only a taciturn disabled army veteran to keep her company. When no one comes to get her after her six months are up, the desperate girl begins sleeping with any local bureaucrat who dangles false promises of influence before her. The story, part indictment of government corruption, part ode to the Chinese countryside, and part love story, earned Chen well-deserved praise and critical respect everywhere but in China, where it was banned. It was a remarkable debut, and led to the opportunity to direct a mainstream Hollywood film, the Winona Ryder/Richard Gere weepie, *Autumn in New York* (2000). Chen did not enjoy the "lack of creative autonomy" in the studio system, and she and Geling Yan are back to work on another project.

Chen still lives in San Francisco, her adopted hometown, with her husband Peter and two young daughters. She is active in the local film community, and most recently starred in Alice Wu's debut feature film, *Saving Face*. Although she spends time in Los Angeles, Chen prefers San Francisco, which, she says, "is a much better place to be unemployed. You can be creative; you can read; you don't have to be beautiful."

"There are only so many roles as empresses ... but I've had a lot of offers to play vampires."

—Joan Chen

FILMOGRAPHY

2000 *Autumn in New York*
1999 *Xiu Xiu: The Sent-Down Girl*

CHRIS COLUMBUS

The majority of films directed by Chris Columbus are about family— about the fear of losing them, and about the experience of finding them. By making films that are entertaining, story-driven, and financially successful, Columbus has proven he can be an A-list Hollywood director without having to live or work in Los Angeles.

Born in Spangler, Pennsylvania, in 1958, Columbus moved with his parents to Warren, Ohio, where he grew up daydreaming and reading comic books. As a means of escape, he became obsessed with movies and was inspired by both *The Godfather* (1972) and *Blazing Saddles* (1974), which he calls the two bookends of what you can do in films. Columbus began reading every book about filmmaking that he could get his hands on, partly motivated by a desire to escape a dreary future. "I was in this Ohio town," he remembers. "Both of my parents were factory workers: My dad worked in an aluminum factory, and my mom worked in an automotive plant. I could either become a filmmaker or be a factory worker for the rest of my life."

Columbus escaped by going to film school at New York University. He sold his first screenplay while still a student, but it was *Gremlins*, a script he wrote for Steven Spielberg's newly formed company, Amblin Entertainment, that seriously started his career as a screenwriter. After that, Columbus wrote *The Goonies* and *Young Sherlock Holmes*. But what the young screenwriter really wanted to do was direct, and he finally got a chance with *Adventures in Babysitting* (1987), a charming farce about the (mis)adventures of a teenager (Elizabeth Shue) and her young charges. The story established what would turn out to be one of the director's biggest strengths: tapping into the fears that children and their parents have about being separated from each other, and making comedy out of it, which he did with even more success in the megahit *Home Alone* (1990), a film which was written by another prominent regional filmmaker, Chicago's bard of eighties adolescence, John Hughes. Made for around $18 million, *Home Alone* brought in almost $500 million and spawned two theatrical sequels. At age 32, Chris Columbus had become one of the industry's most bankable directors.

It was the movie *Mrs. Doubtfire*, however, which first brought the diehard New Yorker to the Bay Area. After filming, he returned to New York, but he missed the slower, more family-friendly, more creative environment of San Francisco. Columbus's production company, 1492 Pictures, is now headquartered in North Beach, just a few blocks away from where Phil Kaufman and Francis Ford Coppola have their offices. "This is the community I want to be a part of," he says. "The filmmakers I grew up admiring are now part of my neighborhood, and that is exciting."

Columbus made two of his next four films, *Nine Months* and *Bicentennial Man*, in his new hometown, but brought his entire family to England to direct the first two *Harry Potter* movies: *Harry Potter and the Sorcerer's Stone* (2001) and *Harry Potter and the Chamber of Secrets* (2002). As a father, he insists on the importance of balancing family and work. "Making movies is a job. It's a wonderful job, but it's still a job. I have four children," he explains. "And I have to give them some time." His most recent labor of love is *Rent*, the film version of the hit Broadway musical, which was filmed largely on Treasure Island. Columbus describes his first viewing of Rent as the most inspirational night he'd ever spent at the theater, and when it came time to cast the film version he cast many of the original Broadway performers who first moved him years ago. Not surprisingly, "Rent" is about an American family, one bound not by traditional blood ties but by love.

Chris Columbus.

HOME ALONE (1990)

The poster for the movie, which has Macaulay Culkin with his hands on his face screaming, is based on the famous painting *The Scream* by Edvard Munch, an apt image for a movie which taps into the primeval childhood terrors: abandonment and fear of strangers. From the moment he first received the script from Hughes, Columbus knew that it was the rich vein that could be mined for comedy, especially because it resonated with his own nightmares as a child that had been brought on by first seeing the definitely-not-for-kids movie *In Cold Blood*.

"I made my family disappear!"

—Kevin McCallister

RIGHT: Kevin McCallister (Macaulay Culkin) is accidently left behind when his family flies to France for Christmas without him. BELOW: Marv Merchants (Daniel Stern) and Harry Lime (Joe Pesci) are idiotic burglers who are outwitted by an 8-year-old.

The child's scars nursed the filmmaker's vision. "For this picture," says Columbus, "I was mostly inspired by old David Lean films, particularly *Oliver Twist* and *Great Expectations*, both told from a child's perspective. No one has shown the terror of being a child in an adult world better than Lean." Culkin played Kevin McCallister, a boy whose parents leave him behind during a hectic morning preparing for a family trip to Paris. At first young Kevin has a field day. He jumps on the bed, digs up some old *Playboys* ("No clothes on anybody," he shudders. "Sickening!"), and makes a kitchen firing range out of the family rifle. Kevin also settles in for a private viewing of a movie called *Angels with Filthy Souls*—which he later uses, hilariously, to frighten the burglars at his doorstep. (He achieves his *ruse de guerre* with nothing but imagination, a VCR, and a remote control.)

The film also played with the slapstick rhythms of a Saturday-morning cartoon, as the two bumbling burglars played by Daniel Stern and an unusually child-friendly Joe Pesci, of course, prove no match for the boy's wiles. By the time his mother (Catherine O'Hara) makes it back to him from Paris, Kevin, a wily Tom to his two clueless Jerrys, has vanquished his foes on his own. As *New York Times* film critic Caryn James wrote, "That's the holiday spirit behind this surprisingly charming film, which may be the first Christmas black comedy for children."

MRS. DOUBTFIRE (1993)

Columbus first knew he wanted to work with the master impresario and Bay Area treasure Robin Williams after seeing his dazzling improvisational work playing a DJ in Barry Levinson's *Good Morning Vietnam*. "It was like catching lightening in a bottle," he says. "I wanted to

CLINT EASTWOOD

From Hollywood bit player to television heartthrob to American icon to action hero and finally, today, to internationally acclaimed director, 75-year-old Clint Eastwood has come closer than almost any other filmmaker in America to maintaining the integrity of his own artistic vision while still being backed by the Hollywood studio system. For years, he has had a handshake financing deal with Warner Brothers, but he lives in Carmel-by-the-Sea. His two most recent films, *Mystic River* and *Million Dollar Baby*, considered to be among his greatest pictures, were a struggle to get green-lighted, even though Eastwood has a well-deserved reputation for bringing home lucrative films under budget. But Eastwood is as tenacious and stubborn today as he was as a young actor with dreams of directing.

Clint Eastwood was born Clinton Eastwood Jr. in 1930 during the Great Depression. His father, a bond salesman forced to take various jobs to support the family, moved the Eastwoods up and down the state of California before settling down in Oakland, where his son graduated from Oakland Technical High School in 1948. A jazz lover like Saul Zaentz, Eastwood—as young as the age of 15—would go to a club in Oakland to hear Dave Brubeck, Charlie Parker, and other musicians play. After high school, Eastwood drifted from job to job, working as a lumberjack, a honky-tonk piano player, and a swimming instructor in the U.S. Army. On the G.I. bill he went to Los Angeles City College before becoming a contract player at Universal in 1955. After Eastwood had acted in a few (mostly science-fiction) movies, a studio executive spotted him in a cafeteria and offered him the second lead in the TV series *Rawhide*. He accepted.

From 1959 to 1966, American television viewers knew Eastwood as Rowdy Yates, a bland hero who only rarely lived up to his name. As the challenge of playing Yates wore off, Eastwood began studying the many directors who worked on the show, learning as much as he could about the craft of filmmaking. When an offer to direct a few episodes himself fell through, he accepted an overseas job working for a European director making Westerns in Italy. The decision proved one of the most fortuitous of his career—Sergio Leone's "spaghetti Westerns," as they came to be called, made Eastwood an international star. When he returned to Hollywood he soon formed his own production company, Malpaso, and began working with the original 1956 *Invasion of the Body Snatchers* director Don Siegel, who both encouraged him to

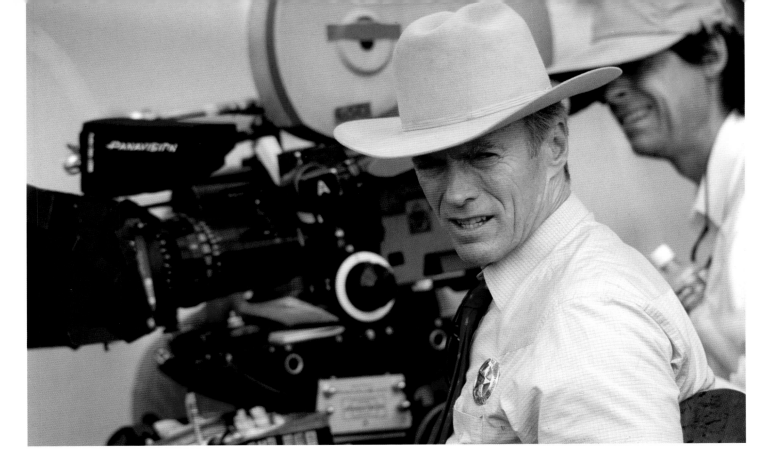

direct and signed his introduction to the Directors Guild. Eastwood's first film, *Play Misty For Me*, was enough of a success to guarantee him more directing work, even if critical respect would be a long time coming. His films were sometimes commercial (*Sudden Impact*), sometimes idiosyncratic (*Bronco Billy*, *Pale Rider*) but always personal, and gradually earned him more critical acclaim in the U.S. (he was always well respected in Europe). Over the years, he has garnered an almost unprecedented level of honor and respect in the business, especially for an actor-turned-director, including Best Picture and Best Director Oscars for *Unforgiven* and *Million Dollar Baby*, Best Picture and Best Director nominations for *Mystic River*, the 1994 Irving Thalberg award, three Golden Globes, the 1988 Cecil B. DeMille, and a lifetime-achievement award from the American Film Institute in 1996. Like other Northern California directors, such as George Lucas, Francis Ford Coppola, and Saul Zaentz, Eastwood has proven that one can make films without being forced to live in Hollywood and play by Hollywood's rules.

"You go by feel. You should know what you are looking for from something and know when it happens. Otherwise, you shouldn't be doing it."

—Clint Eastwood, on directing

PLAY MISTY FOR ME (1971)

For *Play Misty for Me*, the first feature film directed by Eastwood, Universal agreed to let him direct as part of his three-feature deal, but refused to pay him a director's fee. Eastwood was grateful for the chance to prove himself, and agreed to work for a cut of the profit. The gamble paid off: *Play Misty for Me*, an understated chiller, cost less than

TRIVIA

*Eastwood's mentor and the director on the
first two* Dirty Harry *films, Don Siegel, had
a cameo in the first film Eastwood directed.
Eastwood later joked that it was his way of
turning the tables on his own mentor and
"being the boss for a change."*

$800,000, made over $16 million in U.S. box office, was filmed on-location in less than one month, and established him as a director.

In a move he would repeat in most of his films—from *High Plains Drifter* (1973) to *The Outlaw Josey Wales* (1976) to *Sudden Impact* (1983) and, of course, *Unforgiven* (1992)—Eastwood starred as well as directed. He played Dave Garver, a silky-voiced jazz DJ with the well-deserved reputation of being a heartbreaker. One night at his favorite bar, he meets and seduces an attractive

young woman named Evelyn—rather, he *thinks* he's seducing her. It turns out that she is the fan who has been calling him every night with a husky late night request: "Play 'Misty' for me." He succumbs to her wiles even as his common sense blanches at her violent mood swings and instantaneous, obsessive love for him. The movie slowly builds up to something much more uncomfortable when his ex-girlfriend Toby (Donna Mills) steps back into the picture. It's a formula which would be imitated in the much more high-profile Michael Douglas blockbuster *Fatal Attraction*, but while Glenn Close played her villainess as a homicidal vision of the wildly sexual femme fatale, Jessica Walter's Evelyn was a much more heartbreaking and convincing lunatic. Years later, Walters would say, "There's a big trap to playing a woman who's crazy, and that's to playing her crazy." Walters opted for a different strategy, and that was to find the terror inside the woman, and thus elicit our sympathy: "She had to have this man—or die." Evelyn becomes a tragic psychopath, in many ways, a more sympathetic hero than the callow Garver, and her performance anchors the film.

Eastwood showed an immediate and clear sense of vision as a director. Thrifty where it counted (there was almost no budget for wardrobe, makeup, or set design, and most of the movie was shot in Carmel, where Eastwood was guaranteed the enthusiastic help of the locals), he was also willing to spend a great deal of money on what was dearest to him, including shelling out $25,000 for rights to the Errol Garner song

TOP RIGHT: **Jessica Walter plays Evelyn Draper, a crazed fan of disc jockey Dave Garland (Clint Eastwood).**
ABOVE: **Garland playing Evelyn's favorite song.**

"Misty." The film received mixed reviews, although Roger Ebert did praise its cruel efficiency and noticed a key signature of the director's developing style, a skill that he had always had as an actor and would spend the next thirty-odd years honing from the other side of the camera: "He is strong but somehow passive," wrote Ebert. "He possesses strength but keeps it coiled inside."

HIGH PLAINS DRIFTER (1973)

As Eastwood tells it, the treatment for *High Plains Drifter* revolved around a question: What would have happened if the sheriff of *High Noon* had been killed? What would have happened afterwards?

When the drifter rolls into a four-building town in the Old West, long, lean, squinting, and impervious to the hostile looks of the townspeople as he rides through its main street, one could easily be led to believe that this will be a continuation of Eastwood's anecdotal, atmospheric work with Sergio Leone. It starts familiarly enough. The tall stranger heads straight to the bar and asks for "a beer and bottle." When the bartender asks if he needs anything else, he replies, "Just a quiet hour to drink it in." This is the Eastwood that we have come to love: the laconic gunfighter who knows exactly what to say and how to say it in the fewest possible words. But the drifter exhibits a nastiness that we would not expect, a naked sadism that makes it impossible to enjoy the unfolding tension.

One of the first things he does is rape a local strumpet, and the fact that she seems to enjoy it does not lessen his sin—rather, it underscores the sense of corruption and shame that permeates all the action.

After the drifter proves his worth as a gunman—violently, of course—he is hired by the townsmen to protect them from a few outlaws. The outlaws are three brothers who were convicted of the lashing death of the town's former lawman and have just been released from the county jail. It was a death witnessed (and bought

The drifter (Clint Eastwood) comes to Lago, makes a bargain, turns it into Hell and leaves.

The drifter (Clint Eastwood) rides tall in the Southwest frontier of the 1870s.

"What did you say your name was again?"
"I didn't."

—from *High Plains Drifter*

and paid for) by the entire town, and while Eastwood's hero—or villain (we are not yet sure which)—accepts their offer, he makes a series of bizarre demands on the townsmen: first, that they paint the entire town red (this is where the expression comes from); then, that they arm themselves. He appoints a dwarf-size outcast to be the town mayor, humiliates his bosses one by one, and by the time the lawmen he's been hired to work for arrive, almost no one escapes the curse that the stranger's arrival seems to have wrought.

High Plains Drifter is an unpleasant film to sit through, one in which the hero's cruelty is hardly less than that of the town's, and the viewer is implicated in every scene. It's a film whose chief moral outrage is not for the villain, but for the people who watch evil and stand by. Not until the story's end is the drifter's identity revealed, and even then, the credits roll before a flinching eye. Not surprisingly, many reviewers quaffed at the film's violence without, it seems, understanding that the violence formed part and parcel of Eastwood's bitter condemnation of a very specific kind of evil that comes from a combination of greed, cowardice, and groupthink. It would be nineteen years before he delivered the same message in a more palatable way in *Unforgiven*.

UNFORGIVEN (1992)

In the years following *High Plains Drifter*, Eastwood made several more Westerns, including the classics *The Outlaw Josey Wales* and *Pale Rider*. Throughout his career as a director, Eastwood toyed with, subverted, and often undermined his heroic onscreen persona, both the one-

Munny (Eastwood) with his old partner Ned Logan (Morgan Freeman) and The Schofield Kid (Jaimz Woolvett) blurs the line between heroism and villainy.

dimensional good guy of *Rawhide* and the glamorous outlaws of the spaghetti Westerns which made him famous. With *Unforgiven*, however, he not only toyed with those elements, but also smashed them to pieces, in a stunning, elegiac piece of work that even *Gunfighter Nation* writer and Western myth debunker Richard Slotkin praised, saying "I hoped it could be a farewell to the Western."

Eastwood plays Bill Munny, an aging widow and father, who had "killed women and children... killed just about everything that walks or crawls in this world at one time or another." When he finally agrees to pick up a gun again, it seems he's doing so for the right reason: to avenge the cruel disfigurement of a prostitute, for a bounty raised by her fellow prostitute. But is death a fair punishment for disfigurement, no matter how cruel? The prostitutes refuse an attempted financial compensation, and so set in motion a chain of violence which, in true Eastwood style will approach slowly, with time and room to watch its inexorable pull gradually draw in every single character: Little Bill, a local sheriff, who is doing his best to keep law and order in town, but a best that is finally laden with his egotism; Munny's best friend Ned Logan; English Bob, a charming and amoral gunman now selling his story to a hungry press; and of course Munny himself, who has lived the

TOP: **With his wife dead from smallpox, the aging outlaw William "Bill" Munny contemplates his future.**
TOP: **Retired gunslinger Munny tests his aim**
OVERLEAF: **With his children to think of, Munny reluctantly takes on one last job.**

**Sheriff Little Bill (Gene Hackman)
confronts Munny.**

past ten years of his life in search of redemption, but who finds himself, at the film's end, unredeemed, unredeemable, and finally, unforgiven.

To this day, Eastwood claims he never intended to make an anti-Western, but just wanted to tell a good story. Yet by focusing so relentlessly on the moral ambiguities of violence and heroism, which so many traditional westerns have attempted to bypass, Eastwood and screen writer David Webb Peoples (who also, not coincidentally, wrote the equally subversive screenplay for the Ridley Scott classic *Blade Runner*) do just that. Still, Slotkin was right when he points out that what *Unforgiven* shows is that "salvation by violence doesn't really work, that in the end the punishment is worse than the crime." Perhaps because of its nuanced message, *Unforgiven* won four Oscars, including Best Actor in a Supporting Role (Gene Hackman), Best Directing (Clint Eastwood), Best Film Editing (Joel Cox) and Best Picture (Clint Eastwood, Producer).

FILMOGRAPHY

2004	*Million Dollar Baby*
2003	*Mystic River*
2002	*Blood Work*
2000	*Space Cowboys*
1999	*True Crime*
1997	*Midnight in the Garden of Good and Evil*
	Absolute Power
1995	*The Bridges of Madison County*
1993	*A Perfect World*
1992	*Unforgiven*
1990	*The Rookie*
	White Hunter, Black Heart
1988	*Bird*
1986	*Heartbreak Ridge*
1985	*Pale Rider*
1983	*Sudden Impact*
1982	*Honkytonk Man*
	Firefox
1980	*Bronco Billy*
1977	*The Gauntlet*
1976	*The Outlaw Josey Wales*
1975	*The Eiger Sanction*
1973	*Breezy*
	High Plains Drifter
1971	*Play Misty for Me*

A PERFECT WORLD (1993)

The unlikely hero of *A Perfect World*, Kevin Costner's Butch Haynes, is a borderline-sociopathic escaped prisoner who takes a young boy hostage on his run to Alaska. The boy and the convict, both hungry for their fathers, develop a complicated relationship on the way. While the plot sounds like it might have the potential to be a sentimental buddy picture, the film strikes not one wrong or sentimental note. Once again, Eastwood is not afraid to show the weakness in his tough-guy character, playing a small-town law officer who chases Haynes across Texas. He is just doing his job, just as he was only doing his job when he had Haynes sent up for a four-year bid in a tough juvenile prison when Haynes was just a teenager.

It is the kind of film that—were Eastwood a clumsier director—would begin with a voiceover, in which the young boy, now a grown man would solemnly intone, "I spent two days of my life in the company of Butch Haynes. He might not have been the father I never had, but he taught me how to live just the same." The moments in which Butch seems like a potential father for young Phillip, the son of a strict, joyless household (his fam-

ily are Jehovah's Witnesses), are precious but all the more so because we know they can't last.

T.J. Lowther's performance as young Phillip, with his mobile, arresting face, all-scrunched-up lips, wide eyes, and long lashes, is excellent. But it is Costner who shines, in what ought to be considered the best role of his career. Freed from the constraints of a romantic role, Costner endows his Butch with a combination of competence and barely restrained rage, and even though we want to believe in his redemption, we know from the first frame that he won't find the escape he's looking for. He knows that his days are limited, and that even though he is off to Alaska to find his father, he'll probably never get there. His Butch Haynes is tough and principled but, ultimately, as doomed by his boyhood past as by his outlaw status.

A Perfect World is set just days before the Kennedy assassination. Its characters live imperfectly in the "perfect world" idealized by Americans today. Janet Maslin of *The New York Times* praised its "sober intelligence and welcome dearth of empty heroics" and called it that "rare high-powered Hollywood film that is actually about something." The film was not a huge commercial success domestically, but grossed over $100 million overseas. It remains a favorite in the Eastwood canon and a minor classic of the nineties.

"The road behind you, that's your past. Up here in front, that's your future. This here's the present— enjoy it while you can. "

—Butch

PHILIP KAUFMAN

Philip Kaufman graduated from the University of Chicago in 1958 and went on to Harvard Law School for one year before returning to the University of Chicago to begin a master's degree in history. In 1960 he and his wife, Rose, headed west to San Francisco, baby son Peter in tow. One of their first adventures was to trek down to Big Sur to look for Kaufman's hero, the novelist Henry Miller.

Like true San Francisco bohemians, they worked odd jobs (Kaufman even had stints as a mailman and a Fuller Brush salesman). They eventually lived in Europe for a few years, where Philip taught mathematics while working on a novel, and there they fell in love with avant-garde European film of the."New Wave." Inspired by the work of the American independent filmmakers Shirley Clarke and John Cassavetes, Kaufman returned to Chicago in 1962, determined to make independent features in America. He then met Anaïs Nin, who encouraged him to become a filmmaker. In 1963 he took his unfinished novel and, with friends, raised enough money to make the comedy *Goldstein*. The film, shot on a shoe-string budget, about a modern-day prophet wandering the city streets, won the Prix de la Novelle Critique at the 1964 Cannes Film Festival. The following year Kaufman managed to raise money for a second film, *Fearless Frank* (aka *Frank's Greatest Adventure*) starring Jon Voight in his first film. Two years later he was in Hollywood under contract to Universal. While in L.A. he wrote and directed *The Great Northfield Minnesota Raid*, starring Robert Duvall and Cliff Robertson, then in 1973 went to the Arctic to direct *The White Dawn*. Like so many of his peers in southern California, Kaufman became disenchanted with Hollywood and returned to San Francisco to edit *The White Dawn* at American Zoetrope's south of Market offices on Folsom Street.

Kaufman later helped George Lucas develop the story for *Raiders of the Lost Ark*, and then wrote the script to *The Outlaw Josey Wales*, which he directed until actor Clint Eastwood took over the film citing "creative differences." (The move prompted the Directors Guild of America to institute a rule that no DGA member can be replaced by anyone working in any capacity on the same film, now known as "Eastwood's rule.")

Success finally came to Kaufman in 1978 with the smash-hit variation on the 1956 movie *Invasion of the Body Snatchers*, followed by *The Wanderers*, and then *The Right Stuff*, which went on to win four Academy Awards. His most controversial film may have been *Henry and June*, starring Fred Ward and

Philip Kaufman directing *Twisted*.

Maria de Medeiros as his old heroes Henry Miller and Anaïs Nin. The film caused the MPAA to create the first NC-17 rating.

Though his work on *The Unbearable Lightness of Being*, *Henry and June*, and *Quills* shows a European sensibility with sexuality in film, Kaufman's style, moving from genre to genre even within films, makes him a difficult director to classify. But this is both his charm and what makes him such a classic San Francisco personality: "I don't really ascribe to the theory that a distinguished filmmaker, an auteur, makes a movie at 19 with guys shooting guns at each other and is supposed to replicate that movie for the next fifty years.... I'm interested in many things."

"Living up here is great—not being in a L.A. environment where you can get broken down. In San Francisco I don't feel competitive with anybody about making films. My only competition comes with the material and trying to do the best I can with it. In L.A., everybody at the next table's worrying, 'Spielberg's doing what?'"

—Philip Kaufman

INVASION OF
THE BODY SNATCHERS (1978)

Dr. Matthew Bennell (Donald Sutherland) and his lab assistant Elizabeth (Brooke Adams) are puzzled as they examine an unfamiliar blossom.

"… in a way, everything that was being talked about in Body Snatchers *has come to pass … we are now living in a world largely controlled by pods."*

—Philip Kaufman

TRIVIA

Robert Duvall was given an Eddie Bauer arctic coat for his cameo in Invasion of the Body Snatchers. *Kevin McCarthy, the star of the original film, also had a brief appearance—as the hysterical man who throws himself on the windshield of Donald Sutherland's car. In homage to the original 1956 version, Kaufman cast the original director, Don Siegel, as a pod-taxi driver towards the film's end.*

In *Invasion of the Body Snatchers*, where alien invaders mysteriously take over people's bodies and turn them into evil pods, there is another sinister presence lurking onscreen throughout much of the picture: San Francisco's Transamerica Pyramid. The distinctive landmark building seen throughout the film housed the parent company of United Artists, who financed the film; while making the movie, Kaufman and his crew had an ongoing joke of affectionately (or perhaps not so affectionately) calling the building "pod central."

The combination of terror and humor runs through the genre-bending film, which is at once a horror flick, a film noir, a love story, a comedy, and a subtle commentary on late-seventies California culture. It stars Donald Sutherland, Veronica Cartwright (one of Kaufman's favorite actresses and a veteran of the Hitchcock classic *The Birds*), Brooke Adams, Jeff Goldblum, and Leonard Nimoy, lampooning his hyperlogical *Star Trek* character as a pop psychologist turned arch-villain. Sutherland plays a health supervisor who begins by shutting down unsanitary restaurants (the restaurant chosen for the foreboding opening scene is San Francisco's Bimbo's) and ends by trying to fight a civilization-threatening plague. His character is not a dashing, romantic hero but rather a bureaucrat who loves Asian cooking and carries a secret torch for one of his employees, the wide-eyed and lovely Elizabeth Driscoll (Brooke Adams).

Perhaps more than any other film of the seventies, *Invasion of the Body Snatchers* is a true San Francisco film. Kaufman invited local writers like Herb Gold, Curt Gentry, and Rose Kaufman, his wife and sometimes co-writer, to appear in the Leonard Nimoy book-party scene. And Tom Luddy, a close friend of Kaufman's and indispensable figure in Bay Area film history, has a cameo as a pod person. The humor is macabre and its main characters eccentric and likeable, but it is still one of the scariest movies of the seventies. Michael Chapman (*Taxi Driver*, *Raging Bull*) shoots it with noir stylization, and the film is loaded with foreboding, skewed images: people in suits running down the streets for no apparent reason, shots of San Francisco through Sutherland's cracked car window, Robert Duvall in a cameo shot in the film's very first scene as a priest on a playground swing. And of course, the film's last scene, one which even the studio heads, cast, and crew weren't told of until the film's opening night, stands as one of the great classic moments in American Horror.

THE RIGHT STUFF (1983)

Today, *The Right Stuff* is considered by many to be Kaufman's greatest film. Ironically, however, the exhilarating, epic story of the first astronauts and pilots who broke the sound barrier was not a commercial success when it first hit the theaters due to its small-platform "road show" release and to an unfortunate link with the real John Glenn's bid for the presidency. Like Kaufman's earlier cult favorite, *The Wanderers*, which suffered from its release proximity to *The Warriors* (where there was violence and death in the theaters), *The Right Stuff* may not have been successful by Hollywood's box office standards, but it was destined nevertheless to become a classic.

Based on Tom Wolfe's masterful retelling of the early days of the space program, *The Right Stuff*, like *Invasion*, drew on Bay Area locations (Market Street, The Cow Palace, Half Moon Bay) and Bay Area talent (especially Jordan Belson, the sixties experimental filmmaker who did the special effects, and the now-defunct Colossal Pictures, which helped create the believable flying effects). Roger Ebert called *The Right Stuff* his second favorite film of the decade with its "daring blend of styles, from social satire to historical reconstruction to flat-out space opera." The story weaves back and forth from the private lives of the media heroes who manned the first trips in space (including John Glenn, Gus Grissom, Gordon Cooper, Alan Shepard, and Chuck Yaeger—the test pilot who broke the "demon in the

FILMOGRAPHY

2004	*Twisted*
2000	*Quills*
1993	*Rising Sun*
1990	*Henry & June*
1988	*The Unbearable Lightness of Being*
1983	*The Right Stuff*
1979	*The Wanderers*
1978	*Invasion of the Body Snatchers*
1974	*The White Dawn*
1972	*The Great Northfield Minnesota Raid*
1967	*Fearless Frank*
1965	*Goldstein*

LEFT AND ABOVE: Phil Kaufman directing *The Right Stuff*.

"There was a demon that lived in the air.
They said whoever challenged it would die...."

—Voice over

air," the sound barrier) to the politics behind their publicity to the lone-wolf heroism of Yeager. Like the book, the film explores the "American circus" and questions what it means to have the "right stuff." The film was most notably a celebration of courage in the face of danger; it is a tribute to the valor of the test pilots, the astronauts, and the women behind these heroes. *The Right Stuff* was a launching pad for many careers of its ensemble cast, among them Ed Harris, Dennis Quaid, Fred Ward, Sam Shepard, and Scott Glenn. It was nominated for eight Oscars and won four: Sound, Film Editing, Score, and Sound Effects Editing.

TWISTED (2004)

In 2004 Kaufman again returned to shoot a noir thriller entirely in San Francisco—this time starring Ashley Judd, Samuel L. Jackson, and Andy Garcia. In his four-star review, critic Michael Sragow observed, "Kaufman knows the odd corners of the city's misty parks and sea-lion laden piers and lived-in saloons ... he lets you taste the city's lusciousness in packed frame after packed frame ... where cops ... criminals ... and lawyers ... give in to the thick, sensuous environment."

"Everyone...who kisses me...turns up dead...."

—Jessica Shepard (Ashley Judd)

OPPOSITE: **The first seven astronauts selected for the NASA space program making history in *The Right Stuff*.**
LEFT: **Jessica Shepard (Ashley Judd) in *Twisted*.**

JOHN KORTY

Director John Korty.

In 1966, the 30-year-old John Korty, thrilled and stunned by the runaway festival success of his first feature film, *Crazy Quilt*, picked up the ringing telephone in his Marin studio, and a voice he'd never heard before said, "You don't know me, but I live in Texas, and I just saw your movie last night and decided to become a film director." The caller was Terrence Malick, who would go on to direct *Badlands* and the seven-time Academy Award–nominated film *The Thin Red Line*. He was not the only young artist who would be influenced by the pioneering director. It was Korty's modest, but independent production studio in Marin that provided the example for young Francis Ford Coppola and George Lucas to set up shop in the Bay Area. Over the past forty-plus years, countless other young filmmakers have worked on or been inspired by Korty's films.

Korty, an Indiana native, was first influenced by the art of abstract animator Norman McLaren and began making short films at the age of 16. He started his own television-commercial company while still a student at Antioch College, and then for his first job after graduation, moved to Philadelphia to make documentaries for the Quakers. One of them, *The Language of Faces*, won the young filmmaker eleven film-festival prizes, and, in his own words "sort of put me on the map." Korty moved to New York for a year and taught animation at Columbia University. He knew that the big-city life was not for him, however, and in 1963 he went west with a dream of living on the edge of the ocean and rented a small house in Stinson Beach for $125 a month. Though still a young filmmaker, his move to Northern California was the move of an adult, not a teenaged dreamer searching North Beach for inspiration. He expanded his production capacity beyond a wind-up Bolex by buying a Siemens double-system projector, and raised the money for his first feature film, rounding up the funds from forty-three separate investors.

"I'm not that crafty a person," he explains, "but I was crafty enough to figure out that if I had forty-three investors, there was no one investor who could tell me how to make my movie." *Crazy Quilt* was a bittersweet romantic comedy which poked gentle fun the existential crises of a young California couple. Shot in black and white and narrated by an immediately wry and recognizable Burgess Meredith, the movie opened to rave reviews and helped Korty secure funding for his next film, *Funnyman*.

ABOVE: John Korty, David Schickele,
and Sheilah Dorcy on location at the
Palace of the Legion of Honor
in San Francisco for *Crazy Quilt*.
LEFT: Lorabelle, the Visionary Maid,
played by Ina Mela and Henry,
the Illusionless Man, played by
Tom Rosqui in *Crazy Quilt*.
BELOW: John Korty with Carol Androsky
on *Funnyman*.

As with *Crazy Quilt*, Korty took his inspiration from local culture, specifically a San Francisco–based comedy troupe called The Committee. *Funnyman*, starring Peter Bonerz, was made for two-and-a-half times the cost of *Crazy Quilt* at $110,000, with a crew of five people instead of three. After watching Bonerz and his compatriots wisecrack their way through life, Korty decided to build a film around another existential comedy: "How does an actor know when he's acting and when he isn't?" The movie won him more praise and several meetings with Hollywood agents.

"I had big fancy lunches with these guys who came up to San Francisco, and they all wanted me to sign up with their agency. But I told them, 'I made this film, I raised the money for it, and when it was done, you know what? It was my film. I liked that and I want to do it again.'"

R O B
N I L S S O N

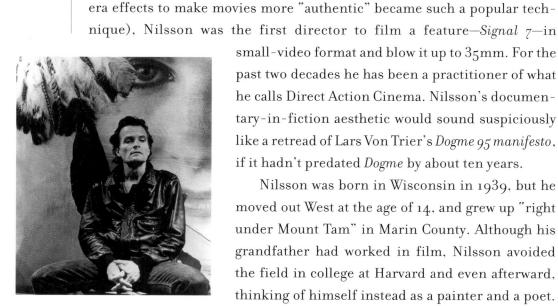

Though the Bay Area has produced some very high profile, mainstream filmmakers, there are dozens of talented local directors whose work is much less well known but no less innovative. These directors are in their own way as essential to the area's vitality as Lucas, Coppola, and Zaentz. Among the most accomplished of these is the multiple-award winning and stubbornly experimental Rob Nilsson. A pioneer of handheld video and an early believer in the democratizing power of digital cinema, Nilsson has been living and working in San Francisco for more than twenty-five years. Influenced by John Cassavetes, who introduced guerilla-style filmmaking (long before using jittery-camera effects to make movies more "authentic" became such a popular technique), Nilsson was the first director to film a feature—*Signal 7*—in small-video format and blow it up to 35mm. For the past two decades he has been a practitioner of what he calls Direct Action Cinema. Nilsson's documentary-in-fiction aesthetic would sound suspiciously like a retread of Lars Von Trier's *Dogme 95 manifesto*, if it hadn't predated *Dogme* by about ten years.

Nilsson was born in Wisconsin in 1939, but he moved out West at the age of 14, and grew up "right under Mount Tam" in Marin County. Although his grandfather had worked in film, Nilsson avoided the field in college at Harvard and even afterward, thinking of himself instead as a painter and a poet. Still, he caught the bug after making a short film with some friends called *The Lesson* while living in Africa. "Luckily for film history," he says today, "the only copy was stolen."

Nilsson codirected his first feature film, *Northern Lights* with John Hanson. The movie is about an uprising among struggling North Dakota Norwegian immigrant farmers during the famine in 1915 and won the Prix de la Camera d'Or at Cannes. After *On The Edge*, a critically acclaimed but, he felt, personally compromised studio venture starring Bruce Dern premiered, Nilsson self-produced *Signal 7*. Presented by Francis Ford Coppola, it achieved worldwide distribution. Next came *Heat and Sunlight*, a passionate and often very hilarious look at the last sixteen hours in an obsessive love affair, which took the Grand Jury Prize at Sundance. Today, Nilsson's rather

LEFT: Recent Rob Nilsson self portrait taken on a location scout for *Cycles*, a feature in development.
BELOW: Steve Burns' poignant poster photo for *Signal 7*. The egg is in reference to the acting exercise the director assigns Speed (Bill Ackridge behind the bubble) during the audition scene.

astonishing achievement (he was the first American director to ever win both awards) may well have propelled him to "A-lister with edge" status, as it did to more recent Sundance honorees like Todd Solendz, David O. Russell, and Terry Zwigoff, who can now command big budgets and big-name stars. But in the pre–Steven Soderbergh seventies and eighties, winning top laurels as an independent filmmaker was an unlikely stepping stone to Hollywood success. Nilsson's films, which push Cassavetes-style, loosely plotted, and improvisation-based (though still scripted) stories forward, make your average Sundance entry look like a Joel Schumacher release. That they did not lead to Hollywood blockbusters is probably something he didn't much mind, though some money might have been nice.

Today, Nilsson has applied his organic, raw directing style to making films with low-profile actors, or, even more likely, nonprofessional performers, whom he prefers to call "players ." He makes movies internationally—in South Africa, Japan, and Jordan—but most consistently, he works locally in San Francisco's Tenderloin district. His interest in collaborating with Tenderloin residents, most of them homeless, grew out of his search for his own homeless younger brother. Nilsson would scour the Tenderloin every day on the way to the editing room where he was finishing up *Heat and Sunlight*, at first looking for a sign of his brother, but finally just captivated by the men and women he did meet. He formed the Tenderloin Action Group (now known as the Tenderloin Y Group) a loosely organized film collective who have developed a nine-part series called 9@Night based on the work they've been doing together in their weekly Wednesday workshops for the past fifteen years.

As of this writing, the 9@Night films have all been shot, and about half have been edited and screened. Nilsson finances them through grants, foundations, and benefit concerts. The scrappy financing style seems appropriate to his vision as a filmmaker. "We're squatters," he says proudly of his troop. "Squatters in the arena of cinema."

FILMOGRAPHY

1996 *Chalk*
1988 *Heat and Sunlight*
1986 *On the Edge*
1986 *Signal 7*
1979 *Nothern Lights*

MICHAEL

RITCHIE

Michael Ritchie was born in Wisconsin in 1938 and raised in Berkeley, where his father was a psychology professor and his mother worked as an art-and-music librarian. He first became interested in directing while studying history and literature at Harvard University. His success with plays like *Oh Dad, Poor Dad, Mama's Hung You in the Closet and I'm Feeling So Sad* got him jobs after graduation in television, where he worked on series like *Dr. Kildare*, *Omnibus*, and *Profiles in Courage*, which brought him to the attention of Robert Redford. His first film, *Downhill Racer*, starred Redford as a self-absorbed ski champion and was notable as much for its light touch as for its thrilling on-ski camera work. In *Downhill Racer* and in his next two films—*The Candidate*, a devastating take-down of American political campaigns, and *Smile*, a withering attack on beauty-pageant culture—Ritchie uses a loose, casual directing style and shows the audience his delicious ability to see that which is ridiculous in the American spirit of competition and winner-worship. Even if he had done nothing else besides this triptych of mock-documentary films in the late sixties and early seventies, he would have earned a reputation as a scathing and important comic director. But he soon followed these sharp satires with more commercial ventures, most notably the unlikely feel-good baseball movie *The Bad News Bears*, a film that managed to profile losers and be heartwarm-

ing at the same time—no mean feat. Ritchie pursued this line with *Semi-Tough*, a football movie starring Burt Reynolds.

Throughout most of the seventies, Ritchie lived and worked in the Bay Area, sharing office space at George Lucas's Parkway facility with Hal Barwood, Matt Robbins, and for a time, Carroll Ballard. His directing style gradually became fluffier and fluffier, with eighties hits like *Fletch*, *Fletch Lives*, and the Eddie Murphy vehicle *The Golden Child*. But even as he made compromises to earn a living, Ritchie never totally lost his

Michael Ritchie at a 4th of July picnic at Skywalker Ranch, 1981.

Carroll Ballard once said that there is no such thing as a good movie that is badly edited. Ritchie, the director of many good movies, was known for shooting fast and loose, and for cutting corners on costs. His almost careless directing style was frequently well served by

the skills of his editor, **RICHARD HARRIS**. Ritchie and Harris worked together for more than twenty years, right up through the film *Fletch Lives* in 1989. Harris ultimately moved on to work with James Cameron. He was nominated for an Oscar for *Terminator 2* and won for film editing (with Conrad Buff and James Cameron) on *Titanic*.

Richard Harris, from editor to winemaker, in Santa Ynez.

FILMOGRAPHY

2000 *The Fantasticks*
1997 *A Simple Wish*
1994 *The Scout*
   Cops and Robbersons
1992 *Diggstown*
1989 *Fletch Lives*
1988 *The Couch Trip*
1986 *The Golden Child*
   Wildcats
1985 *Fletch*
1983 *The Survivors*
1980 *Divine Madness!*
   The Island
1979 *An Almost Perfect Affair*
1977 *Semi-Tough*
1976 *The Bad News Bears*
1975 *Smile*
1972 *The Candidate*
   Prime Cut
1969 *Downhill Racer*

edge. He was one of the first directors to recognize the artistic freedom in directing for television, with his HBO film, *The Positively True Adventures of the Alleged Texas Cheerleader Murdering Mom*, staring Holly Hunter as a hyper-driven backstage mother whose wild ambition and all-American dreams could have been ripped from any of his earlier films. Ritchie won a Director's Guild award for the TV film, and Holly Hunter won an Emmy. Years later, after Ritchie's untimely death of prostate cancer in 2001, Hunter praised both his gifts as a director and his comic sensibilities, "I can say without hesitation that it was the most fun I've ever had on a movie set."

THE CANDIDATE (1972)

NBC's once palliative and now saccharine television show, *The West Wing*, began its four-year journey on national television during the last years of the Clinton administration, asking the question: What would happen if a genuinely honest man ran for president? On TV, Martin Sheen's loveable and liberal Jed Bartlett took office with his integrity intact and ruled in kind for more seasons on NBC.

Michael Ritchie's underplayed and scathing political satire, *The Candidate*, asks the same question, and his far less encouraging answer remains as relevant today as it was in 1972, if not more so. Robert Redford, who coproduced the film, plays Bill McKay, an idealistic, young lawyer who fights for the working person and for environmental protection. McKay has turned his back on his ex-governor father and the corruption his father personifies. Marvin Lucas, a bearded, savvy campaign organizer lures McKay into a campaign for Senate with promises that the campaign will be a new kind, but McKay has no chance against Senator Crocker Jarmon (Don

Bill McKay (Robert Redford) is a candidate for the U.S. Senate from California with no hope of winning.

Porter), the wily incumbent. This is a campaign, promises Lucas, in which McKay will be able to wage political warfare as it ought to be waged, by appealing to the good will, idealism, education, and logic of the next generation.

Little by little, however, McKay finds himself disappearing in the implacable forward momentum of the campaign. All the props which have taken the place of issues are in place: glossy commercials, empty and abstract politics, an absurd attention to the beauty and dressing style of the candidate's wife, and, of course, a constant, worshipful enslavement to public-opinion polls. When his own father is asked how he thinks his son is performing, his father replies, "Who cares? He's cute."

By the film's end whether or not Redford's candidacy results in a victory is beside the point. He has already lost, and he knows it. Written by former McCarthy speechwriter, Jeremy Larner, who won an Oscar for his work, the film skewers the contemporary political process in a way that would be hilarious if it were only a bit less true, and along with *Smile*, stands today as Ritchie's best and most acute film, one which even by itself would guarantee him an honored place in film history.

THE BAD NEWS BEARS (1976)

**Beer drinking Coach Buttermaker
(Walter Matthau) trying to ignore his
pitcher Amanda (Tatum O'Neal).**

*"This quitting thing,
it's a hard habit to break
once you start."*

—Morris Buttermaker

On the surface, *The Bad News Bears* is exactly what it sounds like: a shaggy-dog movie in the grand American "everybody wins" tradition. Walter Matthau plays Morris Buttermaker, an alcoholic, down-on-his luck pitcher who is hired to manage an even more down-on-its-luck little-league baseball team. The kids curse, spit, fight, hurl racial epithets at each other, do everything, in fact, besides catch or throw, and at first Buttermaker has no interest in doing anything to help them. However, he has a secret weapon in the form of young Amanda (Tatum O'Neal), the preteen daughter of an ex-girlfriend, a tiny hellion with a killer throwing arm and, more importantly, deeply held dreams that Buttermaker will come back into her life.

All the expected heartwarming moments take place, and the audience does indeed leave the theater feeling good. But underneath its heartwarming plotline, the film reveals the underside of competition and the destructiveness of the pressure parents put on their children to win. There is a ruthlessness to some of the team's first humiliating losses that make the audience want to look away, and Matthau, a gifted comedian whose specialty

is finding likeability in unlikable characters, does not shy away from making his coach unsympathetic. It's clear from the start that he is just using Amanda for her skills, just as he uses the lonely, desperate boys to keep him in sauce. Instead of helping the boys practice their pitches, he drags them along to his other job, cleaning swimming pools, and he lounges and drinks while they do all the work. He convinces us that there is no real hope for his character, which makes his eventual redemption all the more meaningful and powerful.

There is also a brutal realism in Buttermaker's relationship with Amanda, and the chemistry between the two adds heart. The film came out in 1976, when single parents and feminism were first coming into mainstream movie culture, and Tatum O'Neal's hard-hitting, young tomboy, who just wants to be a fine young lady and find a father, has a heartbreaking wistfulness under her sprightly saves-the-day persona.

The film was Ritchie's first real moneymaker and gave him a new and well-deserved bankability in Hollywood. Film critic Robert Ebert noted the strength of the film, which could also be seen as Ritchie's forte: "He directs scenes for comedy even in the face of his disturbing material, and that makes the movie all the more effective; sometimes we laugh, and sometimes we can't, and the movie's working best when we're silent."

The aging, down-on-his-luck, ex-minor leaguer Coach Buttermaker drives his team of misfits to their next competitive little-league game.

TRIVIA

A very young Tatum O'Neal played a gifted baseball player desperate for love and attention from her father-figure coach, Morris Buttermaker. In real life, the young actress was living in a very similar situation with her own father, whose tumultuous years as her parent she documented in the brutally honest 2004 autobiography Paper Life.

MATTHEW ROBBINS

At the very end of *THX 1138*, a figure climbs out of a trap door and escapes into an unknown future, exultant and triumphant against a sunset sky. That figure is, of course, meant to be THX played by Robert Duvall, but in that last scene, THX is actually George Lucas's old USC classmate Matthew Robbins, who like so many others from that enchanted class became swept up in the early days of American Zoetrope. It is fitting that Robbins should have the film's visual last word because in 1966 the 23-year-old wrote the very first treatment for THX after a conversation with Lucas at a film school party. "I called it *Breakout*," he remembers now, "which was a pretty weak title." Though he didn't know it at the time, he was setting on what would be a pattern in his career: screenwriting as an entrée to filmmaking.

Robbins first came to USC with his college friend Walter Murch, whom he'd met at freshman orientation at John Hopkins University, and with whom he'd lived and studied in Italy and France during their junior year in college. While abroad, the two young men discovered they both loved cinema and motorcycles, and as seniors, they'd applied to film school in California. After graduating from USC, Robbins teamed up with another

Director Matthew Robbins (seated on steps) on the set of *Dragonslayer*.

The dragon from *Dragonslayer.*

classmate, Hal Barwood, and began writing screenplays for an up-and-coming agent named Jeff Berg (now the chairman and CEO of ICM). Berg negotiated a screenwriting contract for Robbins and Barwood that was separate from but later tied in to the original Zoetrope seven-script agreement—thus connecting them early on to American Zoetrope. "I'm still amazed at the entrepreneurial spirit that Francis and George showed at the time," says Robbins. "I mean, I had no idea then that this kind of thing was possible." Though it would be several years before he would move up to San Francisco himself, he was a frequent visitor, driving up in his old Volkswagen bus and staying with Walter and Aggie Murch on their Sausalito houseboat.

Like most of the other projects in Coppola's ill-fated deal, the script Robbins and Barwood wrote, a story about motorcycle racing and smuggling called *The Privateer*, slipped into oblivion. But on the basis of that script, they gained credibility and more paid screenwriting work, which meant, Robbins remembers, that they wrote five more scripts that were never produced, and essentially got paid to hone their craft. Even before the team

FILMOGRAPHY

1991 *Bingo*
1987 *Batteries Not Included*
1985 *The Legend of Billie Jean*
1981 *Dragonslayer*
1978 *Corvette Summer*

TRIVIA

Both Matthew Robbins and Hal Barwood played "returnees" in Steven Spielberg's 1977 hit, Close Encounters of the Third Kind.

Faye (Jessica Tandy) and Frank (Hume Cronyn) lead their fellow tenement dwellers in a battle against their evil landlord in *Batteries Not Included*.

"It's hard to believe, but in those days the USC film students, if we had a reputation at all, it was that we were very slick and influenced by Hollywood filmmaking as opposed to the UCLA filmmakers who were more into personal filmmaking or documentaries. I don't think there was much truth to this, but we kind of liked to believe it because it was so funny to be accused of slickness. We could barely put a film together!"

—Matthew Robbins

TRIVIA

Matthew Robbins first met George Lucas in a darkroom at USC.

struck gold and began working with Steven Spielberg on *The Sugarland Express*, they had developed a hankering to make films on their own. In 1974 they moved into Lucas's Parkway offices in Marin, cowrote *The Bingo Long Traveling All-Stars & Motor Kings* (1976) and *MacArthur* (1977), and made several films together, with Robbins directing and Barwood producing. For *Dragonslayer* (1981), a magical tale of cross-dressing sacrificial virgins, gallant and ambitious heroes, corrupt leaders, and one of the most fearsome dragons to ever grace—or curse—a movie screen, Robbins and Barwood reached back to the sober fantasy of the Brothers Grimm to make a decidedly unchildlike adventure, casting classically trained actors in the romantic leads (the kinds who, though American, pronounce *princess* with the accent on the second syllable) and a pitch-perfect Ralph Richardson as the wizard Ulrich, a wry elder with an acid tongue. In her rave review of the film,

Pauline Kael called attention to the significance of the film-maker's choice: "*Dragonslayer*," she wrote, "recalls reading a fairy tale that has the mixture of happiness and trauma to set your imagination whirling. It's true that almost everything in the film echoed in my memory; it all comes from movies. But it has been transformed and made new; in the terms the picture sets, it is almost completely successful."

In 1987, Robbins directed the sweet, lighthearted flying-saucer comedy *Batteries Not Included*, starring Jessica Tandy and Hume Cronyn (and cowritten by a team that included Brad Bird). Robbins continues to write for Hollywood while staying active in the Bay Area film community, teaching screenwriting workshops and participating in festivals. Robbins doesn't regret his decision to move to the Bay Area. "Being here," he says, "you felt that you belonged to a world that was ambitious artistically and that you could present something to them with a certain cachet that it was going to be, you hoped, different from product."

Faye encounters the alien who has come to help save her building from demolition.

Roger Ebert called Vermithrax Pejorative "one of the meanest, ugliest, most reprehensible creatures" he'd ever seen on film. That Ebert meant this as a compliment owes much to the genius of ILM and especially to **PHIL TIPPETT**, the special-effects supervisor on *Dragonslayer*, and the co-inventor of Go-Motion, an animation technique which used motorized and computerized rods to "blur" the movements of the dragon.

Tippett, a master of stop-motion animation, began working for ILM in 1975, and was largely responsible for the holographic chess characters in *Star Wars* and the tauntauns in *The Empire Strikes Back*. He left ILM in 1983 to found Tippett Studio and was eventually hired to create the dinosaurs for *Jurassic Park*. When Spielberg saw the digital advances being made at ILM, he decided to make the dinosaurs using digital effects instead of stop-motion. Fortunately, Tippett had a mastery of the mechanics and artistry of dinosaur motion, and his Digital-Input-Device was used to bridge the transition of stop-motion to digital animation. He is credited as *Jurassic Park*'s dinosaur supervisor.

Tippett's next major milestone was the hit movie *Starship Troopers* for director Paul Verhoeven, who had it written into his contract that he would only take the job if Tippett were "doing the bugs." Those bugs, which took

Phil Tippett,
master stop-motion animator.

four and a half years to realize, were so successful that Tippett received his sixth nomination in 1997 for an Academy Award and was given the chance to direct the film's sequel. Tippett Studio is now considered one of the premier effects houses in the Bay Area.

HENRY SELICK

Today, in part because of the extraordinary financial successes of such digitally produced films as *Shrek* and *The Incredibles*, computer-generated imagery (CGI) is the new darling of the film industry. Many of the creators working in the medium, however, view CGI as just one of many tools and still revere the masters of animation who worked and continue to work in hand-drawn, stop-motion, and claymation. A digital star, like Brad Bird or John Lasseter, will still speak with awe about animators like the original Disney cel artists, Japan's Hidao Miyazaki (who wrote and directed the highest-grossing film in Japanese box-office history, *Spirited Away* [*Sen To Chihiro Kamikakushi*]), Nick Park (who created *Wallace and Gromit*), the great Ray Harryhausen (who animated the original *King Kong*), and Henry Selick, one of stop-motion's contemporary masters.

Selick is a New Jersey native who traveled west to study at CalArts. Like so many of his classmates, he spent several years working for Disney after graduation, but in 1979 he took an eight-month leave to work on his own films with funding from the National Endowment for the Humanities. (One of those films, a nine-minute short called *Seepage*, which combined stop-motion and watercolor animation to describe a conversation between two people sitting by a swimming pool, won several awards.) Selick returned to Disney, but moved to the Bay Area after a few years to work on more challenging projects, including John Korty's *Twice Upon a Time* (1983), Carroll Ballard's *Nutcracker* (1986), and Walter Murch's underappreciated directorial turn, *Return to Oz* (1986).

Selick started his own company, Selick Projects, in 1986, and made several commercials (most memorable were the ads he did for the Pillsbury Doughboy and Ritz Crackers) and created several station-bumpers for MTV (one of which won a Clio award). His big animation breakthrough was the wildly popular six-minute short he did for MTV in 1990, *Slow Bob in the Lower Dimensions*, which won several awards and reunited him with his old CalArts classmate and quirky Disney cohort, Tim Burton. Since his early days at Disney, Burton had made two blockbuster films, *Beetle Juice* and *Batman*, and he was able to parlay his new it-boy status into winning his previous employer's support for his next project: a full-length feature-film musical with puppets that was based on a poem he'd written years earlier. The poem was called "The Nightmare Before Christmas," and Burton later

Director Henry Selick, one of the leading innovators in stop-motion and other forms of animation, devoted nearly three years to bringing Tim Burton's imaginative vision to the screen with *Tim Burton's The Nightmare Before Christmas*.

James, Ladybug, Spider, and
Grasshopper go on a magical odyssey
after James spills magic crocodile
tongues and a giant peach grows as huge
as a house in *James and the Giant Peach*.

said that he was inspired to write it after marveling at the speed with which
the cheerful Christmas decorations replaced their more sinister Halloween
counterparts in storefront windows.

Disney allocated a modest $15 million for the project and let Burton
name a director. Selick was the perfect choice. Burton admits he had no
patience for the day-to-day grind of stop-motion animation, in which
puppets are manipulated by hand from frame to frame, requiring on average twenty-four full poses per second. The slow pace, he said, "would have
put me in the nuthouse." Selick, on the other hand, loved the intricate
hands-on work, and later called the two and a half grueling years in the
40,000-square-foot warehouse in San Francisco that he took over, the
best and smoothest time he ever spent on a film set. Bouncing around
amongst the twenty-odd soundstages of Skellington Productions, the crew
produced no more than seventy seconds of footage a week using puppets
that had as many as 400 interchangeable heads with different expressions.

Selick has said that he and Burton "come from the same planet" — a
strange, gothic place that looks like a scene from *Snow White and the Seven*

"Tim Burton's
The Nightmare
Before Christmas
is 99% handmade."
—Henry Selick

Dwarfs were Edvard Munch to redraw the Seven Dwarfs. The men shared a similar vision, but as Roger Ebert put it, Selick "made it all work." For inspiration, Selick and cinematographer Pete Kozachik turned to Italian horror films, dark movies from the forties and fifties, such as *Night of the Hunter*, and, says Selick, "everything from German Expressionism to Dr. Seuss."

Danny Elfman composed the score and sang the part of Jack Skellington, the Pumpkin King and most popular guy in Halloween Town. During a late-night walk, Skellington stumbles upon the North Pole and discovers a man even more powerful than he is, who rides through the night and gives presents to children, and this man's name is... Sandy Claws. Skellington decides to give Sandy Claws the year off, takes over the role of Santa, and makes a fine mess of the Christmas holidays—until he is set right by a healthy dose of law enforcement, his own conscience, and the love of a winsome rag doll named Sally (marvelously voiced by Catherine O'Hara). The movie, perhaps the least saccharine and most genuinely celebratory holiday release of the last few decades, brought in $50 million in domestic box office and rave reviews. It was re-released for the winter 2000 holidays and has become a cult film with regular annual reissues and new merchandise tie-ins.

Selick made a second feature film at Skellington Studios—an adaptation of the Roald Dahl classic children's book *James and the Giant Peach*. Although Disney was willing to invest more money for the new film than they had for *The Nightmare Before Christmas*, they were *not* willing to finance Selick's original vision (which would have been to have live actors interacting with stop motion puppets), nor would they finance another full-length stop-motion picture. So Selick decided to blend the two media by telling the opening and ending in live action but animating the middle. "It was a compromise," says Selick today. "It wasn't the ideal way to go." It's true that the movie suffered from a disjointed feel, in large part because the live-action portion couldn't compare to the wonder and magic created by the puppets. But it still boasted one of cinema's sexiest animated spiders (voiced by Susan Sarandon) and several sublime sequences, especially once the peach finally takes flight—plus, *James and the Giant Peach* is still a cult favorite. The director went on to make *Monkeybone* in 2001 and most recently created the stop-motion underwater world for Wes Anderson's 2004 feature, *The Life Aquatic with Steve Zissou*.

Selick is now working with Vinton Studios in Portland, Oregon, and has several films on the way, including *Coraline*, based on the popular Neil Gaiman fantasy. But the Bay Area remains his home. "Let me put it this way," he says firmly, "I'm sure not selling my house."

"There are children throwing snowballs Instead of throwing heads They're busy building toys. And absolutely no one's dead!"

—Jack Skellington

FILMOGRAPHY

2001 *Monkeybone*
1996 *James and the Giant Peach*
1993 *Tim Burton's The Nightmare Before Chrismas*

Jack Skellington, the Pumpkin King of Halloween Town, yearns for something more in *Tim Burton's The Nightmare Before Christmas*.

WAYNE WANG

Wayne Wang was born in Hong Kong in 1949, and raised by traditional Chinese parents who loved American film (he was named after John Wayne). His family sent him to Los Altos Hills in California to attend Foothill College in the late sixties, where he lived on the Quaker-run Hidden Villa Ranch owned by the Duvenecks, legendary figures in the San Francisco Bay Area who believed building relationships between people would lead to a more peaceful and just society. The Quakers encouraged an appreciation of the arts, and Wang was introduced to musicians like the Grateful Dead and Santana, who all hung out on the Ranch. When he told his father he was getting an art degree instead of going to medical school, as he'd originally intended, the checks from his parents quickly stopped coming.

Wang moved from Los Altos to Berkeley to attend graduate school at the California College of Arts and Crafts, and the experience continued to

expose him to new ways of looking at the world. In addition to intense late-night philosophical conversations about the limits of technology with his computer-whiz college roommate, Wang would often take in two movies a night at the Pacific Film Archive, then run by Tom Luddy, who would show every kind of film from the experimental to the mainstream.

Two of Wang's strongest influences were the classic story-based films of Japanese director Yasujiro Ozu and the more provocative and controversial films of Dusan Makavejev, especially the surreal and anarchic *Sweet Movie* (1974). While still in school, Wang shot the experimental film *A Man, A Woman, and a Killer* in Mendocino with two other graduate students, and after finishing he got a job in the film industry working on short documentaries for a local TV station. He returned to Hong Kong to work on a soap opera and, after a stint in television, was assistant director on the 1974 thriller *Golden Needles*.

Wang returned to San Francisco in 1975 and taught English to Chinese immigrants, all the while collecting their stories for a movie he knew he wanted to do about the Chinese community. That movie ended up becoming *Chan is Missing*, a 1982 thriller shot in sixteen-millimeter black-and-white, which explored the cultural schisms and contrasts in the Chinese community. *Chan* was the first all Chinese-American film shot in San Francisco, and Wang made it for $22,500 with grants from the American Film Institute and the National Endowment for the Arts. Ironically, the San Francisco Film Festival rejected the movie, but New York's Museum of Modern Art's "New Directors, New Films" Festival selected it and, suddenly, Wang had a distributor, an opening in New York, and best of all, long lines of theatergoers eager to see his movie.

Chan is Missing put Wang on the map, and gave him the opportunity to direct several more films, including *Dim Sum: A Little Bit of Heart* and *Eat A Bowl Of Tea*. But it was his adaptation of Amy Tan's book *The Joy Luck Club*

"As Sydney Pollack always says, 'You've got one foot in art and one foot in commerce.' I actually consciously choose to deal with that contradiction and conflict, just as I'm one side Chinese and one side American. I want to deal with that conflict and try to push the envelope as much as I can."

—Wayne Wang

FILMOGRAPHY

2005 *Last Holiday*
      Because of Winn-Dixie
2002 *Maid in Manhattan*
2001 *The Center of the World*
1999 *Anywhere But Here*
1998 *Chinese Box*
1995 *Blue in the Face*
1995 *Smoke*
1993 *The Joy Luck Club*
1990 *Life is Cheap...But Toilet Paper
      is Expensive*
1989 *Eat a Bowl of Tea*
1987 *Slam Dance*
1985 *Dim Sum: A Little Bit of Heart*
1982 *Chan is Missing*

**Richard Longman (Peter Sarsgarrd)
gets a lap dance in *Center of the World*.**

(1993) that brought the director his first major commercial success. The complexity of Tan's plot made for a potential quagmire: Four mothers, all immigrants from China, meet for weekly Mah Jong games, during which we hear stories about their troubled relationships with their American-born daughters. The book weaves together the mothers' astonishing, and often tragic, childhoods in China with the struggles of their children, raised between the old world and the new. Wang made the job look easy, weaving together all the disparate narrative threads into a smooth, well-paced, and moving multigenerational saga.

Since directing *The Joy Luck Club*, Wang has alternated mainstream ventures like the Susan Sarandon, Natalie Portman mother-daughter drama *Anywhere But Here* (1999) and *Maid in Manhattan* (2002), starring Jennifer Lopez and Ralph Fiennes, with quirkier independent projects like the 1995 Miramax film *Smoke*. A human drama based on a short story by Brooklyn writer Paul Auster, *Smoke* starred Harvey Keitel, William Hurt and Stockard Channing and was thoroughly rehearsed and precisely composed, "like a concert." Wang shot the film so quickly that they finished ahead of schedule, so he invited personalities like Lou Reed and Jim

Chinese-American mothers and daughters are the core story of the film *The Joy Luck Club*, based upon the novel by Amy Tan and executive produced by Oliver Stone and Janet Yang.

Jarmusch from Manhattan and Brooklyn to come to the cigar-store set from *Smoke* to do a second film, *Blue in the Face*. Wang remembers that making *Blue in the Face*, which was fully improvised, was "like letting mental patients out of the hospital."

Like Philip Kaufman, another San Francisco independent, Wang embraces controversial material, as he did in his wildly underrated *The Center of the World* (2001). The film, set in the dot-com bubble of the late-twentieth-century Internet boom, stars Peter Sarsgaard as Richard Longman, an antisocial programming wunderkind whose company is about to go public. Although the film was not a commercial success, it does succeed as an exposé of the particular way in which human relations were being bought and paid for during this unique and heady time in San Francisco's history.

Wayne Wang's move from China to the Bay Area, more than thirty years ago, set the stage for a life's work that is an example of true "fusion." Culturally, he is a combination of East and West, equally Chinese and American, and as a filmmaker and artist, he jumps back and forth with equal skill between independent and mainstream films. Wang is currently in post-production on the Queen Latifah vehicle *The Last Holiday*, another one of his Hollywood films. His next film will be an independent movie: a story inspired by the writing of humorist David Sedaris about a Chinese-American father and son.

"Coffee and cigarettes, that's like the breakfast of champions."

—Jim Jarmusch as the character Bob in *Blue in the Face*

TERRY ZWIGOFF

"**M**aking a feature film," announced Terry Zwigoff in an interview promoting his hit *Ghost World* in 2001, "was the most stressful, tedious job I've ever had in my life." That's no small statement from a man who had previously worked as a printer, a shipping clerk, a welfare-office worker, and perhaps most thanklessly, as chronicler of his reclusive and difficult bandmate and friend, the underground-comic legend Robert Crumb. While filming that chronicle, a documentary which took nine insolvent years to make, Zwigoff endured constant back pain, which got so excruciating that for one week he slept with a loaded pistol by his head "trying to work up the courage to kill myself." The director is known, both in his work and in his interviews, for a refreshing, if acerbic, lack of Hollywood-speak or California spin:

On Sundance, where *Crumb* won the prize for best documentary:
"I don't ski; I don't have a cellular phone; I don't have a bottle of Evian water. I don't belong here."
On Los Angeles: "It's hell down here. I just hate it."

The Wisconsin-born filmmaker, who moved to San Francisco in 1970, has kinder words for his adopted hometown, calling it "one of the last livable cities in America."

Terry Zwigoff directing *Ghost World*.

Rebecca (Scarlett Johansson) and Enid (Thora Birch) walk the walk in *Ghost World*.

On American culture: "Anything that's authentic and genuine, anything that grew out of any sense of tradition, is wiped out. We're left with this bland monoculture that's swept over the whole country."

On Howard Armstrong, the brilliant and almost-forgotten old-time fiddle player and subject of Zwigoff's first documentary, *Louie Bluie* (1986):"I couldn't get him to play his music right!"

This last was no criticism of Armstrong, the legendary musician who first motivated Zwigoff to make movies, but rather an acknowledgement of his own obsession with integrity and purity. It's a theme that runs through all of his films, and also through his career as a director: After *Crumb* made nearly every critic's top-ten list for 1995 and ignited a major controversy for the Academy when it failed to receive even one Oscar nomination, Zwigoff was flooded with new directing opportunities. He was all set to direct a documentary about Woody Allen but left the project when the film's producers refused to grant him final cut. Then, while shopping the script for *Ghost World* with collaborator Daniel Clowes, an East Bay comic-book writer on whose graphic novel *Ghost World* is based, he refused to accept the studio "actress of the moment" casting choices.

"I can't relate to ninety-nine percent of humanity."

—Seymour
(Terry Zwigoff's alter ego in *Ghost World*.)

Executives everywhere were recommending starlets like Jennifer Love Hewitt, Alicia Silverstone, and Clare Danes, but Clowes and Zwigoff wanted characters who could project the vulnerability and outsider status of Enid and Rebecca. Once a deal was made with United Artists, however, the casting was left up to the director, who chose Scarlett Johansson, then still a gawky teenager with dark hair and baby fat, and *American Beauty*'s Thora Birch, who gained twenty pounds for the role. Finally, after *Ghost World*'s success launched the already-beloved indie director to near-icon status, he refused to pose for a Gap ad which was seeking to feature young hip directors, arguing that (a) he wasn't young, (b) he wasn't hip, and (c) he had just spent six years of his life making a movie that railed against American culture—how could anyone expect him to want to pose for The Gap? As of this writing, Zwigoff has just finished mixing *Art School Confidential*, which stars John Malkovich, Jim Broadbent, and Angelica Huston and skewers the cult of celebrity.

His previous films have taken on "corporate monoculture" (and phony liberalism, and bad musical taste, and bar bands, and well-meaning parents, and therapy, and feminism, and fandom, and just about everything else). The satire is tempered by a keen gift for comedy and by the fact that, beneath their critical stance, the films are usually dominated by a tender and almost naïve belief in redemption. Zwigoff's survivors—Armstrong, Crumb, and the fictional Enid—are all artists, seeking sanity and compassion in a hostile, Styrofoam world. Sometimes they find it through their work and sometimes through love, like Billy Bob Thornton's vituperative, profane drunk in *Bad Santa* (2003), who gets dragged to salvation, kicking screaming and cursing all the way by a lonely kid who steals his heart. Even this potential cliché carries an edge: The boy is no irresistible Punky Brewster but rather a fat, curly-haired outcast who speaks in an unendearing monotone and wears his shorts too tight. Taken as a whole, Zwigoff's oeuvre hardly puts forth a completely misanthropic vision of the world. As Crumb admits in the documentary while playing one of his beloved 78s, "When I listen to old music, it's one of the few times I

LEFT TO RIGHT: **Sophia Myles, Max Minghella, Dan Clowes, and Terry Zwigoff** on the set of *Art School Confidential*.

WEIRD SEX · OBSESSION · COMIC BOOKS

CRUMB

DAVID LYNCH presents a TERRY ZWIGOFF film "CRUMB"
Cinematography: MARYSE ALBERTI · Editor: VICTOR LIVINGSTON
Music: DAVID BOEDDINGHAUS · Sound: SCOTT BREINDEL · Coproducer: NEAL HALFON
Executive Producers: LAWRENCE WILKINSON, ALBERT BERGER, LIANNE HALFON
Produced by LYNN O'DONNELL & TERRY ZWIGOFF · Directed by TERRY ZWIGOFF

The release poster for Zwigoff's 1995 documentary on R. Crumb.

actually have a kind of love of humanity. You can hear the best part of the soul of the common people, you know, their way of expressing their connection to eternity or whatever you want to call it." Lest the viewer get too comfortable, Crumb follows up with a more pessimistic train of thought, insisting that "people can't express themselves that way anymore." But it's too late to retract the flash of idealism. Like Zwigoff, he's shown us his cards, and given us a moment of grace, a fleeting connection with "whatever you want to call it."

TRIVIA

According to Robert Crumb, neither he nor his wife ever expected Zwigoff's movie Crumb *to get released, let alone become one of the first genuine documentary "hits." The film tested the men's twenty-five-year friendship, but soon after the film was released, they were back collaborating on a new screenplay. And a few years later, the artwork in Enid's sketchbook in* Ghost World *was drawn by Crumb's then-teenaged daughter Sophie.*

FILMOGRAPHY

2005   *Art School Confidential*
2003   *Bad Santa*
2001   *Ghost World*

FILMOGRAPHIES

American Zoetrope

FEATURE FILMS

Apocalypse Now
(released August 15, 1979)
An American Zoetrope Production
A United Artists Pictures Release
Produced by Francis Ford Coppola
Co-Produced by Gray Frederickson,
  Fred Roos, Tom Sternberg
Directed by Francis Ford Coppola
Screenplay by Francis Ford Coppola,
  John Milius
Narration written by Michael Herr
Cinematography by Vittorio Storaro
Edited by Lisa Fruchtman, Gerald B. Greenberg,
  Richard Marks, Walter Murch
Original Music by Carmine Coppola,
  Francis Ford Coppola, Mickey Hart
Production Design by Dean Tavoularis
Art Direction by Angelo P. Graham
Costume Design by Charles E. James
Sound by Walter Murch (design); Mark Berger,
  Richard Beggs, Nathan Boxer

Featured Cast
Sam Bottoms, Marlon Brando, Aurore Clement,
Robert Duvall, Albert Hall, Dennis Hopper,
Laurence Fishburne, Harrison Ford, Frederic
Forrest, Christian Marquand, Martin Sheen

Awards
8 Academy Award nominations, 2 wins:
Actor In a Supporting Role—Robert Duvall
Art Direction—Dean Tavoularis, Angelo Graham,
  George R. Nelson
✔ Cinematography—Vittorio Storaro
Director—Francis Ford Coppola
Film Editing—Richard Marks, Walter Murch,
  Gerald B. Greenberg, Lisa Fruchtman
Picture—Francis Ford Coppola, Fred Roos,
  Gray Frederickson, Tom Sternberg
✔ Sound—Walter Murch, Mark Berger,
  Richard Beggs, Nathan Boxer
Writing—Screenplay Based on Material
  from Another Medium—John Milius,
  Francis Ford Coppola

4 Golden Globes nominations, 3 wins:
✔ Actor in a Supporting Role–Motion Picture—
  Robert Duvall (tied with Melvyn Douglas
  for *Being There*)
✔ Director–Motion Picture—Francis Ford Coppola
Motion Picture—Drama
✔ Original Score—Motion Picture—
  Carmine Coppola, Francis Ford Coppola

Assassination Tango
(released March 28, 2003)
An American Zoetrope Production
A United Artists Release
Executive Produced by Francis Ford Coppola,
  Linda Reisman
Produced by Robert Duvall, Rob Carliner
Co-Produced by Steven Brown, Raúl Outeda
Directed by Robert Duvall
Screenplay by Robert Duvall
Cinematography by Félix Monti
Edited by Stephen Mack
Original Music by Luis Bacalov
Production Design by Stefania Cella
Art Direction by Sara Parks

Costume Design by Beatriz De Benedetto
Sound by Benjamin Cheah

Featured Cast
Rubén Blades, Kathy Baker, Robert Duvall,
Luciana Pedraza

Awards
Deauville Film Festival 2003:
Grand Special Prize—Robert Duvall (nominated)

Barfly
(released December 18, 1987)
Golan-Globus Production
A Cannon Films Release
"The Cannon Group, Inc.
  Francis Ford Coppola Presents"
Executive Produced by Yoram Globus,
  Menahem Golan
Produced by Fred Roos, Tom Luddy,
  Barbet Schroeder
Directed by Barbet Schroeder
Screenplay by Charles Bukowski
Cinematography by Robby Müller
Edited by Éva Gárdos
Original Music by Jack Baran; Steve Cropper,
  Donald Dunn (song "Hip Hug-Her")
Production Design by Bob Ziembicki
Set Decoration by Lisa Dean
Costume Design by Milena Canonero
Sound by Robert Fitzgerald, Hari Ryatt
  (sound supervisors)

Featured Cast
Faye Dunaway, Alice Krige, J.C. Quinn,
Mickey Rourke, Frank Stallone

Awards
1 Golden Globe nomination:
Performance by an Actress in a Motion
  Picture–Drama—Faye Dunaway

Cannes Film Festival:
Palme d'Or–Barbet Schroeder (nominated)

The Black Stallion
(released October 17, 1979)
A Zoetrope Studios Production
A United Artists Release
Executive Produced by Francis Ford Coppola
Produced by Fred Roos, Tom Sternberg
Directed by Carroll Ballard
Screenplay by Melissa Mathison,
  Jeanne Rosenberg, William D. Wittliff
Based on the novel by Walter Farley
Cinematography by Caleb Deschanel
Edited by Robert Dalva
Original Music by Carmine Coppola
Art Direction by Aurelio Crugnola, Earl Preston
Sound by Alan Splet (supervising sound editor)

Featured Cast
Hoyt Axton, Teri Garr, Michael Higgins,
Clarence Muse, Kelly Reno, Mickey Rooney

Awards
2 Academy Award nominations, 1 Special
  Achievement Award:
Actor in a Supporting Role—Mickey Rooney
Film Editing—Robert Dalva

✔ Special Achievement Award–Sound Editing—
  Alan Splet

1 Golden Globe nomination:
Original Score–Motion Picture—
  Carmine Coppola

The Black Stallion Returns
(released March 25, 1983)
A Zoetrope Studios Production
An MGM/UA Release
Executive Produced by Francis Ford Coppola
Produced by Tom Sternberg, Fred Roos,
  Doug Claybourne
Directed by Robert Dalva
Screenplay by Jerome Kass, Richard Kletter
Based on the novel by Walter Farley
Cinematography by Carlo Di Palma
Edited by Paul Hirsch
Original Music by Georges Delerue
Art Direction by Aurelio Crugnola
Costume Design by Danda Ortona
Sound by Roman Coppola, Mario Bramonti,
  Gary Weir, Tom Bullock

Featured Cast
Teri Garr, Allen Goorwitz, Kelly Reno,
Vincent Spano, Woody Strode

Bram Stoker's Dracula
(released November 13, 1992)
An American Zoetrope/Osiris Films Production
A Columbia Pictures Release
Executive Produced by Michael Apted,
  Robert O'Connor
Produced by Francis Ford Coppola,
  Fred Fuchs, Charles B. Mulvehill
Co-Produced by James V. Hart, John P. Veitch
Directed by Francis Ford Coppola
Screenplay by James V. Hart
Based on the novel by Bram Stoker
Cinematography by Michael Ballhaus
Edited by Anne Goursaud, Glen Scantlebury,
  Nicholas C. Smith
Music Composed by Wojciech Kilar, Annie
  Lennox (song "Love Song for a Vampire")
Production Design by Thomas E. Sanders
Art Direction by Andrew Precht
Costume Design by Eiko Ishioka
Sound by Tom C. McCarthy (supervising
  sound editor), Leslie Shatz (sound designer),
  David E. Stone (supervising sound editor)

Featured Cast
Anthony Hopkins, Gary Oldman,
Keanu Reeves, Winona Ryder

Awards
4 Academy Award nominations, 3 wins:
Art Direction—Thomas Sanders, Garrett Lewis
✔ Costume Design—Eiko Ishioka
✔ Makeup—Greg Cannom, Michèle Burke,
  Matthew W. Mungle
✔ Sound Effects Editing—Tom C. McCarthy,
  David E. Stone

Buddy
(released June 6, 1997)
An American Zoetrope, Jim Henson

Jack

(released August 9, 1996)
An American Zoetrope Production
A Hollywood Pictures Release
Executive Produced by Doug Claybourne
Produced by Francis Ford Coppola,
  Fred Fuchs, Ricardo Mestres
Directed by Francis Ford Coppola
Screenplay by James DeMonaco, Gary Nadeau
Cinematography by John Toll
Edited by Barry Malkin
Original Music by Michael Kamen,
  Bryan Adams
Production Design by Dean Tavoularis
Art Direction by Angelo Graham
Costume Design by Aggie Guerard Rodgers
Sound by John Nutt (supervising sound editor),
  Kim Aubry (postproduction supervisor),
  Kyrsten Camaglia, Agamemnon Andrianos,
  Christopher Brooks

Featured Cast
Bill Cosby, Fran Drescher, Brian Kerwin,
Diane Lane, Jennifer Lopez, Robin Williams

Jeepers Creepers

(released August 31, 2001)
An American Zoetrope Production/
  Cinerenta-Cinebeta Production
An MGM/UA Release
Executive Produced by Francis Ford Coppola,
  Willi Baer, Eberhard Kayser, Mario Ohoven,
  Linda Reisman
Produced by Tom Luse, Barry Opper
Co-Produced by J. Todd Harris
Directed by Victor Salva
Screenplay by Victor Salva
Cinematography by Don E. FauntLeRoy
Edited by Ed Marx
Original Music by Bennett Salvay
Production Design by Steven Legler
Art Direction by Kevin Egeland
Costume Design by Emae Villalobos
Sound by James P. Lay (supervising sound
  editor), Andy Rosenthal (sound effects editor),
  Angelo Palazzo (sound designer, editor)

Featured Cast
Jonathan Breck, Eileen Brennan, Justin Long,
Gina Philips

Jeepers Creepers 2

(released August 29, 2003)
An American Zoetrope Production
An MGM/UA Release
In association with Myriad Pictures
Executive Produced by Francis Ford Coppola,
  Bobby Rock, Kirk D'Amico, Lucas Foster
Co-Executive Produced by
  Philip von Alvensleben
Produced by Tom Luse
Directed by Victor Salva
Screenplay by Victor Salva
Cinematography by Don E. FauntLeRoy
Edited by Ed Marx
Original Music by Bennett Salvay
Production Design by Peter Jamison
Art Direction by Nanci Roberts
Costume Design by Jana Stern
Sound by Paul B. Clay (supervising sound
  editor), Patrick O'Sullivan (sound effects editor)

Featured Cast
Jonathan Breck, Ray Wise

John Grisham's The Rainmaker

(released November 21, 1997)
An American Zoetrope Production
A Paramount Pictures Release
Executive Produced by Michael Douglas,
  Fred Fuchs
Produced by Steven Reuther
Co-Produced by Georgia Kacandes
Directed by Francis Ford Coppola
Screenplay by Francis Ford Coppola
Narration written by Michael Herr
Based on the novel by John Grisham
Cinematography by John Toll
Edited by Barry Malkin, Melissa Kent
Original Music by Elmer Bernstein
Production Design by Howard Cummings
Art Direction by Robert K. Shaw, Jr.
Costume Design by Aggie Guerard Rodgers
Sound by David A. Cohen, Larry Hoki,
  Jennifer L. Ware, Michael Kirchberger

Featured Cast
Matt Damon, Claire Danes, Danny DeVito,
Mary Kay Place, Mickey Rourke, Jon Voight

Awards
1 Golden Globe nomination:
  Actor in a Supporting Role—Jon Voight

Lost in Translation

(released October 3, 2003)
An American Zoetrope/
  Elemental Films Production
A Tohokashinsha Film Company Ltd. Production
A Focus Features Release
Executive Produced by Francis Ford Coppola,
  Fred Roos
Produced by Sofia Coppola, Ross Katz,
  Callum Greene
Co-Produced by Stephen Schible
Directed by Sofia Coppola
Screenplay by Sofia Coppola
Cinematography by Lance Acord
Edited by Sarah Flack
Original Music by Kevin Shields, Jean-Benoît
  Dunckel, Nicolas Godin, Roger Joseph
  Manning, Jr., Bryan Mills, Brian Reitzell,
  Justin Stanley, William Storkson
Production Design by K.K. Barrett, Anne Ross
Costume Design by Nancy Steiner
Sound Design by Richard Beggs

Featured Cast
Anna Faris, Fumihiro Hayashi,
Scarlett Johansson, Bill Murray, Giovanni Ribisi

Awards
4 Academy Award nominations, 1 win:
  Actor in a Leading Role—Bill Murray
  Director—Sofia Coppola
  Picture—Ross Katz, Sofia Coppola
✔ Writing–Original Screenplay—Sofia Coppola

5 Golden Globe nominations, 3 wins:
✔ Actor in a Motion Picture–Musical or Comedy—
  Bill Murray
  Actress in a Motion Picture–Musical or
  Comedy—Scarlett Johansson
  Director Motion Picture—Sofia Coppola
✔ Motion Picture–Musical or Comedy
✔ Screenplay–Motion Picture—Sofia Coppola

Mary Shelley's Frankenstein

(released November 4, 1994)

An American Zoetrope Production
A TriStar Pictures Release
In association with Japan Satellite Broadcasting,
  Inc., the IndieProd Company
Executive Produced by Fred Fuchs
Produced by James V. Hart, John Veitch,
  Francis Ford Coppola
Co-Produced by Kenneth Branagh, David Parfitt
Directed by Kenneth Branagh
Screenplay by Steph Lady, Frank Darabont
Based on the novel by Mary Shelley
Cinematography by Roger Pratt
Edited by Andrew Marcus
Original Music by Patrick Doyle
Production Design by Tim Harvey
Art Direction by Desmond Crowe, John Fenner
Costume Design by James Acheson
Sound by Campbell Askew, Roy Prendergast
  (supervising sound editor), Colin Miller
  (sound effects editor), Ross Adams

Featured Cast
Kenneth Branagh, Helena Bonham Carter,
John Cleese, Robert De Niro, Ian Holm,
Tom Hulce, Aidan Quinn

Awards
1 Academy Award nomination:
  Makeup—Daniel Parker, Paul Engelen,
  Carol Hemming

My Family/Mi Familia

(released May 3, 1995)
An American Zoetrope
  Anna ThomasNewComm Production
A New Line Cinema Release
In association with Majestic Films
Executive Produced by Francis Ford Coppola,
  Guy East, Lindsay Law, Tom Luddy,
  Sergio Molina (Mexico Unit)
Produced by Anna Thomas
Directed by Gregory Nava
Screenplay by Gregory Nava, Anna Thomas
Story by Gregory Nava
Cinematography by Edward Lachman,
  Jason Poteet
River Cinematography by Carroll Ballard
Edited by Nancy Richardson
Original Orchestral Music by Mark McKenzie
Folkloric Music Score by Pepe Avila
Production Design by Barry Robison
Art Direction by Troy Myers, Adam Lustig
Costume Design by Tracy Tynan
Sound by Marian Wilde (supervising sound
  editor), Ethan Van der Ryn (sound effects
  editor), Rolf Johnson

Featured Cast
Elpidia Carrillo, Jenny Gago, Esai Morales,
Constance Marie, Edward James Olmos,
Eduardo Lopez Rojas, Jimmy Smits

Awards
1 Academy Award nomination:
  Makeup—Ken Diaz, Mark Sanchez

No Such Thing

(released March 29, 2002)
An American Zoetrope Production
An MGM/UA Release
In association with The Icelandic Film
  Corporation, True Fiction Pictures
Executive Produced by Francis Ford Coppola,
  Linda Reisman, Willi Baer
Produced by Fridrik Thor Fridriksson,

Hal Hartley, Cecilia Kate Roque
Directed by Hal Hartley
Screenplay by Hal Hartley
Cinematography by Michael Spiller
Edited by Steve Hamilton
Original Music by Hal Hartley
Production Design by Árni Páll Jóhannsson
Art Direction by Ed Check, Einar Unnsteinsson
Costume Design by Frank L. Fleming,
  Helga I. Stefánsdóttir
Sound by Jennifer Ralston, Steve Hamilton

Featured Cast
Robert John Burke, Julie Christie, Helen Mirren,
Sarah Polley

One from the Heart
(released February 11, 1982)
A Zoetrope Studios Production
A Columbia Pictures Release
Executive Produced by Bernard Gersten
Produced by Gray Frederickson, Fred Roos
Co-Produced by Armyan Bernstein
Directed by Francis Ford Coppola
Screenplay by Armyan Bernstein,
  Francis Ford Coppola
Cinematography by Vittorio Storaro,
  Ronald Victor Garcia
Edited by Rob Bonz, Rudi Fehr, Anne Goursaud,
  Michael Magill, Randy Roberts
Original Music by Tom Waits
Production Design by Dean Tavoularis
Art Direction by Angelo P. Graham
Costume Design by Ruth Morley
Sound by Richard Beggs (sound designer),
  Leslie Shatz (supervising sound editor),
  Richard Burrow, Teresa Eckton

Featured Cast
Frederic Forrest, Teri Garr, Raul Julia, Lainie
Kazan, Nastassia Kinski, Harry Dean Stanton

Awards
1 Academy Award nomination:
Music-Original Song Score, Its Adaptation or
  Adaptation Score—Tom Waits

The Outsiders
(released March 25, 1983)
A Zoetrope Studios Production
A Warner Bros. Release
Executive Produced by Francis Ford Coppola
Produced by Gray Frederickson, Fred Roos
Directed by Francis Ford Coppola
Screenplay by Kathleen Knutsen Rowell
Based on the novel by S.E. Hinton
Cinematography by Stephen H. Burum
Edited by Anne Goursaud
Original Music by Carmine Coppola
Production Design by Dean Tavoularis
Set Decoration by Gary Fettis
Costume Design by Marjorie Bowers
Sound Design by Richard Beggs, Anthony Milch,
  Michael D. Wilhoit

Featured Cast
Tom Cruise, Matt Dillon, Emilio Estevez,
Leif Garrett, C. Thomas Howell, Diane Lane,
Rob Lowe, Ralph Macchio, Patrick Swayze

Peggy Sue Got Married
(released October 10, 1986)
A Paul R. Gurian/Zoetrope Studios Production
A TriStar Pictures Release

Executive Produced by Barrie M. Osborne
Produced by Paul R. Gurian
Directed by Francis Ford Coppola
Screenplay by Jerry Leichtling, Arlene Sarner
Cinematography by Jordan S. Cronenweth
Edited by Barry Malkin
Original Music by John Barry
Production Design by Dean Tavoularis
Art Direction by Alex Tavoularis
Costume Design by Theadora Van Runkle
Sound by Richard Bryce Goodman,
  Michael Kirchberger

Featured Cast
Nicolas Cage, Catherine Hicks, Barry Miller,
Kathleen Turner

Awards
3 Academy Award nominations:
Actress in a Leading Role—Kathleen Turner
Cinematography—Jordan Cronenweth
Costume Design—Theadora Van Runkle

2 Golden Globe nominations:
Actress in a Motion Picture–Musical or
  Comedy—Kathleen Turner
Motion Picture–Musical or Comedy

Pumpkin
(released June 28, 2002)
An American Zoetrope Production
A United Artists Release
Executive Produced by Willi Baer,
  Francis Ford Coppola, Linda Reisman
Produced by Karen Barber, Albert Berger,
  Christina Ricci, Andrea Sperling, Ron Yerxa
Co-Produced by Melanie Backer
Directed by Anthony Abrams,
  Adam Larson Broder
Screenplay by Adam Larson Broder
Cinematography by Tim Suhrstedt
Edited by Richard Halsey, Sloane Kevin
Original Music by John Ottoman
Production Design by Richard Sherman
Set Decoration by Paul Roome
Costume Design by Edi Giguere
Sound by Christopher Sheldon
  (supervising sound editor), Eddie Kim,
  Amanda Goodpaster

Featured Cast
Sam Ball, Brenda Blethyn, Marisa Coughlan,
Hank Harris, Christina Ricci, Dominique Swain

Awards
Sundance Film Festival:
Grand Jury Prize Dramatic Film—
  Anthony Abrams, Adam Larson (nominated)

The Rain People
(released August 27, 1969)
An American Zoetrope Production
A Warner Bros./Seven Arts Release
Produced by Ronald Colby, Bart Patton
Associate Produced by George Lucas,
  Mona Skager
Directed by Francis Ford Coppola
Screenplay by Francis Ford Coppola
Cinematography by Bill Butler
Edited by Barry Malkin
Original Music by Carmine Coppola,
  Ronald Stein
Art Direction by Leon Ericksen
Sound by Walter Murch (sound montage),
  Nathan Boxer (sound)

Featured Cast
James Caan, Robert Duvall, Shirley Knight,
Marya Zimmet

Awards
San Sebastián International Film Festival:
Gran Concha de Oro (Golden Seashell) Award
  for Picture—Francis Ford Coppola
Gran Concha de Oro (Golden Seashell) Award
  for Director—Francis Ford Coppola

Rumble Fish
(released October 21, 1983)
A Zoetrope Studios Productions
An MCA/Universal Pictures Release
Executive Produced by Francis Ford Coppola
Produced by Fred Roos, Doug Claybourne
Directed by Francis Ford Coppola
Screenplay by Francis Ford Coppola,
  S.E. Hinton
Based on the novel by S.E. Hinton
Cinematography by Stephen H. Burum
Edited by Barry Malkin
Original Music by Stewart Copeland; Stan
  Ridgway (end title song "Don't Box Me In")
Production Design by Dean Tavoularis
Costume Design by Marjorie Bowers
Sound Design by Richard Beggs, Edward Beyer,
  Leslie Shatz, Randy Thom

Featured Cast
Nicholas Cage, Matt Dillon, Dennis Hopper,
  Diane Lane, Mickey Rourke, Diana Scarwid,
  Vincent Spano

Awards
1 Golden Globe nomination:
Original Score–Motion Picture—
  Stewart Copeland

The Secret Garden
(released August 13, 1993)
An American Zoetrope Production
A Warner Bros. Release
Executive Produced by Francis Ford Coppola
Produced by Fred Fuchs, Tom Luddy,
  Fred Roos
Directed by Agnieszka Holland
Screenplay by Caroline Thompson
Based on the novel by Frances
  Hodgson Burnett
Cinematography by Roger Deakins,
  Jerzy Zielinski
Edited by Isabelle Lorente, Dede Allen
Production Design by Stuart Craig
Original Music by Zbigniew Preisner
Art Direction by Peter Russell, John King
Costume Design by Marit Allen
Sound by Jennifer L. Ware (supervising sound
  editor), Pat Jackson

Featured Cast
Andrew Knott, Kate Maberly, Hayden Prowse,
Maggie Smith

Sleepy Hollow
(released November 19, 1999)
A Scott Rudin/American Zoetrope Production
A Paramount Pictures Release
Executive Produced by Francis Ford Coppola,
  Larry Franco
Produced by Scott Rudin, Adam Schroeder
Co-Produced by Kevin Yagher
Directed by Tim Burton

Screenplay by Andrew Kevin Walker
Based on the story by Washington Irving
Cinematography by Emmanuel Lubezki
Edited by Chris Lebenzon, Joel Negron
Original Music by Danny Elfman
Production Design by Rick Heinrichs
Art Direction by Ken Court, John Dexter,
  Andrew Nicholson, Les Tompkins
Costume Design by Colleen Atwood
Sound by Skip Lievsay (supervising sound editor)

Featured Cast
Johnny Depp, Casper Van Dien,
Michael Gambon, Jefferey Jones,
Christina Ricci, Miranda Richardson

Awards
3 Academy Award nominations, 1 win:
✔ Art Direction–Set Decoration—Rick Heinrichs
  (art director), Peter Young (set decorator)
Cinematography—Emmanuel Lubezki
Costume Design—Colleen Atwood

The Spirit of '76
(released October 12, 1990)
A Columbia Pictures Release,
  a Black Diamond Production
Executive Produced by Roman Coppola,
  Fred Fuchs
Produced by Susie B. Landau, Daniel Talpers
Directed by Lucas Reiner
Screenplay by Roman Coppola
Cinematography by Stephen Lighthill
Edited by Glen Scantlebury
Original Music by David Nichtern
Production Design by Daniel Talpers
Art Direction by Isabella Kirkland
Costume Design by Sofia Coppola
Sound by Jennifer L. Ware (supervising sound
  editor), Donny Blank (sound effects editor)

Featured Cast
Gerald V. Casale, David Cassidy, Olivia D'Abo,
Mark Mothersbaugh

The Third Miracle
(released December 29, 1999)
An American Zoetrope Production
A Sony Pictures Classics Release, a Haft
  Entertainment Production
Executive Produced by Francis Ford Coppola,
  Ashok Amritraj, Andrew Stevens
Produced by Fred Fuchs, Steven Haft,
  Eie Samaha
Co-Produced by Don Carmody
Directed by Agnieszka Holland
Screenplay by John Romano, Richard Vetere
Based on the novel by Richard Vetere
Cinematography by Jerzy Zielinski
Edited by David J. Siegel
Original Music by Jan A.P. Kaczmarek
Production Design by Robert de Vico
Set Decoration by Wayne Jacques
Costume Design by Denise Cronenberg
Sound by Tim Kimmel (sound effects editor),
  John Brasher

Featured Cast
Charles Haid, Ed Harris, Anne Heche, Armin
Mueller-Stahl, Michael Rispoli, Barbara Sukowa

The Virgin Suicides
(released April 21, 2000)
An American Zoetrope Production

A Paramount Classics Release
In association with 2Films Ltd., Muse
  Productions, Eternity Pictures
Executive Produced by Willi Baer, Fred Fuchs
Produced by Julie Constanzo, Francis Ford
  Coppola, Dan Halsted, Chris Hanley
Co-Produced by Fred Roos, Gary Scott Marcus
Directed by Sofia Coppola
Screenplay by Sofia Coppola
Based on the novel by Jeffrey Eugenides
Cinematography by Edward Lachman
Edited by Melissa Kent, James Lyon
Original Music by Jean Benoit Dunckel,
  Nicholas Godin (as Air), Richard Beggs
Production Design by Jasna Stefanovic
Art Direction by Jon P. Goulding
Costume Design by Nancy Steiner
Sound Design by Richard Beggs,
  Galen Walker

Featured Cast
Danny DeVito, Kirsten Dunst, Scott Glenn,
Josh Hartnett, Michael Pare, Giovanni Ribisi,
Kathleen Turner, James Woods

Wait Until Spring, Bandini
(released June 29, 1990)
A Dusk CFC-Zoetrope Studios Production
An Orion Pictures Release
Executive Produced by Christian Charret,
  Cyril de Rouvre, Giorgio Silvagni
Co-Executive Produced by Maurits De Prins,
  Amedeo Pagani
Produced by Fred Roos, Tom Luddy,
  Erwin Provoost
Directed by Dominique Deruddere
Screenplay by Dominique Deruddere
Based on the novel by John Fante
Cinematography by Jean-François Robin
Edited by Ludo Troch
Original Music by Angelo Badalamenti,
  Paolo Conte
Production Design by Bob Ziembicki
Art Direction by Roger Crandall
Costume Design by Shay Cunliffe
Sound by Philippe Ravoet

Featured Cast
Michael Bacall, Faye Dunaway, Joe Mantegna,
Ornella Muti,

Wind
(released September 11, 1992)
A Columbia TriStar Release
Executive Produced by Francis Ford Coppola,
  Fred Fuchs
Produced by Tom Luddy, Mata Yamamoto
Directed by Carroll Ballard
Screenplay by Rudy Wurlitzer, Mac Gudgeon
Cinematography by John Toll, Axel Sand
Edited by Michael Chandler, Ruby Yand
Original Music by Basil Poledouris
Production Design by Lawrence Eastwood
Art Direction by Paul W. Gorfine
Costume Design by Marit Allen
Sound by Alan Splet (supervising sound editor),
  Ann Kroeber, Jeffrey Stephens

Featured Cast
Jennifer Grey, Rebecca Miller, Matthew Modine,
Cliff Robertson, Stellan Skarsgärd,
Jack Thompson

DOCUMENTARIES

Hearts of Darkness:
A Filmmaker's Apocalypse
(1991)
Directed by Fax Bahr, Eleanor Coppola,
  George Hickenlooper

Awards
4 Emmy Award nominations, 2 wins:
✔ Outstanding Individual Achievement–
  Informational Programming–Picture Editing—
  Michael Greer (editor), Jay Miracle (editor)
✔ Outstanding Individual Achievement–
  Informational Programming–Directing—
  George Hickenlooper (director), Fax Bahr
  (director), Eleanor Coppola (director)
  Outstanding Individual Achievement–
  Informational Programming–Writing—Fax Bahr
  (writer), George Hickenlooper (writer)
  Outstanding Informational Special—
  Doug Claybourne (executive producer),
  Fred Roos (executive producer), George
  Zaloom (producer), Les Mayfield (producer)

National Board of Review, USA:
Won NBR Award—Documentary

Koyaanisqatsi
(1983)
Directed by Godfrey Reggio
Executive Produced by Francis Ford Coppola
Film Score by Philip Glass

SHORTS
Directed by Francis Ford Coppola

Rip Van Winkle
premiered on HBO's Faerie Tale Theatre (1985)

New York Stories
"Life Without Zoe" segment
(1989)
Produced by Fred Roos, Dean Tavoularis,
  Fred Fuchs
Directed by Francis Ford Coppola
Screenplay by Francis Ford Coppola,
  Sofia Coppola
Cinematography by Vittorio Storaro
Edited by Barry Malkin
Original Music by Carmine Coppola
Production Design by Geoffrey Kirkland
Set Decoration by George DeTitta, Jr.
Costume Design by Sofia Coppola
Sound by Michael Kirchberger (supervising
  sound editor)

Francis Ford Coppola, George Lucas Collaborations

FEATURE FILMS

American Graffiti
(released August 1, 1973)
A Lucasfilm Ltd./Coppola Company Production
A Universal Pictures Release
Produced by Francis Ford Coppola
Co-Produced by Gary Kurtz
Directed by George Lucas
Screenplay by George Lucas, Gloria Katz,
  Willard Huyck
Directors of Photography: Ron Eveslage,
  Jan D'Alquen
Edited by Verna Fields, Marcia Lucas
Art Direction by Dennis Clark
Visual Consultant: Haskell Wexler
Set Decoration by Douglas Freeman
Costume Design by Aggie Guerard Rodgers
Sound Montage by Walter Murch

Featured Cast
Candy Clark, Richard Dreyfuss, Ronny Howard,
Wolfman Jack, Paul LeMat, Charlie Martin
Smith, Mackenzie Phillips, Cindy Williams

Awards
5 Academy Award nominations:
Actress in a Supporting Role—Candy Clark
Director—George Lucas
Film Editing—Verna Fields, Marcia Lucas
Picture—Francis Ford Coppola, Gary Kurtz
Writing-Story, Screenplay Based on Factual
  Material or Material Not Previously Published
  or Produced—George Lucas, Gloria Katz,
  Willard Huyck

4 Golden Globe nominations, 2 wins:
Director–Motion Picture—George Lucas
✔ Most Promising Newcomer–Male—Paul Le Mat
Motion Picture Actor–Musical or Comedy—
  Richard Dreyfuss
✔ Motion Picture–Musical or Comedy

AFI 100 Years 100 Films, ranked #77

Mishima: A Life in Four Chapters
(released September 13, 1985)
A Francis Ford Coppola and George Lucas
  Presentation
A Zoetrope Studios, Filmlink International,
  Lucasfilm Ltd. Production
A Warner Brothers Release
Executive Produced by Francis Ford Coppola,
  George Lucas
Produced by Mata Yamamoto, Tom Luddy
Directed by Paul Schrader
Screenplay by Paul Schrader, Leonard Schrader,
Narrated by Roy Scheider
Cinematography by John Bailey
Edited by Michael Chandler
Original Music by Philip Glass
Production Design by Eiko Ishioka
Costume Design by Etsuko Yagyu
Sound Design by Leslie Shatz

Featured Cast
Yasosuke Bando, Toshiyuki Nagashima,
Ken Ogata, Kenji Sawada

Awards
2 Cannes Film Festival Nominations, 1 win:
✔ Artistic Contribution—John Bailey
  (cinematographer), Eiko Ishioka (production
  designer/costume designer), Philip Glass
  (composer)
Palme d'Or—Paul Schrader (nominated)

THX 1138
(released March 11, 1971; director's cut released
  September 10, 2004)
An American Zoetrope Production
A Warner Bros. Release
Executive Produced by Francis Ford Coppola
Produced by Lawrence Sturhahn
Directed by George Lucas
Screenplay by George Lucas, Walter Murch
Story by George Lucas
Cinematography by Albert Kihn, David Myers
Edited by George Lucas
Original Music by Lalo Schifrin
Art Direction by Michael Haller
Costume Design by Donald Longhurst
Sound Montage by Walter Murch
Sound by Jim Manson, Louis Yates
  (location sound)

Featured Cast
Don Pedro Colley, Robert Duvall,
Maggie McOmie, Donald Pleasence, Ian Wolfe

Tucker: The Man and His Dream
(released August 12, 1988)
A Lucasfilm Ltd. Production
A Paramount Pictures Release
Executive Produced by George Lucas
Produced by Fred Fuchs, Fred Roos
Directed by Francis Ford Coppola
Screenplay by Arnold Schulman, David Seidler
Cinematography by Vittorio Storaro (AIC)
Edited by Priscilla Nedd-Friendly
Original Music by Joe Jackson
Production Design by Dean Tavoularis
Art Direction by Alex Tavoularis
Set Decoration Armin Ganz
Costume Design by Milena Canonero
Sound by Richard Beggs (sound designer),
  Gloria S. Borders (supervising sound editor),
  Randy Thom

Featured Cast
Joan Allen, Jeff Bridges, Frederic Forrest,
Martin Landau, Mako, Dean Stockwell

Awards
3 Academy Award nominations:
Actor in a Supporting Role—Martin Landau
Art Direction-Set Decoration—Dean Tavoularis,
  Armin Ganz
Costume Design—Milena Canonero

1 Golden Globe nomination, 1 win:
✔ Performance by an Actor in a Supporting Role
  in a Motion Picture—Martin Landau

DOCUMENTARIES

Filmmaker
(1968)
(About the making of *The Rain People* directed
  by Francis Ford Coppola)
Written, directed, photographed, and edited by
  George Lucas

SHORTS

Captain EO
(released at Disneyland September 13, 1986)
A George Lucas Presentation
Executive Produced by George Lucas
Produced by Rusty Lemorande
Directed by Francis Ford Coppola
Screenplay by George Lucas
Cinematography Consultant: Vittorio Storaro
Edited by Walter Murch, Lisa Fruchtman
Original Music by Michael Jackson (songs),
  James Horner
Art Direction by Geoffrey Kirkland
Set Decoration by John Sweeney
Sound by Gary Rydstrom (sound design),
  Gary Summers, Shawn Murphy

Featured Cast
Anjelica Huston, Michael Jackson

FRANCIS FORD COPPOLA, GEORGE LUCAS EXECUTIVE PRODUCERS

Kagemusha, The Shadow Warrior
(1980)
A 20th Century Fox Release
A film by Akira Kurosawa
Executive Produced (international version)
  by George Lucas, Francis Ford Coppola
Directed by Akira Kurasawa

Awards
2 Academy Award nominations:
Foreign Language Film
Art Direction-Set Decoration—Yoshirô Muraki

1 Golden Globe nomination:
Foreign Film

Cannes Film Festival:
Palme d'Or—Akira Kurosawa (tied with
  All That Jazz)

Powaqqatsi
(1988)
A Cannon Group Release
A Francis Ford Coppola, George Lucas
  Presentation.
A film by Godfrey Reggio
Directed by Godfrey Reggio

The Saul Zaentz Company

FEATURE FILMS

Amadeus

(released September 26, 1984)
A Saul Zaentz Company Production
An Orion Pictures Release
Produced by Saul Zaentz
Executive Produced by Michael Hausman,
  Bertil Ohlsson
Directed by Milos Forman
Screenplay by Peter Shaffer
Based on the play by Peter Shaffer
Cinematography by Miroslav Ondricek
Edited by Michael Chandler, Nena Danevic
Music by W.A. Mozart, J.S. Bach,
  G.B. Pergolesi, Antonio Salieri
Production Design by Patrizia Von Brandenstein
Art Direction by Karel Cerny
Costume Design by Theodor Pistek
Sound by John Nutt (supervising sound editor),
  Mark Adler (music editor), C.J. Appel (sound
  effects editor), Tom Bellfort (sound effects edi-
  tor), Mark Berger (supervising rerecording
  mixer), Jay Boekelheide (sound effects
  editor), Tim Holland (sound effects editor),
  B.J. Sears (sound editor)

Featured Cast

F. Murray Abraham, Elizabeth Berridge,
Simon Callow, Roy Dotrice, Christine Ebersole,
Tom Hulce, Jeffrey Jones, Charles Kay

Awards

11 Academy Award nominations, 8 wins:
✔ Picture—Saul Zaentz
✔ Actor in a Leading Role—F. Murray Abraham
✔ Sound—Mark Berger, Thomas Scott,
  Todd Boekelheide, Christopher Newman
✔ Makeup—Paul LeBlanc, Dick Smith
✔ Director—Milos Forman
✔ Costume Design—Theodor Pistek
✔ Writing-Screenplay Based on Material from
  Another Medium—Peter Shaffer
✔ Art Direction-Set Decoration—
  Patrizia von Brandenstein, Karel Cerny
  Actor in a Leading Role—Tom Hulce
  Cinematography—Miroslav Ondrícek
  Film Editing—Nena Danevic, Michael Chandler

6 Golden Globe nominations, 4 wins:
✔ Motion Picture-Drama—Saul Zaentz
✔ Actor in a Motion Picture-Drama—
  F. Murray Abraham
✔ Director-Motion Picture—Milos Forman
✔ Screenplay-Motion Picture—Peter Shaffer
  Actor in a Motion Picture-Drama—Tom Hulce
  Actor in a Supporting Role in a Motion Picture—
  Jeffrey Jones

AFI 100 Years 100 Films, ranked #53

At Play in the Fields of the Lord

(released December 6, 1991)
A Saul Zaentz Company Production
A Universal Pictures Release
Produced by Saul Zaentz
Executive Produced by David Nichols,
  Francisco Ramalho, Jr.
Directed by Hector Babenco
Screenplay by Hector Babenco,

Jean-Claude Carrière
Based on the novel by Peter Matthiessen
Cinematography by Lauro Escorel
Edited by William M. Anderson,
  Armen Minasian, Louise Innes
Original Music by Zbigniew Preisner
Production Design by Clovis Bueno
Costume Design by Rita Murtinho
Sound by Mark Berger (supervising
  rerecording mixer), Pat Jackson (sound effects
  editor), Ann Kroeber (sound effects editor),
  David Parker and Todd Boekelheide
  (rerecording mixers)

Featured Cast

Kathy Bates, Tom Berenger, Daryl Hannah,
John Lithgow, Aidan Quinn, Tom Waits

1 Golden Globe Nomination:
Original Score-Motion Picture—
  Zbigniew Preisner

The English Patient

(released November 6, 1996)
A Saul Zaentz/Tiger Moth Production
A Miramax Films Release
Produced by Saul Zaentz
Associate Produced by Paul Zaentz,
  Steve Andrews
Executive Produced by Scott Greenstein,
  Bob Weinstein, Harvey Weinstein
Directed by Anthony Minghella
Screenplay by Anthony Minghella
Based on the novel by Michael Ondaatje
Cinematography by John Seale
Edited by Walter Murch
Original Music by Gabriel Yared
Art Direction by Aurelio Crugnola
Set Decoration by Aurelio Crugnola,
  Stephanie McMillan
Costume Design by Ann Roth, Gary Jones
Sound by Pat Jackson (supervising
  sound editor)

Featured Cast

Naveen Andrews, Juliette Binoche,
Willem Dafoe, Ralph Fiennes, Colin Firth,
Jürgen Prochnow, Kristin Scott Thomas,
Julian Wadham

Awards

12 Academy Award nominations, 9 wins:
✔ Picture—Saul Zaentz
✔ Actress in a Supporting Role—Juliette Binoche
✔ Art Direction-Set Decoration—Stuart Craig,
  Stephanie McMillan
✔ Director—Anthony Minghella
✔ Sound—Walter Murch, Mark Berger,
  David Parker, Christopher Newman
✔ Film Editing—Walter Murch
✔ Costume Design—Ann Roth
✔ Cinematography—John Seale
✔ Music-Original Score—Gabriel Yared
  Actor in a Leading Role—Ralph Fiennes
  Actress in a Leading Role—
  Kristin Scott Thomas
  Writing-Screenplay Based on Material from
  Another Medium—Anthony Minghella

7 Golden Globe nominations, 2 wins:
✔ Motion Picture-Drama—Saul Zaentz

✔ Original Score-Motion Picture—Gabriel Yared
  Actor in a Motion Picture-Drama—
  Ralph Fiennes
  Director-Motion Picture—Anthony Minghella
  Screenplay-Motion Picture—Anthony Minghella
  Actress in a Motion Picture-Drama—
  Kristin Scott Thomas
  Actress in a Supporting Role in a Motion
  Picture—Juliette Binoche

J.R.R. Tolkien's The Lord of the Rings

(released November 15, 1978)
A Saul Zaentz Production
A United Artists Release
Produced by Saul Zaentz
Directed by Ralph Bakshi
Screenplay by Chris Conkling, Peter S. Beagle
Based on the novels by J.R.R. Tolkien
  (*The Fellowship of the Ring*, *The Two Towers*)
Cinematography by Timothy Galfas
Edited by Donald W. Ernst
Original Music by Leonard Rosenman
Special Costumes Designed and Constructed
  by William Barbe, Lynne Betner
Sound by Jim Henrikson (music editor)

Awards

1 Golden Globe nomination:
Original Score-Motion Picture—
  Leonard Rosenman

The Mosquito Coast

(released November 22, 1986)
A Jerome Hellman Production
A Warner Bros. Release
"The Saul Zaentz Company Presents"
Produced by Jerome Hellman
Executive Produced by Saul Zaentz
Directed by Peter Weir
Screenplay by Paul Schrader
Based on the novel by Paul Theroux
Cinematography by John Seale
Edited by Thom Noble
Original Music by Maurice Jarre
Production Design by John Stoddart
Art Direction by John Wingrove
Set Decoration by John Anderson
Costume Design by Gary Jones
Sound by Alan Splet (supervising sound
  editor), Richard Hymns, John Benson,
  Jay Boekelheide, Pat Jackson (sound
  effects editors)

Featured Cast

Harrison Ford, Andre Gregory,
Helen Mirren, River Phoenix, Martha Plimpton,
Conrad Roberts

2 Golden Globe nominations:
Actor in a Motion Picture-Drama—
  Harrison Ford
Original Score-Motion Picture—Maurice Jarre

One Flew Over the Cuckoo's Nest

(released November 15, 1975)
A Fantasy Films Production
A United Artists Release

Produced by Saul Zaentz, Michael Douglas
Directed by Milos Forman
Screenplay by Lawrence Hauben, Bo Goldman
Based on the novel by Ken Kesey
Cinematography by Haskell Wexler, Bill Butler
Film Editing by Richard Chew (supervisor)
Original Music by Jack Nitzsche
Production Design by Paul Sylbert
Art Direction by Edwin O'Donovan
Costume Design by Agnes Rodgers
Sound by Mark Berger (postproduction sound
  director), Pat Jackson, Mary McGlone, Robert
  Rutledge, Veronica Selver (sound editors)

Featured Cast
Louise Fletcher, Jack Nicholson, William Redfield
  (Additional cast not on one sheet includes
  Danny DeVito, Christopher Lloyd,
  Will Sampson)

Awards
9 Academy Award nominations, 5 wins:
✔ Picture—Saul Zaentz, Michael Douglas
✔ Actor in a Leading Role—Jack Nicholson
✔ Actress in a Leading Role—Louise Fletcher
✔ Director—Milos Forman
✔ Writing-Screenplay Adapted From Other
  Material—Lawrence Hauben, Bo Goldman
  Film Editing—Richard Chew, Lynzee Klingman,
  Sheldon Kahn
  Actor in a Supporting Role—Brad Dourif
  Cinematography—Haskell Wexler, Bill Butler
  Music-Original Score—Jack Nitzsche

6 Golden Globe nominations, 6 wins:
✔ Motion Picture-Drama—Saul Zaentz,
  Michael Douglas
✔ Acting Debut in a Motion Picture-Male—
  Brad Dourif
✔ Actor in a Motion Picture-Drama—
  Jack Nicholson
✔ Actress in a Motion Picture-Drama—
  Louise Fletcher
✔ Director-Motion Picture—Milos Forman
✔ Screenplay-Motion Picture—Lawrence Hauben,
  Bo Goldman

AFI 100 Greatest American Movies of All Time
  list, ranked #20

Payday
(released April 4, 1973)
A PFC Production
In association with Fantasy Productions
A Cinerama Releasing Presentation
Directed by Daryl Duke
Screenplay by Don Carpenter
Executive Produced by Ralph J. Gleason
Produced by Don Carpenter and Martin Fink
Cinematography by Richard C. Glouner
Edited by Richard Halsey
Original Music by Ed Bogas, Tommy McKinney,
  Shel Silverstein, Ian Tyson, and Sylvia Tyson

Featured Cast
Ahna Capri, Cliff Emmich, Michael C. Gwynne,
Elayne Heilveil, Jeff Morris, Rip Torn

Awards
1974 National Society of Film Critics Awards:
Richard and Hilda Rosenthal Foundation Award
  for a person working in cinema whose
  contribution to film art has not yet received
  due public recognition—Daryl Duke

1974 Writers Guild of America:

WGA Award for Drama Written Directly for the
  Screen—Don Carpenter (nominated)

Screened at 1973 Cannes Film festival but not
  in competition.

Three Warriors
(released July 1978)
A Saul Zaentz Production
A United Artists Release
Produced by Saul Zaentz, Sy Gomberg
Executive Produced by Terry Morse, Jr.
Directed by Kieth Merrill
Screenplay by Sy Gomberg
Cinematography by Bruce Surtees
Film Edited by Irving Saraf (supervisor),
  Bonnie Koehler
Original Music by Merrill B. Jenson
Art Direction by Steven P. Sardanis
Set Decoration by Raphael Bretton
Costume Design by Aggie Guerard Rodgers
Postproduction Sound Mixing by Mark Berger,
  William Mumford

Featured Cast
Christopher Lloyd, Lois Red Elk, McKee "Kiko"
Red Wing, Randy Quaid, Charles White Eagle

The Unbearable
Lightness of Being
(released February 5, 1988)
A Saul Zaentz Company Production
An Orion Pictures Release
Produced by Saul Zaentz
Executive Produced by Bertil Ohlsson
Directed by Philip Kaufman
Screenplay by Jean-Claude Carrière,
  Philip Kaufman
Based on the novel by Milan Kundera
Cinematography by Sven Nykvist
Supervising Film Editor Walter Murch
Edited by Vivien Hillgrove Gilliam, B.J. Sears,
  Stephen A. Rotter
Original Music by Mark Adler (original music),
  Ernie Fosselius (Swiss music)
Production Design by Pierre Guffroy
Costume Design by Ann Roth
Sound Editing by Alan Splet (supervisor)
Rerecording Mixing by Mark Berger
  (supervisor), David Parker, Todd Boekelheide

Featured Cast
Juliette Binoche, Daniel Day-Lewis, Erland
Josephson, Pavel Landovsky, Derek de Lint,
Donald Moffat, Daniel Olbrychski, Lena Olin,
Stellan Skarsgard

Awards
2 Academy Award nominations:
Writing-Screenplay Based on Material from
  Another Medium—Jean-Claude Carrière,
  Philip Kaufman
Cinematography—Sven Nykvist

2 Golden Globe nominations:
Motion Picture-Drama—Saul Zaentz
Actress in a Supporting Role in a Motion
  Picture—Lena Olin

ADDITIONAL AWARDS

1996
Irving G. Thalberg Memorial Award

1998
American Cinema Editors
Golden Eddie Filmmaker of the Year Award

1996
BAFTA Film Award–Film–for *The English Patient*
  (shared with Anthony Minghella)

2003
Academy Fellowship

Film by the Sea International Film Festival
Lifetime Achievement Award

Lucasfilm Ltd.

FEATURE FILMS

Howard the Duck

(released August 1, 1986)
A Lucasfilm Ltd./Universal Pictures Production
A Universal Pictures Release
Executive Produced by George Lucas
Produced by Gloria Katz
Co-Produced by Robert Latham Brown
Directed by Willard Huyck
Screenplay by Willard Huyck, Gloria Katz
Based on the Comic Books by Steve Gerber
Cinematography by Richard H. Kline
Edited by Michael Chandler, Sidney Wolinsky
Original Music by John Barry; Songs
  by Thomas Dolby, Sylvester Levay,
  Lea Thompson
Production Design by Peter Jamison
Art Direction by Mark Billerman, Blake Russell
Set Decoration by Phil Abramson
Costume Design by Joe I. Tompkins
Sound by Ben Burtt, Richard Hymns,
  Gary Summers, Randy Thom

Featured Cast
Jeffrey Jones, Tim Robbins, Lea Thompson

Indiana Jones and the Last Crusade

(released May 24, 1989)
A Lucasfilm Ltd. Production
A Paramount Pictures Release
Executive Produced by George Lucas,
  Frank Marshall
Produced by Robert Watts
Directed by Steven Spielberg
Screenplay by Jeffrey Boam
Story by George Lucas, Menno Meyjes
Cinematography by Douglas Slocombe
Edited by Michael Kahn
Original Music by John Williams
Art Direction by Stephen Scott
Set Decoration by Peter Howitt
Costume Design by Joanna Johnston,
  Anthony Powell
Sound by Ben Burtt, Tony Dawe,
  Shawn Murphy, Gary Summers

Featured Cast
Sean Connery, Walter Donovan, Alison Doody,
Denholm Elliott, Harrison Ford, Julian Glover,
John Rhys-Davies

Awards
3 Academy Award nominations, 1 win:
Original Score—John Williams
Sound—Ben Burtt, Gary Summers,
  Shawn Murphy, Tony Dawe
✔ Sound Effects Editing—Ben Burtt, Richard Hymns

1 Golden Globe nomination:
Actor in a Supporting Role—Sean Connery

Indiana Jones and the Temple of Doom

(released May 23, 1984)
A Lucasfilm Ltd. Production
A Paramount Pictures Release
Executive Produced by George Lucas,
  Frank Marshall
Produced by Robert Watts
Directed by Steve Spielberg
Screenplay by Willard Huyck, Gloria Katz
Story by George Lucas
Cinematography by Douglas Slocombe
Edited by Michael Kahn
Original Music by John Williams
Production Design by Elliot Scott
Art Direction by Roger Cain, Alan Cassie
Set Decoration by Peter Howitt
Costume Design by Anthony Powell
Sound by Ben Burtt, Richard Hymns,
  Gary Summers, Randy Thom

Featured Cast
Kate Capshaw, Harrison Ford, Amrish Puri,
Ke Huy Quan, Roshan Seth, Philip Stone

Awards
2 Academy Award nominations, 1 win:
Original Score—John Williams
✔ Visual Effects—George Gibbs, Dennis Muren,
  Michael J. McAlister, Lorne Peterson

Labyrinth

(released June 27, 1986)
A Lucasfilm Ltd./Henson
  Associates Production
A TriStar Pictures Release
Executive Produced by George Lucas,
  David Lazer
Produced by Eric Rattray
Directed by Jim Henson
Screenplay by Dennis Lee, Jim Henson,
  Terry Jones
Cinematography by Alex Thompson
Edited by John Grover
Original Music by David Bowie, Trevor Jones
Production Design by Elliot Scott
Art Direction by Terry Ackland-Snow,
  Roger Cain, Peter Howitt, Michael White
Costume Design by Ellis Flyte, Brian Froud
Sound by Robert Hathaway, Peter Sutton

Featured Cast
David Bowie, Jennifer Connelly

Latino

(released November 21, 1985)
A Lucasfilm Ltd. Production
A Cinecom International Release
Produced by Benjamin Berg
Directed by Haskell Wexler
Screenplay by Haskell Wexler
Cinematography by Newton Thomas Sigel
Edited by Robert Dalva
Original Music by Diane Louie
Costume Design by Nubia Bermudez,
  Julián González
Sound by Ken Fischer, Mary Helen Leasman,
  Randy Thom

Featured Cast
Robert Beltran, Annette Cardona,
Ricardo López, Julio Medina, Tony Plana,
Luis Torrentes

More American Graffiti

(released August 3, 1979)
A Lucasfilm Ltd./Universal Production
A Universal Pictures Release
Executive Produced by George Lucas
Produced by Howard Kazanjian
Directed by Bill Norton
Screenplay by Bill Norton
Based on characters by George Lucas,
  Gloria Katz, Willard Huyck
Cinematography by Caleb Deschanel
Edited by Tina Hirsch, Dwayne Dunham
Art Direction by Ray Storey
Set Decoration by Kurt Von Koss
Costume Design by Aggie Guerard Rodgers
Sound by Ben Burtt, Greg Landaker,
  Steve Maslow, Bill Varney

Featured Cast
Candy Clark, Bo Hopkins, Ron Howard,
Paul Le Mat, Mackenzie Phillips, Charlie Martin
Smith, Cindy Williams

Radioland Murders

(released October 21, 1994)
A Lucasfilm Ltd. Production
A Universal Pictures Release
Executive Produced by George Lucas
Produced by Rick McCallum, Fred Roos
Directed by Mel Smith
Screenplay by Willard Huyck, Gloria Katz,
  Jeff Reno, Ron Osborn
Cinematography by David Tattersall
Edited by Paul Trejo
Original Music by Ray Bauduc, Joel McNeely
Production Design by Gavin Bocquet
Art Direction by Peter Russell
Set Decoration by Jim Ferrell
Costume Design by Peggy Farrell
Sound by Tom Bellfort, Carl Rudisill,
  Christopher Scarabosio, Dan Wallin

Featured Cast
Ned Beatty, Brian Benben, Scott Michael
Campbell, Michael Lerner, Christopher Lloyd,
Mary Stuart Masterson, Michael McKean,
Jeffrey Tambor, Stephen Tobolowsky

Raiders of the Lost Ark

(released June 12, 1981)
A Lucasfilm Ltd. Production
A Paramount Pictures Release
Executive Produced by Howard Kazanjian,
  George Lucas
Produced by Frank Marshall
Directed by Steven Spielberg
Screenplay by Laurence Kasdan
Story by Philip Kaufman, George Lucas
Cinematography by Douglas Slocombe
Edited by Michael Kahn
Original Music by John Williams
Production Design by Norman Reynolds
Art Direction by Leslie Dilley
Set Decoration by Michael Ford
Costume Design by Deborah Nadoolman
Sound by Richard L. Anderson, Ben Burtt,
  Roy Charman, Gregg Landaker, Steve Maslow,
  Bill Varney

Featured Cast
Karen Allen, Denholm Elliott, Harrison Ford,
Paul Freeman, Ronald Lacey, John Rhys-Davies

Awards
9 Academy Award nominations, 5 wins:
✔ Art Direction-Set Decoration—Norman
 Reynolds, Leslie Dilley, Michael Ford
 Cinematography—Douglas Slocombe
 Director—Steven Spielberg
✔ Film Editing—Michael Kahn
 Original Score—John Williams
 Picture—Frank Marshall
✔ Sound—Roy Charman, Gregg Landaker,
 Steve Maslow, Bill Varney
✔ Special Achievement Award for Sound Effects
 Editing—Ben Burtt, Richard L. Anderson
✔ Visual Effects—Richard Edlund, Kit West,
 Bruce Nicholson, Joe Johnston

1 Golden Globe nomination:
Director-Motion Picture—Steven Spielberg

AFI 100 Years 100 Films, ranked #60

Star Wars: Episode I
The Phantom Menace
(released May 19, 1999)
A Lucasfilm Ltd. Production
A 20th Century Fox Film Corp. Release
Executive Produced by George Lucas
Produced by Rick McCallum
Directed by George Lucas
Screenplay by George Lucas
Cinematography by David Tattersall
Edited by Ben Burtt, Paul Martin Smith
Original Music by John Williams
Production Design by Gavin Bocquet
Set Decoration by Peter Walpole
Costume Design by Trisha Biggar
Sound by Ben Burtt, Tom Bellfort, Tom Johnson,
 John Midgley, Shawn Murphy, Gary Rydstrom

Featured Cast
Pernilla August, Kenny Baker, Anthony Daniels,
Jake Lloyd, Ian McDiarmid, Ewan McGregor,
Liam Neeson, Frank Oz, Natalie Portman

Awards
3 Academy Award nominations:
Sound—Tom Johnson, John Midgley,
 Shawn Murphy, Gary Rydstrom
Sound Effects Editing—Ben Burtt, Tom Bellfort
Visual Effects—Rob Coleman, John Knoll,
 Denis Muren, Scott Squires

Star Wars: Episode II
Attack of the Clones
(released May 16, 2002)
A Lucasfilm Ltd. Production
A 20th Century Fox Film Corp. Release
Executive Produced by George Lucas
Produced by Rick McCallum
Directed by George Lucas
Screenplay by George Lucas
Cinematography by David Tattersall
Edited by Ben Burtt
Original Music by John Williams
Production Design by Gavin Bocquet
Set Decoration by Peter Walpole
Costume Design by Trisha Biggar
Sound by Ben Burtt, Shawn Murphy,
 Gary Rydstrom, Matthew Wood

Featured Cast
Kenny Baker, Hayden Christensen,
Anthony Daniels, Samuel L. Jackson,
Christopher Lee, Ian McDiarmid,
Ewan McGregor, Frank Oz, Natalie Portman

Awards
1 Academy Award nomination:
Visual Effects—Rob Coleman, Pablo Helman,
 John Knoll, Ben Snow

Star Wars: Episode III
Revenge of the Sith
(released May 19, 2005)
A Lucasfilm Ltd. Production
A 20th Century Fox Film Corp. Release
Executive Produced by George Lucas
Produced by Rick McCallum
Directed by George Lucas
Screenplay by George Lucas
Cinematography by David Tattersall
Edited by Ben Burtt, Roger Barton
Original Music by John Williams
Production Design by Gavin Bocquet
Art Direction by Ian Gracie, Phil Harvey,
 David Lee, Peter Russell
Set Decoration by Richard Roberts
Costume Design by Trisha Biggar
Sound by Paul Brincat, Ben Burtt,
 Shawn Murphy, Christopher Scarabosio,
 Matthew Wood

Featured Cast
Kenny Baker, Hayden Christensen,
Anthony Daniels, Samuel L. Jackson,
Christopher Lee, Ian McDiarmid,
Ewan McGregor, Frank Oz, Natalie Portman

Star Wars: Episode IV
A New Hope
(released May 25, 1977)
A Lucasfilm Ltd. Production
A 20th Century Fox Film Corp. Release
Executive Produced by George Lucas
Produced by Gary Kurtz
Directed by George Lucas
Screenplay by George Lucas
Cinematography by Gilbert Taylor
Edited by Richard Chew, Paul Hirsch,
 Marcia Lucas
Original Music by John Williams
Production Design by John Barry
Art Direction by Leslie Dilley, Norman Reynolds
Set Decoration by Roger Christian
Costume Design by John Mollo
Sound by Derek Ball, Ben Burtt, Don
 MacDougall, Bob Minkler, Ray West

Featured Cast
Kenney Baker, Peter Cushing, Anthony Daniels,
Carrie Fisher, Harrison Ford, Alec Guinness,
Mark Hamill, Peter Mayhew, David Prowse

Awards
11 Academy Award nominations, 7 wins:
 Actor in a Supporting Role—Alec Guinness
✔ Art Direction-Set Decoration—John Barry,
 Roger Christian, Leslie Dilley,
 Norman Reynolds
✔ Costume Design—John Mollo
 Director—George Lucas
✔ Editing—Richard Chew, Paul Hirsch,
 Marcia Lucas
 Picture—Gary Kurtz
✔ Original Score—John Williams
 Screenplay Written Directly for the Screen—
 George Lucas
 Sound—Derek Ball, Don MacDougall,
 Bob Minkler, Ray West
✔ Special Achievement Award for Sound Effects—
 Ben Burtt

✔ Visual Effects—Robert Blalack, Richard Edlund,
 Grant McCune, John Stears

4 Golden Globe nominations, 1 win:
 Actor in a Supporting Role—Alec Guinness
 Director-Motion Picture—George Lucas
 Motion Picture—Drama
✔ Original Score—John Williams

AFI 100 Years 100 Films, ranked #15

Star Wars: Episode V
The Empire Strikes Back
(released May 21, 1980)
A Lucasfilm Ltd. Production
A 20th Century Fox Film Corp. Release
Executive Produced by George Lucas
Produced by Gary Kurtz
Directed by Irvin Kershner
Screenplay by Leigh Brackett,
 Lawrence Kasdan
Story by George Lucas
Cinematography by Peter Suschitzky
Edited by Paul Hirsch
Original Music by John Williams
Art Direction by Leslie Dilley, Harry Lange,
 Alan Tompkins
Set Decoration by Michael Ford
Costume Design by John Mollo
Sound by Ben Burtt, Gregg Landaker,
 Steve Maslow, Peter Sutton, Bill Varney

Featured Cast
Kenny Baker, Anthony Daniels, Carrie Fisher,
Harrison Ford, Alec Guinness, Mark Hamill, Peter
Mayhew, Frank Oz, David Prowse,
Billy Dee Williams

Awards
4 Academy Award nominations, 2 wins:
 Art Direction-Set Decoration—Leslie Dilley,
 Michael Ford, Harry Lange, Norman Reynolds,
 Alan Tompkins
 Original Score—John Williams
✔ Sound—Gregg Landaker, Steve Maslow,
 Peter Sutton, Bill Varney
✔ Special Achievement Award for Visual Effects—
 Richard Edlund, Brian Johnson,
 Dennis Muren, Bruce Nicholson

1 Golden Globe nomination:
Original Score—John Williams

Star Wars: Episode VI
Return of the Jedi
(released May 25, 1983)
A Lucasfilm Ltd. Production
A 20th Century Fox Film Corp. Release
Executive Produced by George Lucas
Produced by Howard Kazanjian
Co-Produced by Jim Bloom, Robert Watts
Directed by Richard Marquand
Screenplay by Lawrence Kasdan, George Lucas
Story by George Lucas
Cinematography by Alan Hume
Edited by Sean Barton, Duwayne Dunham,
 Marcia Lucas
Original Music by John Williams, Joseph
 Williams (Jizzwailer music)
Art Direction by Fred Hole, James Schoppe
Set Decoration by Michael Ford, Harry Lange
Costume Design by Aggie Guerard Rodgers,
 Nilo Rodis-Jamero
Sound by Ben Burtt, Tony Dawe,
 Gary Summers, Randy Thom

Featured Cast
Kenny Baker, Anthony Daniels, Mark Hamill,
Harrison Ford, Carrie Fisher, Alec Guinness,
James Earl Jones, Peter Mayhew,
Ian McDiarmid, Frank Oz, David Prowse,
Sebastian Shaw, Billy Dee Williams

Awards
5 Academy Award nominations, 1 win:
Art Direction-Set Decoration—
  Michael Ford, Fred Hole, Norman Reynolds,
  James L. Schoppe
Original Score—John Williams
Sound—Ben Burtt, Tony Dawe, Gary Summers,
  Randy Thom
Sound Effects Editing—Ben Burtt
✔ Special Achievement Award for Visual Effects—
  Richard Edlund, Dennis Muren, Ken Ralston,
  Phil Tippett

Twice Upon a Time
(released August 5, 1983)
A Lucasfilm Ltd./Korty Films Production
A Warner Bros. Release
Executive Produced by George Lucas
Produced by Bill Couturié
Directed by John Korty, Charles Swenson
Screenplay by Bill Couturié, Suella Kennedy,
  John Korty, Charles Swenson
Edited by Jennifer Gallagher
Original Music by Dawn Atkinson,
  Tom Ferguson, Bruce Hornsby, John Hornsby,
  Maureen McDonald, Ken Melville,
  David Moordigian
Art Direction by Harley Jessup
Sound by John Benson, Walt Kraemer,
  Michael Minkler, Dale Strumpell

Featured Cast
Voice talent by Hamilton Camp, James Cranna,
Marshall Efron, Paul Frees, Judith Kahan
Kampmann, Lorenzo Music, Julie Payne

Willow
(released May 20, 1988)
A Lucasfilm Ltd., Imagine
  Entertainment Production
An MGM Release
Executive Produced by George Lucas
Produced by Nigel Wooll
Directed by Ron Howard
Screenplay by Bob Dolman
Story by George Lucas
Cinematography by Adrian Biddle
Edited by Daniel Hanley, Michael Hill,
  Richard Hiscott
Original Music by James Horner
Production Design by Allan Cameron
Art Direction by Tim Hutchinson, Jim Pohl,
  Tony Reading, Kim Sinclair, Malcolm Stone
Costume Design by Barbara Lane
Sound by Ben Burtt, Richard Hymns,
  Shawn Murphy, Gary Summers

Featured Cast
Billy Barty, Warwick Davis, Val Kilmer,
Jean Marsh, Joanne Whalley

Awards
2 Academy Award nominations:
Sound Effects Editing—Ben Burtt,
  Richard Hymns
Visual Effects—Christopher Evans,
  Michael J. McAlister, Dennis Muren, Phil Tippett

SHORT FILMS

The Adventures of André & Wally B.
(1984)
2 minutes
A Computer Graphics Project,
  Computer Division, Lucasfilm Ltd.
Concept and Direction by Alvy Ray Smith
Forest Design and Rendering by William Reeves
Character Design and Animation by
  John Lasseter
Sound Design by Ben Burtt (Sprocket Systems).

ACADEMY OF MOTION PICTURE ARTS & SCIENCES SCIENTIFIC & TECHNICAL AWARDS

1977
Development of a facility uniquely oriented
toward visual effects photography—
John C. Dykstra

1981
Development of a Motion Picture Figure Mover
for animation photography—Dennis Muren and
Stuart Ziff

Concept and engineering of a beam splitter
optical composite motion picture printer—
Richard Edlund and ILM

Engineering of the Empire Motion Picture
Camera System—Richard Edlund and ILM

1987
Development of a Wire Rig Model Support
Mechanism used to control the movements
of miniatures in special effects—
Tadeuz Krzanowski

1992
Development and first implementation in feature
motion pictures of the MORF system for digital
metamorphosis of high-resolution images—
Douglas Smythe and the Computer Graphics
Department at ILM

1993
Concept and development of the Digital
Motion Picture Retouching System for
removing visible rigging, dirt/damage artifacts
from original motion picture imagery—
Mark Leather, Les Dittert, Douglas Smythe, and
George Joblove

1994
Development work on a linear array CCD
(Charge Coupled Device) film input scanning
system—Lincoln Hu and Michael Mackenzie

Pioneering work in the field of film input
scanning—Scott Squires (shared with
Gary Demos, Dan Cameron of Information
International, David DiFrancesco, and
Gary Starkweather of Pixar)

1995
Pioneering efforts in the creation of the
ILM digital film compositing system—Douglas
Smythe, Lincoln Hu, Douglas S. Kay, ILM

1996
Development of the Viewpaint 3D Paint System
for film production work—John Schlag,

Brian Knep, Zoran Kacic-Alesic, and
Thomas Williams

Development of a system to create and control
computer-generated fur, hair in motion
pictures—Jeffery Yost, Christian Rouet,
David Benson, and Florian Kainz

Creation and development of the Direct Input
Device—Brian Knep, Craig Hayes, Rick Sayre,
and Thomas Williams

1998
Pioneering work in motion-controlled, silent
camera dollies—Michael MacKenzie,
Mike Bolles, Udo Pampel, and Joseph Fulmer

Design and development of the "Caricature"
Animation Software System—Cary Phillips

Pioneering work in the design of digital signal
processing, its application to audio editing for
film—James A. Moorer

2001
Development of the ILM creature Dynamics
System—John Anderson, Jim Hourihan,
Cary Phillips, and Sebastian Marino

Development of the ILM Motion, Recovery
System (MARS)—Dr. Steve Sullivan and
Eric Schafer

Research, systems integration resulting in the
improvement of motion picture loudspeaker
systems—Tomlinson Holman

2003
Development of practical methods for
rendering skin, other translucent materials using
subsurface scattering techniques—
Christophe Hery, Ken McGaugh, and Joe Letteri

Pixar Animation Studios

FEATURE FILMS

A Bug's Life

(released November 20, 1998)
Walt Disney Pictures presents
 a Pixar Animation Studios film
Directed by John Lasseter
Co-directed by Andrew Stanton
Original story by John Lasseter,
 Andrew Stanton, Joe Ranft
Screenplay by Andrew Stanton, Donald McEnery
 and Bob Shaw
Produced by Darla K. Anderson and Kevin Reher
Original Music by Randy Newman
Supervising Technical Direction by William
 Reeves and Eben Ostby
Supervising Animation by Glenn McQueen
 and Rich Quade
Director of Photography Sharon Calahan
Edited by Lee Unkrich
Production Design by William Cone
Art Direction by Tia W. Kratter and Bob Pauley
Sound Design by Gary Rydstrom

Awards

1 Academy Award nomination:
Original Musical or Comedy Score—
 Randy Newman

Finding Nemo

(released May 30, 2003)
Walt Disney Pictures presents
 a Pixar Animation Studios film
Directed by Andrew Stanton
Co-directed by Lee Unkrich
Screenplay by Andrew Stanton, Bob Peterson
 and David Reynolds
Produced by Graham Walters
Executive Produced by John Lasseter
Original Music by Thomas Newman
Directors of Photography Sharon Calahan and
 Jeremy Lasky
Edited by David Ian Salter
Supervising Technical Direction by Oren Jacob
Production Design by Ralph Eggleston
Supervising Animator Dylan Brown
Character Art Director Ricky Vega Nierva
Shading Art Director Robin Cooper
Environment Art Director Anthony Christov,
 Randy Berrett
Sound Design by Gary Rydstrom

Awards

4 Academy Award nominations, 1 win:
✔ Animated Feature Film
Original Screenplay—Andrew Stanton,
 Bob Peterson and Dave Reynolds
Sound Editing—Gary Rydstrom and
 Michael Silvers
Music Score—Thomas Newman

1 Golden Globe nomination:
Picture—Musical or Comedy

The Incredibles

(released November 5, 2004)
Walt Disney Pictures presents
 a Pixar Animation Studios film
Written and Directed by Brad Bird
Produced by John Walker

Executive Produced by John Lasseter
Original Music by Michael Giacchino
Story Supervised by Mark Andrews
Directors of Photography Andrew Jimenez,
 Patrick LinandJanet Lucroy
Edited by Stephen Schaffer
Supervising Technical Direction by Rick Sayre
Supervising Animation by Tony Fucile,
 Steven Clay Hunter and Alan Barillaro
Production Design by Lou Romano
Art Direction by Ralph Eggleston
Sound Design by Randy Thom

Awards

4 Academy Award nominations, 2 wins:
✔ Animated Feature Film
Original Screenplay—Brad Bird
✔ Achievement in Sound Editing—Michael Silvers
 and Randy Thom
Achievement in Sound Mixing—Randy Thom,
 Gary A. Rizzo and Doc Kane

1 Golden Globe nomination:
Picture—Musical or Comedy

Monsters, Inc.

(released November 2, 2001)
Walt Disney Pictures presents
 a Pixar Animation Studios film
Directed by Pete Docter
Co-directed by Lee Unkrich, David Silverman
Screenplay by Andrew Stanton, Daniel Gerson
Original Story by Pete Docter, Jill Culton,
 Jeff Pidgeon, Ralph Eggleston
Produced by Darla K. Anderson
Executive Produced by John Lasseter and
 Andrew Stanton
Music by Randy Newman
Film Editor Jim Stewart
Story Supervised by Bob Peterson
Supervising Technical Direction
 by Thomas Porter
Supervising Animation by Glenn McQueen
 and Rich Quade
Production Design by Harley Jessup
 and Bob Pauley
Art Direction by Tia W. Kratter
 and Dominique Louis
Set Dressing Supervisor Sophie Vincelette
Sound Design by Gary Rydstrom

Awards

4 Academy Award nominations, 1 win:
✔ Original Song ("If I Didn't Have You")—
 Randy Newman
Animated Feature Film—John Lasseter
 and Pete Docter
Sound Editing—Gary Rydstrom
 and Michael Silvers
Original Score—Randy Newman

Toy Story

(released November 22, 1995)
Walt Disney Pictures presents
 a Pixar Animation Studios film
Directed by John Lasseter
Screenplay by Joss Whedon, Andrew Stanton,
 Joel Cohen, Alex Sokolow
Story by John Lasseter, Pete Docter,
 Andrew Stanton, Joe Ranft

Produced by Bonnie Arnold
 and Ralph Guggenheim
Executive Produced by Edwin Catmull
 and Steve Jobs
Original Music by Randy Newman (including
 songs); Klaus Lage (German version only)
Edited by Robert Gordon and Lee Unkrich
Supervising Technical Direction
 by William Reeves
Supervising Animation by Pete Docter
Art Direction by Ralph Eggleston
Sound Design by Gary Rydstrom

Awards

3 Academy Award nominations, 1 special
 achievement award:
✔ Special Achievement Award—John Lasseter
Original Musical or Comedy Score—
 Randy Newman
Original Song ("You've Got a Friend in Me")—
 Randy Newman
Screenplay Written Directly for the Screen —
 Andrew Stanton, John Lasseter, Pete Docter,
 Joe Ranft, Joss Whedon, Joel Cohen,
 Alec Sokolow

2 Golden Globe nominations:
Picture—Musical or Comedy
Original Song ("You Got A Friend In Me")—
 Randy Newman

Toy Story 2

(released November 24, 1999)
Walt Disney Pictures presents
 a Pixar Animation Studios film
Directed by John Lasseter
Co-directed by Lee Unkrich, Ash Brannon
Produced by Helene Plotkin,
 Karen Robert Jackson
Executive Produced by Sarah McArthur
Original Story by John Lasseter, Pete Docter,
 Ash Brannon, Andrew Stanton
Screenplay by Andrew Stanton, Rita Hsiao,
 Doug Chamberlin, Chris Webb
Original Music by Randy Newman
Supervising Technical Direction
 by Galyn Susman
Supervising Animation by Glenn McQueen
Director of Photography Sharon Calahan
Film Editors Edie Bleiman, David Ian Salter,
 Lee Unkrich
Production Design by William Cone,
 Jim Pearson
Sound Design by Gary Rydstrom

Awards

1 Academy Award nomination:
Original Song ("When She Loved Me")—
 Randy Newman

2 Golden Globe nominations, 1 win:
✔ Picture—Musical or Comedy
Original Song ("When She Loved Me")—
 Randy Newman

SHORT FILMS

Boundin'
(2003)
4:40 min.
A Pixar Animation Studios production
Directed by Bud Luckey
Co-directed by Roger Gould
Screenplay by Bud Luckey
Produced by Osnat Shurer
Executive Produced by John Lasseter
Original Music and Lyrics by Bud Luckey
Production Design by Bud Luckey
Cinematography by Jesse Hollander
Edited by Steve Bloom
Sound Design by Tom Myers
Supervising Animation by Doug Sweetland

Awards
1 Academy Award nomination:
Short Film–Animated—Bud Luckey

For the Birds
(2000)
3:31 min.
A Pixar Animation Studios production
Directed by Ralph Eggleston
Produced by Karen Dufilho
Executive Producer by John Lasseter
Edited by Jennifer Taylor, Tom Freeman
Sound Design by Tom Myers
Supervising Animation by James Ford Murphy

Awards
1 Academy Award nomination, 1 win:
✔ Short Film–Animated—Ralph Eggleston

Geri's Game
(1997)
4:56 min.
A Pixar Animation Studios production
Directed by Jan Pinkava
Screenplay by Jan Pinkava
Produced by Karen Dufilho
Executive Produced by Edwin Catmull
  and John Lasseter
Music by Gus Viseur et son Orshestre
Edited by Jim Kallett
Sound Design by Tom Myers

Awards
1 Academy Award nomination, 1 win:
✔ Short Film–Animated—Jan Pinkava

Jack-Jack Attack
(2005)
4:42 min.
Walt Disney Pictures presents
  a Pixar Animation Studios film
Written and Directed by Brad Bird
Produced by Osnat Shurer
Executive Produced by John Lasseter
Edited by Stephen Schaffer
Sound Design by Skywalker Sound

Knick Knack
(1989)
3:47 min.
A Pixar Animation Studios production
Directed by John Lasseter
A film by John Lasseter, Eben Ostby,
  William Reeves, Ralph Guggenheim,
  Craig Good, Don Conway, Flip Phillips,

Yael Miló, Tony Apodaca, Deirdre Warin
Music by Bobby McFerrin
Sound Design by Gary Rydstrom

Luxo Jr.
(1986)
2:08 min.
A Pixar Animation Studios production
Directed by John Lasseter
Story, Design, Models and Animation
  by John Lasseter
Sound by Gary Rydstrom

Awards
1 Academy Award nomination:
Short Film–Animated—John Lasseter

Mike's New Car
(2002)
3:45 min.
Walt Disney Pictures presents a Pixar Animation
  Studios film
Directed by Pete Docter and Roger Gould
Original Story by Pete Docter
Story by Jeff Pidgeon, Roger Gould, Rob Gibbs
Produced by Gale Gortney
Executive Produced by John Lasseter
Music Composed by Randy Newman
Edited by Robert Grahamjones
Sound Design by Tom Myers

Awards
1 Academy Award nomination:
Short Film–Animated—Pete Docter
  and Roger Gould

One Man Band
(2005)
4:30 min.
A Pixar Animation Studios production
Written and Directed by Andrew Jimenez
  and Mark Andrews
Produced by Osnat Shurer
Original Music by Michael Giacchino
Edited by Steve Bloom
Supervising Animation by Angus MacLane

Red's Dream
(1987)
4:10 min.
A Pixar Animation Studios production
Written, directed and animated by John
  Lasseter
Music by David Slusser
Sound Design by Gary Rydstrom

Tin Toy
(1988)
5:08 min.
A Pixar Animation Studios production
Directed by John Lasseter
Screenplay by John Lasseter
Story by John Lasseter
Sound by Gary Rydstrom
Computer Graphics by Tony Apodaca, Pat
  Hanrahan, Jeff Hilgert, Jim Lawson, Sam
  Leffler, Jeffrey Mock, Darwyn Peachey
  (RenderMan team), Don Conway & Ralph
  Guggenheim (output scanning), Eben Ostby
  and William Reeves (animation, modeling),
  Craig Good & John Lasseter (animation &
  modeling)

Technical direction by Eben Ostby
  and William Reeves

Awards
1 Academy Award nomination, 1 win:
✔ Short Film–Animated—John Lasseter, William
  Reeves

ACADEMY OF MOTION PICTURE ARTS & SCIENCES SCIENTIFIC & TECHNICAL AWARDS

1991
For the design and development of the CAPS
production system for feature film animation—
Thomas Hahn, Peter Nye, and Michael Shantzis
(shared with The Walt Disney Feature Animation
Department)

1992
For the development of RenderMan software
which produces images used in motion picture
from 3D computer descriptions of shape and
appearance—Loren Carpenter, Rob Cook,
Ed Catmull, Tom Porter, Pat Hanrahan,
Tony Apodaca, and Darwyn Peachey

1994
For their pioneering work in the field of Digital
Scanning—David DiFrancesco (and others from
ILM and I.I.)

1995
For their pioneering inventions in digital image
compositing—Alvy Ray Smith, Ed Catmull,
Thomas Porter, and Tom Duff

1996
For the original concept and the development
of particle systems used to create computer
generated visual effects in motion pictures—
William Reeves

For the creation and development of the Direct
Input Device, an encoded armature which allows
stop-motion animators to bring their skills and
artistry directly into computer animation—Rick
Sayre

1997
For the development of the Marionette three-
dimensional computer animation system—
Eben Ostby, William Reeves, Samuel J. Leffler
and, Tom Duff

For their pioneering efforts in the development
of digital paint systems—Richard Shoup,
Alvy Ray Smith, and Thomas Porter

1998
For his pioneering efforts in the development of
laser film recording technology (PixarVision)—
David DiFrancesco

2000
For their significant advancements to the field
of motion picture rendering as exemplified in
Pixar's RenderMan—Rob Cook, Loren Carpenter,
and Ed Catmull

Pacific Data Images

PDI / DREAMWORKS ANIMATION

Antz

(released October 12, 1998)
DreamWorks Pictures Presents
A PDI Production
Executive Produced by Penney Finkelman Cox,
  Sandra Rabins, Carl Rosendahl
Produced by Brad Lewis, Aron Warner,
  Patty Wooton
Directed by Eric Darnell and Tim Johnson
Screenplay by Todd Alcott, Chris Weitz,
  Paul Weitz

Featured Cast

Woody Allen, Dan Aykroyd, Anne Bancroft,
Jane Curtin, Danny Glover, Gene Hackman,
Jennifer Lopez, Grant Shaud, Sylvester Stallone,
Sharon Stone, Christopher Walken

Madagascar

(released May 27, 2005)
DreamWorks Animation presents
A PDI/DreamWorks Production
Produced by Teresa Cheng, Mireille Soria
Directed by Eric Darnell and Tom McGrath
Screenplay by Mark Burton, Billy Frolick

Featured Cast

Jada Pinkett Smith, Chris Rock,
David Schwimmer, Ben Stiller

Shrek

(released May 18, 2001)
DreamWorks Pictures Presents
A PDI/DreamWorks Production
Executive Produced by Penney Finkelman Cox,
  Sandra Rabins
Co-Executive Produced by David Lipman
Produced by Jeffrey Katzenberg, Aron Warner,
  John H. Williams
Co-Produced by Ted Elliott, Terry Rossio
Directed by Andrew Adamson and Vicky Jenson
Screenplay by Ted Elliott & Terry Rossio, Joe
  Stillman, Roger S.H. Schulman
Based on the book, *Shrek!* by William Steig

Featured Cast

Cameron Diaz, John Lithgow, Eddie Murphy,
Mike Myers

Awards

2 Academy Award nominations, 1 win:
✔ Animated Feature—Aron Warner
Writing, Screenplay Based on Material
  Previously Produced or Published—Ted Elliott,
  Terry Rossio, Joe Stillman, Roger S.H. Schulman

1 Golden Globe nomination:
Motion Picture–Musical or Comedy

1 Cannes Film Festival nomination:
Golden Palm (Palme d'Or)—Vicky Jenson,
  Andrew Adamson

Shrek 2

(released May 17, 2004)
DreamWorks Pictures Presents

A PDI/DreamWorks Production
Executive Produced by Jeffrey Katzenberg
Produced by David Lipman, Aron Warner,
  John H. Williams
Directed by Andrew Adamson, Kelly Asbury,
  and Conrad Vernon
Screenplay by Andrew Adamson, Joe Stillman,
  J. David Stem, David N. Weiss

Featured Cast

Julie Andrews, Antonio Banderas, John Cleese,
Cameron Diaz, Rupert Everett, Eddie Murphy,
Mike Myers, Jennifer Saunders

Awards

2 Academy Award nominations:
Animated Feature Film—Andrew Adamson
Achievement in Music Written for Motion
  Pictures, Original Song—Adam Duritz
  (composer/lyricist), Charles Gillingham,
  Jim Bogios, David Immerglück, Matthew
  Malley, David Bryson (composers), Dan Vickrey
  (lyricist) for the song "Accidentally In Love"

1 Golden Globe nomination:
Original Song–Motion Picture ("Accidentally In
  Love")—Adam Duritz (composer), Dan Vickrey
  (lyricist)

1 Cannes Film Festival 2004 nomination:
Golden Palm (Palme d'Or)—Andrew Adamson,
  Kelly Asbury, Conrad Vernon

PDI SHORT FILMS

Burning Love

(1988)
4 minutes
Directed by Roger Gould and Howard Baker

Chromosaurus

(1984)
40 seconds
Created by Don Venhaus

Fat Cat on a Diet

(1999)
4 minutes
Produced by Judy Conner
Directed by Raman Hui

Fishing

(2000)
4 minutes
Directed by David Gainey

Gabola the Great

(1997)
2 minutes
Directed by Tim Cheung

Gas Planet

(1992)
3 minutes
Executive Produced by Carl Rosendahl
Directed by Eric Darnell

Locomotion

(1990)
4 minutes
Directed by Steve Goldberg

Max's Place

(1984)
1 minute
Directed by Adam Chin

Metropopular

(2001)
6:30 minutes
Produced by Laura Lockwood and Jason Heapy
Directed by Jonah Hall

Millennium Bug

(1988)
2 minutes
Created by Lee Lanier

Opéra Industriel

(1988)
2 minutes
Directed by Adam Chin and Rich Cohen

Shrek 4-D

(2003)
12 minutes
Produced by Jeffrey Katzenberg and
  David Lipman
Directed by Simon J. Smith
Screenplay by David Lipman, based on
  characters by William Steig

Sleepy Guy

(1994)
4 minutes
Executive Produced by Carl Rosendahl
Directed by Raman Hui

Sprout

(2002)
3:17 minutes
Produced by Michael Garner
Directed by Scott B. Peterson

INDEX

A

Abraham, F. Murray, 77, 88, 89
Abyss, The (Cameron, 1989), 105
Academy Awards (Oscars)
  Amadeus, 81, 89
  American Graffiti, 102, 105, 110, 111
  American Zoetrope, 27
  Apocalypse Now, 49
  The Black Stallion, 47
  A Bug's Life, 159
  Ben Burtt, 139
  The Candidate, 226
  The Conversation, 43
  Eastwood, 203
  The English Patient, 81, 83, 94, 95
  Finding Nemo, 164
  Geri's Game, 151
  The Godfather, 29, 41
  The Godfather Part II, 29, 45
  The Incredibles, 153, 167
  Indiana Jones and the Last Crusade, 132
  Indiana Jones and the Temple of Doom,
    124, 125
  Industrial Light and Magic, 103, 105, 109
  Kaufman, 212
  Korty, 221
  Lasseter, 151
  Lost in Translation, 35, 73
  Lucas (Thalberg Award), 105
  Lucasfilm Ltd., 101
  Monsters, Inc., 163
  Randy Newman, 163
  One Flew Over the Cuckoo's Nest, 79, 87
  Pacific Data Images, 171
  Pixar Animation Studios, 149
  Raiders of the Lost Ark, 118
  Saul Zaentz Company, 77, 83
  Shrek, 175, 181
  Shrek 2, 182
  Skywalker Sound, 105
  Star Wars: Episode IV A New Hope, 103, 113
  *Star Wars: Episode V The Empire Strikes
    Back*, 116
  Star Wars: Episode VI Return of the Jedi,
    104, 122
  Star Wars: Episode I The Phantom Menace,
    136
  Star Wars: Episode II Attack of the Clones,
    140
  Tin Toy, 152, 153
  Tippett, 231
  Toy Story, 153, 157
  Toy Story 2, 161
  Tucker: The Man and His Dream, 130
  Unforgiven, 210
  Willow, 129
Ackridge, Bill, 223
Adams, Brooke, 214, 214
Adventures in Babysitting (Columbus, 1987),
  194
Adventures of André and Wally B., The
  (Lasseter, 1984), 104, 108–9, 108, 151, 151

Allen, David, 129
Allen, Karen, 118, 118
Allen, Tim, 156, 156
Allen, Woody, 19, 30
  Antz, 178, 179, 179
  Take the Money and Run, 17, 27
  Zwigoff and, 241
Amadeus (Forman, 1984), 79–81, 88–89,
  88, 89
Amadeus: The Director's Cut (Forman, 2002),
  83
American Graffiti (Lucas, 1973), 29, 101, 102,
  104–5, 104, 110–11, 110, 111
  awards and honors for, 102, 106
  Lucas-Coppola collaboration on, 32
  production disputes over, 15
American Zoetrope, 27, 29, 29, 31
  Apocalypse Now, 48–49, 48, 49
  The Black Stallion, 46–47, 46, 47
  The Black Stallion Returns, 50–51, 50, 51
  Bram Stoker's Dracula, 60–61, 60, 61
  chronology of, 29, 31, 33, 35
  The Conversation, 42–43, 42, 43
  CQ, 70–71, 70, 71
  establishment of, 18, 104
  The Godfather, 38–41, 40–41
  The Godfather Part II, 44–45, 44, 45
  The Godfather III, 58–59, 58, 59
  John Grisham's The Rainmaker, 66–67,
    66, 67
  Korty and, 221
  later history of, 31–33
  Lost in Translation, 72–73, 72, 73
  Murch and, 96
  My Family, 64–65, 64, 65
  Niebaum-Coppola Estate Winery stage
    of, 34, 35
  opening of, 30
  The Outsiders, 52–53, 52, 53
  Peggy Sue Got Married, 56–57, 56, 57
  Robbins and, 228
  Rumble Fish, 54–55, 54, 55
  The Secret Garden, 62–63, 62, 63
  Sentinel Building, 33
  THX 1138, 36–37, 36, 37
  The Virgin Suicides, 68–69, 68, 69
Anderson, Gilbert M. (Max Aronson), 13
Anderson, Henry, 174
Anderson, Scott, 173
Anderson, Wes, 234
Andrews, Julie, 182
Andrews, Naveen, 95
Androsky, Carol, 219
animated films
  The Adventures of André and Wally B.,
    108–9, 108, 151, 151, 152
  Antz, 178–79, 178, 179
  A Bug's Life, 158–59, 158, 159
  Finding Nemo, 164–65, 164, 165
  The Incredibles, 166–67, 166, 167
  Monsters, Inc., 162–63, 162, 163
  of Pacific Data Images, 171–75

  Pacific Data Images's short films, 176–77,
    176, 177
  of Pixar Animation Studios, 149–54
  Pixar's short films, 155, 155
  Selick's, 232–34
  Shrek, 180–81, 180, 181
  Shrek 2, 182–83, 182, 183
  Toy Story, 156–57, 156, 157
  Toy Story 2, 160–61, 160, 161
  Twice Upon a Time, 120–21, 120, 121
Antonioni, Michelangelo, 42
Antz (Darnell, Johnson, 1998), 173, 175,
  178–79, 178, 179
Anywhere But Here (Wang, 1999), 238
Apocalypse Now (Coppola, 1979), 31, 48–49,
  48, 49
Apocalypse Now: Redux (Coppola, 1999), 48
Apur Sansar (Ray, 1959), 64
Armstrong, Howard, 241
Art School Confidential (Zwigoff), 242, 242
Assassination Tango (Duvall, 2003), 35
Atkinson, Rowan, 135
At Play in the Fields of the Lord (Babenco,
  1991), 80, 81, 83
At Play in the Fields of the Lord (novel,
  Matthiessen), 78
Auster, Paul, 238
Austin, 19
Autobiography of Miss Jane Pittman, The
  (television movie; Korty, 1974), 220, 221
Autumn in New York (Chen, 2000), 193

B

Babenco, Hector, 80, 81, 83
Backdraft (Howard, 1991), 105
Back to the Future (Zemeckis, 1985), 56
Bacon, Lloyd, 15
Bad News Bears, The (Ritchie, 1976), 224,
  226–27, 226, 227
Bad Santa (Zwigoff, 2003), 16, 242
Baker, Howard, 173
Baker, Kenny, 141
Bakshi, Ralph, 79
Ballard, Carroll, 18, 29, 186–88, 186, 187,
  189, 225
  American Zoetrope, 31
  The Black Stallion, 31, 46–47
  on Coppola, 30
  Coppola and, 32
  Fly Away Home, 190–91
  Never Cry Wolf, 188–90
  The Nutcracker: The Motion Picture, 232
Baltimore, 19
Banderas, Antonio, 175, 183
Barwood, Hal, 18, 102, 229–30
Batman (Burton, 1989), 232
Batman Forever (Schumacher, 1995), 173
Batman Returns (Burton, 1992), 173
Batteries Not Included (Robbins, 1987), 230,
  231, 231
Beckerman, Barry, 31
Beetle Juice (Burton, 1988), 232

Beier, Thad, *173*
Bell, Geoffrey, 13
Belson, Jordan, 16
Benben, Brian, 135, *135*
Bendich, Al, 78
Benson, Sheila, 123
Berg, Jeff, 229
Berkeley Cinema Guild and Studio, 16
Berridge, Elizabeth, 88, *89*
Bertolucci, Bernardo, 192
Beyond This Winter's Wheat (Ballard, 1965), 187
Bicentennial Man (Columbus, 1999), 195
Bielenberg, Ken, *174*, 182, 183
Big Rock Ranch, 107, *107*
Bingo Long Traveling All-Stars & Motor Kings, The (Badham, 1976), *230*
Binoche, Juliette
    The English Patient, 95, *95*
    The Unbearable Lightness of Being, 80, 92, 93, *93*
Birch, Thora, *241*, 242
Bird, Brad, 151, 153, 231, 166–67, *167*
Black and White (music video; 1991), *173*
Black Stallion, The (Ballard, 1979), 29, *32*, 46–47, *46*, *47*, 187, 188
Black Stallion Returns, The (Dalva, 1983), 31, 50–51, *50*, *51*
Blank, Les, 16
Blowup (Antonioni, 1966), 42
Blue in the Face (Wang, 1995), 239
Body Heat (Kasdan, 1981), 103
Bogdanovich, Peter, 17
Bonerz, Peter, 219
Bottoms, Sam, *49*
Bouchez, Elodie, 71
Boundin' (Luckey, Gould, 2003), 155, *155*
Bowie, David, 104, 126, *126*, 127, *127*
Brackett, Leigh, 116
Brakhage, Stan, 16
Bram Stoker's Dracula (Coppola, 1992), 27, 33, 60–61, *60*, *61*
Brando, Marlon, 45
    Apocalypse Now, 48–49, *49*
    The Godfather, 29, *41*, 157
Breaking the Habit (Korty, 1964), 120
Bridges, Jeff, *130*, 131, *131*
Broadbent, Jim, 242
Brooks, Albert, 165, *165*
Broughton, James, 16
Brubeck, Dave, 77, 78
Bruce, Lenny, 77, 82
Bug's Life, A (Lasseter, 1998), 151, 158–59, *158*, *159*, 178
Bullitt (Yates, 1968), 16–17
Burke, Patti, 175
Burnett, Francis Hodgson, 62, 63
Burning Love (Arquelos, 1988), 176
Burns, George, 135
Burns, Steve, *223*
Burton, Tim, 151, 232–34, *232*
Burtt, Ben, 113, 136, 138–39, *138*
Burum, Stephen H., 54

C

Caen, Herb, 17

Cage, Nicholas, *56*, 57
Cagney, James, 15
Calahan, Sharon, *174*
California Institute for the Arts (CalArts), 150–51
California Motion Picture Corporation, 13–14
Cameron, James, 113
Canby, Vincent
    on *Apocalypse Now*, 48
    on *The Black Stallion Returns*, 51
    on *Bram Stoker's Dracula*, 61
    on *The Godfather*, 41
    on *Raiders of the Lost Ark*, 119
    on *Star Wars: Episode IV A New Hope*, 113
Candidate, The (Ritchie, 1972), 224–26, *225*
Canyon Cinema Group, 101
Capri, Ahna, *85*
Capshaw, Kate, 124
Captain EO (Coppola, 1986), 33
Carpenter, Don, 78, 79, 85
Carpenter, Loren, *109*
Carrey, Jim, 57
Carrillo, Elpidia, *64*
Cartwright, Veronica, 214
Cassavetes, John, 212, 222
Castaway (Zemeckis, 2004), 47
Catmull, Edwin, 108, *109*, 149–52, *150*, 154
Cazale, John, *41*
Center of the World, The (Wang, 2001), 238, 239
Champlin, Charles, 41, 117, 118
Chan is Missing (Wang, 1982), 237, *237*
Channing, Stockard, 238
Chaplin, Charlie, 13, 176
Chapman, Michael, 214
Chen, Joan, 18, 192–93, *192*, *193*
Chin, Adam, *173*
Choy, Curtis, *237*
Christensen, Hayden, 35, 140, *141*, *142*, 143
Christie, Julie, 17
Chromosaurus (Venhaus, 1984), 176, *176*
Chuang, Richard, 171, 172, 173–174, *173*, *174*
Cin, Michael, *237*
City (magazine), 29, 31
Clarke, Shirley, 212
Claybourne, Doug, *187*
Cleese, John, 182
Close, Glenn, 204
Close Encounters of the Third Kind (Spielberg, 1977), 229
Clowes, Daniel, *241*, 242, *242*
Clownhouse (Coppola, 1989), 33
Cohen, Rich, *173*
Coleman, Ron, 141
Columbus, Christopher, 18, 194–95, *195*
    Harry Potter and the Sorcerer's Stone, 198–99
    Home Alone, 195–96
    Mrs. Doubtfire, 196–98
Computer Games Division (Lucasfilm Ltd.), 103, 104
Computer Graphics Group (Lucasfilm Ltd.), *109*, 149, 151
    see also Pixar Animation Studios
Connelly, Jennifer, 126, *126*, 127

Conner, Bruce, 16
Connery, Sean, 94, *132*, 133
Conrad, Joseph, 49
Conversation, The (Coppola, 1974), 29, 42–43, *42*, *43*
Cook, Rob, *109*
Cook, Roderick, *80*
Cooper, Kevin, 35
Copeland, Stewart, 55
Coppola, Carmine, 31, 33, 45, 47
Coppola, Eleanor, 29, 30, 33, *35*, 49
Coppola, Francis Ford, 15, 27–29, 35
    American Zoetrope, 18, *31*, 34–35
    Apocalypse Now, 48–49, 49
    Ballard and, 46, 187, *187*
    Bram Stoker's Dracula, 60–61, *61*
    The Conversation, 42–43
    Dalva and, 51
    early career of, 27–30
    The Godfather, 40–41, *41*
    The Godfather Part II, 44–45, *44*
    The Godfather III, 58–59, *59*
    John Grisham's The Rainmaker, 66–67
    joint productions with Lucas, 101
    Kagemusha: The Shadow Warrior, *32*
    Korty and, 218, 220–21
    Lucas and, 32, 103–4
    Murch and, 96
    The Outsiders, 52–53
    Peggy Sue Got Married, 56–57
    The Rain People, *103*
    Rumble Fish, 54–55
    on San Francisco artistic scene, 24
    Signal 7, 222
    THX 1138, 30
    Tucker: The Man and His Dream, 130–31
Coppola, Gio, 30, *35*
Coppola, Roman, 33, 35, *35*
    CQ, 70–71, *71*
Coppola, Sofia, 35
    The Godfather, 41
    The Godfather III, 58–59, *59*
    Lost in Translation, 72–73, *73*
    New York Stories, 33
    The Virgin Suicides, 68–69, *68*
Coppola, Talia, 41
Coraline (Selick), 234
Corbett, Jim, 15
Corliss, Roger, 141
Corman, Roger, 27, 71
Costner, Kevin, 210, *210*
Cotton Club, The (Coppola, 1984), 31, 33
Couturie, Bill, 121
Cox, Joel, 210
CQ (Coppola, 2002), 35, 70–71, *70*, *71*
Crabbe, Buster, 119
Craig, Stuart, 63, 199
Crazy Quilt, The (Korty, 1965), 17–18, 218, 219, *219*
Creedence Clearwater Revival, 77, 78
Cronyn, Hume, 230, 231
Crowe, Russell, 128
Cruise, Tom, 53, *53*
Crumb, Robert, 79, 240, 242–43, *243*
Crumb (Zwigoff, 1994), 16, 241, 243, *243*
Crystal, Billy, 163, *163*

Culkin, Macaulay, 195, 196, *196*
Cupid Angling (Douglass, 1918), 14
Cusack, Joan, *160*, *161*
Cycles (Nilsson, in production), *223*

D

Dafoe, Willem, 95, *164*, 165
Dahl, Roald, 234
Dalva, Robert, 18, *51*
   American Zoetrope, *31*
   The Black Stallion, 31
   The Black Stallion Returns, 50–51
   Coppola and, 32
Damon, Matt, 66, *66*, 67
Daniels, Anthony, *123*, 137, *141*
Daniels, Jeff, *190*
Darnell, Eric, *174*, *179*
Darnton, Nina, 127
Davies, Jeremy, 70
Davis, Warwick, 128, *128*
Day-Lewis, Daniel, *80*, 93, *93*
DeGeneres, Ellen, 165, *165*
de Medeiros, Maria, 213
De Niro, Robert, 35
   The Godfather Part II, 44–45, *45*
Dennehy, Brian, *188*, 189
Depardieu, Gerard, 71
Dern, Bruce, 17, 222
Deschanel, Caleb, 30, 31, 187, 191
   American Graffiti, *102*
   The Black Stallion, 46–47
Desmond, Paul, 77
DeVito, Danny, 67, *67*, 79, 87
Diaz, Cameron, *180*, 182
Dillon, Matt
   The Outsiders, 53, *53*
   Rumble Fish, 54, *54*, 55
Dim Sum: A Little Bit of Heart (Wang, 1985), 237
Di Palma, Carlo, 51
Directors Guild of America, 212
Dirty Harry (Siegel, 1971), 16–17
Disney Studios, *see* Walt Disney Studios
Dixon, Jamie, *173*
D.O.A. (Mate, 1949), 15–16
Docter, Pete, 152, 157, 161–63
Doody, Alison, *132*, 133
Dorey, Sheilah, *219*
Douglas, Kirk, 78, 87
Douglas, Michael, 79, 87, 204
Douglass, Leon F., 14
Dourif, Brad, *79*, 87
Downhill Racer (Ritchie, 1969), 224
Dracula (Coppola, 1992),
   see Bram Stoker's Dracula
Dragonslayer (Robbins, 1981), 228, 229, 230–31
DreamWorks Animation SKG, *172*, *173*, *175*, 178
Dreyfuss, Richard, *110*, 111
Droids (television series), 104
Duell, William, 79
Duke, Daryl, 78, 85
Duma (Ballard, 2003), *187*
Dunst, Kirsten, 68
Duvall, Robert, 58

Assassination Tango, 35
The Conversation, 43
The Godfather, 41
The Great Northfield Minnesota Raid, 212
Invasion of the Body Snatchers, 214
THX 1138, 36–37, *37*, 228
Dykstra, John, 113

E

Eastwood, Clint, 18, 202–3, *203*
   Dirty Harry, 16
   High Plains Drifter, 205–6
   The Outlaw Josey Wales, 212
   A Perfect World, 210–11
   Play Misty for Me, 203–5
   Unforgiven, 206–10
"Eastwood's rule," 212
Easy Rider (Kovacs, 1969), 18, 29
Eat A Bowl Of Tea (Wang, 1989), 237
Ebert, Roger
   on *Amadeus*, 89
   on *Antz*, 179
   on *The Bad News Bears*, 227
   on *Dragonslayer*, 231
   on *Harry Potter and the Sorcerer's Stone*, 199
   on *Indiana Jones and the Temple of Doom*, 125
   on *Peggy Sue Got Married*, 57
   on *Play Misty for Me*, 205
   on *The Secret Garden*, 63
   on *Selick*, 234
   on *Shrek*, 181
   on *Star Wars: Episode I The Phantom Menace*, 137
   on *Tim Burton's The Nightmare Before Christmas*, 234
   on *Toy Story*, 157
   on *Toy Story 2*, 161
   on *The Unbearable Lightness of Being*, 93
Edelstein, Dave, 165
Edlind, Richard, 113
Eisner, Michael, 95
Elfman, Danny, 234
Ellington, Duke, 78
English Patient, The (Minghella, 1996), 77, 81, *81*, 83, 94–96, *94*, *95*, *97*
English Patient, The (novel, Ondaatje), 94, 95
Entis, Glenn, 171, *172*, 173, *173*
Epstein, Rob, 16
Escape Artist, The (Deschanel, 1982), 31
Essanay Film Manufacturing Company, 13–14
Estevez, Emilio, 53
E.T.: The Extra-Terrestrial (Spielberg, 1982), 103
Eugenides, Jeffrey, 68, 69
Ewok Adventure, The (television movie; Korty, 1984), 104, 221
Ewoks (television series), 104

F

Fantasy Films, 79–81
Fantasy Records
   bought by Concord Records, 83

   bought by Zaentz, 82
   music and comedy produced by, 77
   One Flew Over the Cuckoo's Nest financed by, 87
   Payday financed by, 85
   Zaentz working for, 78
Fantasy Studios, 82
Farley, Chris, 181
Fat Cat on a Diet (Hui, 1999), 177, *177*
Fearless Frank (*Frank's Greatest Adventure*; Kaufman, 1967), 212
Ferlinghetti, Lawrence, 77
Field, Sally, 197, *197*
Fiennes, Ralph, *81*, 94–95, *94*, *95*, *97*, 238
Fincher, David, 121
Finding Nemo (Stanton, 2003), 153, 164–65, *164*, *165*
Finian's Rainbow (Coppola, 1968), 18, 27, 103
Fink, Martin, 78
Fisher, Carrie, *105*, 106, 116–17, *117*, *123*
Fishing (Gainey, 2000), 177, *177*
Fletch (Ritchie, 1985), 224
Fletcher, Louise, 87
Fletch Lives (Ritchie, 1989), 224
Fly Away Home (Ballard, 1996), 190–91, *190*, *191*
Foley, David, 159
Fonda, Peter, 29
Ford, Harrison
   Apocalypse Now, 49
   The Conversation, 43
   Indiana Jones and the Last Crusade, 132–33, *132*, *133*
   Indiana Jones and the Temple of Doom, 124–25, *124*, *125*
   The Mosquito Coast, *80*, 90–91, *90*, *91*
   Raiders of the Lost Ark, 118–19, *118*, *119*
   Star Wars: Episode IV A New Hope, *105*, 113, 114–115
   Star Wars: Episode V The Empire Strikes Back, 116–17, *117*
   Star Wars: Episode VI Return of the Jedi, 122
Forman, Milos, 79–81, 86–89
Forrest, Frederic, 43, 49
For the Birds (Eggleston, 2000), 151–53, 155, *155*
Foss, Bill, *173*
Foster, Nick, 173
Frank' Greatest Adventure (*Fearless Frank*; Kaufman, 1967), 212
Freeborn, Stuart, *117*
Freeman, Morgan, 206
Friedman, Jeffrey, 16
Fritz the Cat (Bakshi, 1972), 79
Frost, Robert, 53
Frost, Sadie, 60
Fuchs, Fred, 35
Funnyman (Korty, 1967), 18, 218–19

G

Gabola The Great (Cheung, 1997), 176, *176*
Gaiman, Neil, 234
Garcia, Andy, 58, 217
Garner, Errol, 204
Gas Planet (Darnell, 1992), 176, *176*

Gentleman Jim (Walsh, 1941), 15
Gentry, Curt, 214
George Lucas Education Foundation
  (GLEF), 105
Gere, Richard, *193*
Geri's Game (Pinkava, 1997), 151, 155, *155*
Getz, Stan, 78
Ghost World (Zwigoff, 2001), 16, 240–43,
  240, 241
Giannini, Giancarlo, 71
Giarratana, Deb, *174*
Gibbs, Mary, 162, *162*
Ginsberg, Allen, 77, 82
Gleason, Ralph J., 78, 79
Glover, Danny, 67
Glusker, Shari, *173*
Godfather, The (Coppola, 1972), 15, 29,
  38–39, 40–41, *40, 41*, 157
Godfather, The (novel, Puzo), 41, 44
Godfather Part II, The (Coppola, 1974), 29,
  32, 44–45, *44, 45*
Godfather III, The (Coppola, 1990), 33,
  58–59, *58, 59*
Gold, Herb, 214
Goldberg, Steve, *173*
Goldblum, Jeff, 135, 214
Golden Child, The (Ritchie, 1986), 224
Golden Needles (Clouse, 1974), 237
Goldman, Walter, 112
Goldstein (Kaufman, 1965), 212
Gomberg, Sy, 79
Good, Craig, *109*
Goodman, John, *162*, 163
Good Morning Vietnam (Levinson, 1987), 196
Gordon, Hilary, *91*
Gordon, Rebecca, *91*
Gould, Alexander, *164*
Gould, Roger, *173*
Graham, Bill, 30
Granz, Norman, 77, 85
Great Northfield Minnesota Raid, The
  (Kaufman, 1972), 212
Great Train Robbery (Porter, 1903), 13
Greed (Von Stroheim, 1923), 14–15
Gremlins (Dante, 1984), 194
Grey, Jennifer, 35
Grignon, Rex, *173*, *174*
Grisham, John, 66
Guaraldi, Vince, 77, 78
Guinness, Sir Alec, 113, *113*

H

Hackman, Gene
  The Conversation, 42–43, *42, 43*
  Unforgiven, 210, *210*
Hairspray (Waters, 1988), 19
Hamill, Mark, *105, 112, 113, 114–15*, 117, *123*
Hammett, Dashiell, 15
Hammett (Wenders, 1982), 31
Hanks, Tom, 156, *156*, 160
Hanson, John, 222
Harris, Richard (actor), 199
Harris, Richard (film editor), 225
Harryhausen, Ray, 232
Harry Potter and the Chamber of Secrets
  (Columbus, 2002), 195

Harry Potter and the Sorcerer's Stone
  (Columbus, 2001), 195, 198–99, *198, 199,*
  200–201
Harvest (Ballard, 1966), 187
Hayashi, Marc, *237*
Heapy, Todd, *174*
Hearts of Darkness: A Filmmaker's Apocalypse
  (Coppola, 1991), 33
Heat and Sunlight (Nilsson, 1988), 222, *222*
Heaven and Earth (Stone, 1993), 192
Heilveil, Elayne, *85*
Henry and June (Kaufman, 1990), 212–13
Henson, Jim, 126–27, *126*, 173
Herr, Michael, 49
High Plains Drifter (Eastwood, 1973), 205–6,
  205, 206
Hinton, S.E., 31, 52–54
Hitchcock, Alfred, 16
Hoffman, Dustin, 197
Holland, Agniezka, 62–63
Holly, Buddy, 56
Home Alone (Columbus, 1990), 194–96, *196*
Hopkins, Robert, 15
Hopper, Dennis, 29, *49*
Howard, Ron
  American Graffiti, *110*, 111
  Willow, 128–29, *129*
Howard the Duck (Huyck, 1986), 104
Howell, C. Thomas, 53
Hughes, Howard, 157
Hughes, John, 19, 194
Hui, Raman, *174*
Hulce, Tom, 77, *80*, 88, *88, 89*
Hunter, Holly, *167*, 225
Huntley, Tim, *31*
Hurt, William, 238
Huston, Angelica, 242
Huston, John, 15
Huyck, Willard, 134

I

Ilyin, Nick, *173*
Imogen Cunningham, Photographer
  (Korty, 1970), 29
Incredibles, The (Bird, 2004), 19, 153,
  166–67, *166, 167*
Indiana Jones and the Last Crusade
  (Spielberg, 1989), 105, 132–33, *132, 133*
Indiana Jones and the Temple of Doom
  (Spielberg, 1984), 104, 124–25, *124, 125*
Indiana Jones series of films, 106
Industrial Light and Magic (ILM), 102, 103,
  105, 172, 231
Ingram, Rex, 15
Interior, Lux, 61
internet, 106, 107
Invasion of the Body Snatchers (Kaufman,
  1978), 31, 212, 214–15, *214*
Invasion of the Body Snatchers (Siegel, 1956),
  202, 214
I Remember Mama (Stevens, 1948), 15
Ishioka, Eiko, 60
Ittimanqnaq, Zachary, *188*

J

Jack (Coppola, 1996), 35

Jack-Jack Attack (Bird, 2005), 155, *155*
Jackson, Michael, 173
Jackson, Samuel L., 217
Jacob, Oren, 164
Jaglom, Henry, 17
Jakob, Dennis, *31*
James, Caryn, 133, 196
James, Rusty, 54
James and the Giant Peach (Selick, 1996),
  233, 234
Jarmusch, Jim, 239
Jobs, Steve, 108, 149–52, *150*, 154, 171
Johansson, Scarlett, 73, *73*, 241, 242
John Grisham's The Rainmaker (Coppola,
  1997), 66–67, *66, 67*
Johnson, Tim, 172, *173, 174*, 175, 179
Jones, Jeffrey, *80*, 88
Jones, Terry, 126
Jorah, Samson, 188, *188*
Josephson, Erland, 92
Joy Luck Club, The (Wang, 1993), 237–38,
  237, 239
Judd, Ashley, 217, *217*
Jurassic Park (Spielberg, 1993), 231

K

Kael, Pauline, 90
  on *The Autobiography of Miss Jane Pittman*,
    221
  on Ballard, 188
  on *The Black Stallion*, 47
  Broughton and, 16
  on *Indiana Jones and the Temple of Doom*,
    125
  on *Payday*, 79, 85
Kagemusha: The Shadow Warrior (Kurosawa,
  1980), 31, *32*, 103
Kamiya, Gary, 95
Kasdan, Lawrence, 103, 116
Katz, Gloria, 134
Katzenberg, Jeffrey, 152, 175, 178, 179, 182
Kauffman, Stanley, 79
Kaufman, Paul, 119
Kaufman, Philip, 212–13
  American Graffiti, 110–11, *110*
  Ballard and, 188
  Invasion of the Body Snatchers, 31,
    214–215, *214*
  The Right Stuff, 16, 18, 215–17, *215, 217*
  Star Wars series, 109
  Twisted, *213*, 217, *217*
  The Unbearable Lightness of Being, 80,
    92–93
  The Wanderers, 118
Kaufman, Rose, 212, 214
Kaufman, Sam, 119
Kay, Charles, *80*
Kazanjian, Howard, *102*, 122
Keaton, Diane, 58
Keitel, Harvey, 48, 238
Kempley, Rita, 129
Kershner, Irvin, 116–17, *117*
Kesey, Ken, 30, 78, 86
Kilmer, Val, 128–29, *129*
Kirby, Bruno, 45
Kitchens, Colin Michael, *188*

Knick Knack (Lasseter, 1989), 149, 155, *155*
Knightley, Kiera, *136*
Knoll, John, 136
Knott, Andrew, *62*
Korty, John, 17–18, 28, 218–21, *218, 219, 220*
   American Zoetrope, *31*, 104
   Imogen Cunningham, Photographer, 29
   Twice Upon a Time, 103, 120–21, 232
Korty Films, 120–21
Kovacs, Laszlo, 17–18
Kozachik, Pete, 234
Krim, Arthur, 79
Kundera, Milan, 92
Kurosawa, Akira, 30–31, *32*

L

Labyrinth (Henson, 1986), 104, 126–27, *126, 127*
Lacey, Ronald, 118
Lachman, Edward, 68
Ladd, Alan, Jr., 105, 112, 120
Lady from Shanghai, The (Wells, 1948), 15
Land Before Time (Bluth, 1988), 105
Lane, Diane, 53–54, *53, 54*
Language of Faces, The (Korty), 218
Larner, Jeremy, 226
Lasseter, John, *109*, 146, 150
   The Adventures of André and Wally B., 108–9
   A Bug's Life, 158–59
   The Incredibles, 166
   Monsters, Inc., 163
   Pixar Animation Studios and, 150–54
   Toy Story, 156–57
   Toy Story 2, 160–61
Lassick, Sydney, 79
Last Emperor, The (Bertolucci, 1987), 192
Last Halloween, The (television program, 1991), 173, *174*
Last Holiday, The (Wang), 239
Latifah, Queen, 239
Latino (Wexler, 1985), 104
Lawton, William, 13
Lean, David, 196
Leary, Denis, *159*
Leffler, Sam, *109*
Le Mat, Paul, *104*
Leone, Sergio, 202, 205
Leopard, The (Visconti, 1963), 14
Lerner, Michael, *135*
Lessler, Larry, *173*
Lester, Richard, 17
Letterman Digital Arts Center, 107, 109, *109*
Levinson, Barry, 19
Lewis, Brad, *174*
Life Aquatic with Steve Zizzou, The (Selick, 2004), 234
Lindvall, Angela, *70, 71*
Line-Up, The (Siegel, 1958), 16
Linklater, Richard, 19
Lishman, Bill, 191
Lithgow, John, *81, 180*
Little Flower (Zhang, 1978), *see Xiao Hua*
Little Lord Fauntleroy (novel, Burnett), 63
Lloyd, Christopher, 87, *135*

Lloyd, Jake, *136, 137*
Locatelli, Al, *31*
Locomotion (Goldberg, 1990), 176
Loos, Anita, 15
Lopez, Jennifer, 64, 238
Lord of the Rings, The (Bakshi, 1978), 79
Los Angeles, 12
Lost in Translation (Coppola, 2003), 35, 72–73, *72, 73*
Louie Bluie (Zwigoff, 1986), 16, 241
Lowe, Rob, 35, 53, *53*
Lowther, T.J., 211
Lucas, George, 15, *101*
   American Graffiti, 102
   American Zoetrope, 18, 31
   Apocalypse Now, 48
   Catmull hired by, 151
   Coppola and, 27–28, 32, 41, 103–4
   as film student, 101–3
   Indiana Jones and the Last Crusade, 132, *133*
   Indiana Jones and the Temple of Doom, 124, *125*
   Kagemusha: The Shadow Warrior, 32
   Kaufman and, 212
   Korty and, 218, 220–221
   Labyrinth, 126, *126*
   Murch and, 96
   Radioland Murders, 134–35, *135*
   Raiders of the Lost Ark, 118, *119*
   The Rain People, 103
   Robbins and, 230
   Howard and, 128
   on San Francisco filmmakers, 98
   Spielberg and, 133
   Star Wars: Episode IV A New Hope, 104, 112–13
   Star Wars: Episode V The Empire Strikes Back, 116–17
   Star Wars: Episode VI Return of the Jedi, 122, *122, 123*
   Star Wars: Episode I The Phantom Menace, 136–37, *136*
   Star Wars: Episode II Attack of the Clones, 35, 140–41
   Star Wars: Episode III Revenge of the Sith, 142–43, *142*
   Star Wars series, 105–6
   THX 1138, 29–31, *30*, 36–37, *37*, 228
   Tucker: The Man and His Dream, 130
   Twice Upon a Time, 120
LucasArts Entertainment, 105
LucasArts Games, 106
Lucasfilm Commercial Productions, 105
Lucasfilm Ltd., 101–6
   The Adventures of André and Wally B., 108–9, *108, 109*
   American Graffiti, 110–11, *110, 111*
   chronology of, 101–7
   Computer Graphics Group, 149, 151
   incorporation of, 29
   Indiana Jones and the Last Crusade, 132–33, *132, 133*
   Indiana Jones and the Temple of Doom, 124–25, *124, 125*
   Labyrinth, 126–27, *126, 127*

Radioland Murders, 134–35, *134, 135*
Raiders of the Lost Ark, 118–19, *118, 119*
Star Wars: Episode IV A New Hope, 105–6, 112–13, *112, 114*
Star Wars: Episode V The Empire Strikes Back, 116–17, *116, 117*
Star Wars: Episode VI Return of the Jedi, 122–23, *122, 123*
Star Wars: Episode I The Phantom Menace, 136–37, *136, 139*
Star Wars: Episode II Attack of the Clones, 140–41, *140, 141*
Star Wars: Episode III Revenge of the Sith, 142–43, *142, 145*
Tucker: The Man and His Dream, 130–31, *130, 131*
Twice Upon a Time, 120–21, *120, 121*
Willow, 128–29, *128, 129*
Lucas On-Line, 106–107
Luddy, Tom, 214, 237
Luxo Jr. (Lasseter, 1986), 149, *149*, 152, *152, 155*
Lynch, David, 192

M

Maberly, Kate, *63*
MacArthur (Sargent, 1977), 230
Macchio, Ralph, 53
MacKenna's Gold (Thompson, 1969), 103
Madagascar (Darnell, McGrath, 2005), 168–69, *170*
Maid in Manhattan (Wang, 2002), 238
Makavejev, Dusan, 237
Malick, Terrence, 218
Malkovich, John, 242
Maltese Falcon, The (Huston, 1941), 15
Man, a Woman, and a Killer, A (Wang, 1975), 237
Mantegna, Joe, *59*
Marquand, Richard, 122–23, *122*
Marshall, Garry, 17
Mary Shelley's Frankenstein (Branagh, 1994), 33, 35
Maslin, Janet
   on *A Bug's Life*, 159
   on *Fly Away Home*, 191
   on *A Perfect World*, 211
   on *Star Wars: Episode V The Empire Strikes Back*, 117
   on *Star Wars: Episode VI Return of the Jedi*, 122–23
   on *Star Wars: Episode I The Phantom Menace*, 136, 137
   on *Toy Story*, 157
   on *Tucker: The Man and His Dream*, 130–31
Masterson, Mary Stuart, 135
Mate, Rudolph, 16
Matthau, Walter, 226–27, *226, 227*
Matthiessen, Peter, 78, 188
Max's Place (Chin, 1984), 176
Maxwell, Delle, *173*
McCarthy, Kevin, 214
McClure, Michael, 16
McDiarmid, Ian, *143*
McFadden, Cheryl (Gates), 127
McGregor, Ewan

Star Wars: Episode I The Phantom Menace, 137, *137*

Star Wars: Episode II Attack of the Clones, 140, *141*

Star Wars: Episode III Revenge of the Sith, *142*, *143*, *143*

McKean, Michael, *134*, 135

McLaren, Norman, 218

McOmie, Maggie, 37

McQueen, Glenn, *174*

McQueen, Steve, 16

McTeague (novel, Norris), 14

Mela, Ina, *219*

Merrill, Keith, *78*

Metropopular (Hall, 2001), 177, *177*

MGM Studios, 14–15

Michelena, Beatriz, 13

Mi Familia (Nava, 1995), *see My Family/ Mi Familia*

Mike's New Car (Docter, Gould, 2002), 155, *155*

Milius, John, 29, 30, *31*, 48

Millennium Bug (Lanier, 1998), 177, *177*

Miller, Henry, 212, 213

Million Dollar Baby (Eastwood, 2004), 202

Mills, Donna, 204

Minghella, Anthony, *83*, 94–95

Minghella, Max, 242

Mirren, Helen, 35, *90*, *91*

Mishima: A Life in Four Chapters (Schrader, 1985), 33, 104

Mitchell, Elvis, 163, 181

Miyazaki, Hidao, 232

Moderns, The (Rudolph, 1988), 57

Molina, Alfred, 118, *119*

Monkeybone (Selick, 2001), 234

Monsters, Inc. (Docter, 2001), 151, 162–63, *162*, *163*

Moore, Demi, 94–95

Morales, Esai, 64–65

Moran of the Lady Letty (Melford, 1922), 14

More American Graffiti (Norton, 1979), 103

Morris, Anita, *135*

Mosquito Coast, The (Weir, 1986), 35, 80–81, *80*, 90–91, *90*, *91*, 132–133

Mosquito Coast, The (novel, Theroux), 90

Moy, Wood, *237*

Mozart, Wolfgang Amadeus, 80, 88–89, *88*, *89*

Mrs. Doubtfire (Columbus, 1993), 194, 196–98, *197*

Mulligan, Gerry, *77*, 78

Munch, Edvard, 195

Murch, Walter, 28, 96, *96*
    American Zoetrope, 18, *31*
    The Conversation, 43, *43*
    Coppola and, 32, *51*
    Crumb, 19
    The Godfather Part II, 45
    Lucas and, 102
    Return to Oz, 232
    Robbins and, 228, 229
    THX 1138, 31, 36, 37, 104, 110

Muren, Dennis, 116, 129, 136

Murphy, Eddie, 181, *181*, 224

Murray, Bill, 72–73, *72*, *73*

Muybridge, Eadweard, 12–13, 18

My Dinner With Andre (Malle, 1981), 108

Myers, Mike
    Shrek, 180, 181, *181*
    Shrek 2, 175, 182

My Family/Mi Familia (Nava, 1995), 64–65, *64*, *65*

Myles, Sophia, 242

Mystic River (Eastwood, 2003), 202

N

Napoleon (Gance, 1981), 31

Narita, Hiro, 189

Nava, Gregory, 64–65, *64*

Neeson, Liam, 137, *137*

Nelson, Craig T., *167*

Nelson, Randy, 154

Never Cry Wolf (Ballard, 1983), 188–90, *188*, *189*

Newman, Randy, 156, 163

New York, 19

New York Stories (Coppola, 1989), 33

Nicholson, Jack, 17
    One Flew Over the Cuckoo's Nest, 79, *79*, 86, 87, *87*

Niebaum-Coppola Estate Vineyards and Winery, 31, 34, *34*, *35*, 107

Nightmare Before Christmas, The (Selick, 1993), *see Tim Burton's The Nightmare Before Christmas*

Nilsson, Rob, 19, 222–23, *222*, *223*

Nimoy, Leonard, 214

Nin, Anaïs, 212, 213

9½ Weeks (Lyne, 1986), 93

9@Night (films), 223

Nine Months (Columbus, 1995), 195

Norris, Frank, 14, 19

North, Edmund H., 29

Northern Lights (Nilsson and Hanson, 1979), 222

No Such Thing (Hartley, 2002), 35

Nutcracker: The Motion Picture, The (Ballard, 1986), 187, 232

O

O'Connor, Kevin J., 57, *57*

O'Hara, Catherine, 196, 234

Oldman, Gary, *60*

Olin, Lena, 93, *93*

Olmos, Edward James, 65

Ondaatje, Michael, 80–81, 94, 95

Ondricek, Miroslav, 89

O'Neal, Tatum, 226–27, 226

One Flew Over the Cuckoo's Nest (Forman, 1975), 79, *79*, 86–87, *86*, *87*

One Flew Over the Cuckoo's Nest (novel, Kesey), 78, 86–87

One from the Heart (Coppola, 1982), 31

One Man Band (Jimenez, Andrews, 2005), 155, *155*

On the Edge (Nilsson, 1986), 222

Opéra Industriel (Chin, Cohen, 1988), 176

Organization, The (Medford, 1971) 17

Osborn, Ron, 134

Oscars, *see Academy Awards*

Ostby, Eben, *109*

Outlaw Josey Wales, The (Kaufman, 1976), 212

Outrage (television movie; Ackerman, 1998), 35

Outsiders, The (Coppola, 1983), 31, 52–54, *52*, *53*

Outsiders, The (novel, Hinton), 52

Overton, Rick, 128

Oz, Frank, 137, 140–41, *140*

Ozu, Yasujiro, 237

P

Pacific Data Images, 171–75
    Antz, 178–79, *178*, *179*
    chronology of, 171, 173, 175
    short films of, 176–77, *176*, *177*
    Shrek, 180–81, *180*, *181*
    Shrek 2, 182–83, *182*, *183*

Pacino, Al, 58–59, *58*

Palrang, Joe, *173*

Paquin, Anna, 191, *191*

Park, Nick, 232

Park, Ray, 137, *137*

Patton (Schaffner; 1970), 29

Payday (Duke, 1973), 78–79, *79*, 84, 85, *85*

Peggy Sue Got Married (Coppola, 1986), 33, 56–57, *56*, *57*

Peoples, David Webb, 18, 210

Perfect World, A (Eastwood, 1993), 210–11, *211*

Pesci, Joe, 196, *196*

Petulia (Lester, 1968), 17

Phoenix, River, *90*, *91*, *91*, 132–33

Picker, David, 101

Pierce, David Hyde, *159*

Pixar Animation Studios, 149–54, *154*
    A Bug's Life, 158–59, *158*, *159*
    chronology of, 149, 151, 153
    Finding Nemo, 164–65, *164*, *165*
    The Incredibles, 166–67, *166*, *167*
    Monsters, Inc., 162–63, *162*, *163*
    Pacific Data Images and, 173
    short films of, 155, *155*
    Star Wars: Episode VI Return of the Jedi, 103
    Toy Story, 156–57, *156*, *157*
    Toy Story 2, 160–61, *160*, *161*

Pixar Technology, 108

Pixar University, 154

Play Misty for Me (Eastwood, 1971), 203–5, 204

Pleasance, Donald, 37

Poitier, Sidney, 17, 30

Pollak, Kevin, 128

Poltergeist (Spielberg, 1982), 132

Porter, Don, 226

Porter, Edwin S., 13

Portman, Natalie
    Anywhere But Here, 238
    Star Wars: Episode I The Phantom Menace, *136*, 137
    Star Wars: Episode II Attack of the Clones, *141*
    Star Wars: Episode III Revenge of the Sith, *142*

Positively True Adventures of the Alleged Texas Cheerleader Murdering Mom, The (television movie; Ritchie, 1993), 225

Powaqqatsi (Reggio, 1988), 33, 105
Privateer, The (film never made), 229
Prowse, David, *123*
Prowse, Heydon, *62*
Psych-Out (Rush, 1968), 17
Puri, Amrish, *125*
Puzo, Mario, 41, *44*

Q

Qing, Jiang, 192
Quan, Ke Huy, 124
Quills (Kaufman, 2000), 213

R

Radcliffe, Daniel, 199, *199*
Radioland Murders (Smith, 1994), 106, 134–35, *134*, *135*
Raiders of the Lost Ark (Spielberg, 1981), 103, 118–19, *118*, *119*, 160, 212
Rainmaker, The (Coppola, 1997), see *John Grisham's The Rainmaker*
Rainmaker, The (novel, Grisham), 66
Rain People, The (Coppola, 1969), 18, 27, 30, 96, 103, *103*
Ranft, Joe, 152, 157, 159, *159*
Ratbastard Protective Association, 16
Ray, Satyajit, 64
Red's Dream (Lasseter, 1987), 149, 155, *155*
Redford, Robert, 224–26, *225*
Reed, Jim, 238–39
Reeves, Keanu, 60
Reeves, William, 108, *109*
Reggio, Godfrey, 33
Reno, Jeff, 134
Reno, Kelley
  The Black Stallion, 46, *46*, 47
  The Black Stallion Returns, 50, *50*
Rent (Columbus, 2005), 195
Return to Oz (Murch, 1986), 232
Reynolds, Burt, 224
Rhys-Davies, Jonathan, 118–19
Ribisi, Giovanni, 69, 73
Richardson, Ralph, 230
Right Stuff, The (Kaufman, 1983), 16, 18, 212, 215–17, *215*, *217*
Ritchie, Michael, 18, 102, 224–26, *224*
  The Bad News Bears, 226, *226*, 227
  The Candidate, 225–26, *225*
Robbins, Matthew, 18, 102, 228–31, *228*
Roberts, Conrad, *91*
Robertson, Cliff, 212
Rodriguez, Robert, 19
Rooney, Mickey, 46, 47
Roos, Fred, 29, 52
Rosendahl, Carl, 168, 171–73, *172*, *173*, *174*, *175*
  Antz, 178–79
Rosqui, Tom, 219
Rota, Nino, 45
Rourke, Mickey, 54, *54*, 55, 67
Rowling, J.K., 199
Rubicon (Coppola, 1985), 33
Rudolph, Alain, 57
Rumble Fish (Coppola, 1983), 31, 53–55, *54*, *55*
Rumble Fish (novel, Hinton), 54

Rush, Richard, 17
Russo, Rianni, *40*
Ryder, Winona, 58, 60, *60*
Rygiel, Jim, *173*

S

Sahl, Mort, 77, 82
Salesin, David, *109*
Sampson, Will, 86, 87
Sarandon, Susan, 234, 238
Saroyan, William, 15
Sarsgaard, Peter, *238*, 239
Saul Zaentz Company, The, 19, *82*
  Amadeus, *74–75*, 88–89, *88*, *89*
  chronology of, 77, 79, 81, 83
  The English Patient, *94–95*, *94*, *95*
  The Mosquito Coast, *90–91*, *90*, *91*
  One Flew Over the Cuckoo's Nest, 86–87, *86*, *87*
  Payday, 84, 85, *85*
  The Unbearable Lightness of Being, *92–93*, *92*, *93*
Saul Zaentz Film Center, 82–83, *82*
Saunders, Jennifer, 183
Schiavelli, Vincent, *79*
Schickle, David, *219*
Schneider, Elsa, 133
Schneider, Roy, 67
Schrader, Paul, 90
Schwartzman, Jason, 71
Scorsese, Martin, 44
Scott, A.O., 69, 143
Scott, George C., 17
scratch voices, 159
Secret Garden, The (Holland, 1993), 33, 62–63, *62*, *63*
Secret Garden, The (novel, Burnett), 62, 63
Sedaris, David, 239
Selick, Henry, 121, 151, 232–34, *232*
Selick, Tom, 118
Selick Projects, 232
Semi-Tough (Ritchie, 1977), 224
Sentinel Building, 29, 32, *33*
Seepage (Selick, 1979), 232
Seven Arts, see Universal/Seven Arts
Shaffer, Peter, 79
Sheen, Martin, 31, 48, *49*, 225
Shire, Talia, *40*, 58, *59*
Shrek (Adamson, Jenson, 2001), 175, 180–81, *180*, *181*
Shrek 2 (Adamson, Asbury, Vernon, 2004), 175, *175*, 182–83, *182*, *183*
Shrek 4-D (Smith, 2003), 177
Shue, Elizabheth, 194
Siegel, Don, 16, 202–4, 214
Signal 7 (Nilsson, 1986), 19, 222, *223*
Silverman, David, 162
Silvers, Michael, 153
Silverstein, Shel, 85
Simon, David, 19
Simpsons, The (television series), 173–75, *174*
Skywalker Ranch, *98–99*, 103–7, *106*, *107*
Skywalker Sound, 105, 109
Sleepy Guy (Hui, 1994), 176
Slotkin, Richard, 207
Slow Bob in the Lower Dimensions (television

short; Selick, 1990), 232
Smile (Ritchie, 1975), 224
Smith, Alvy Ray, 108, *109*, 151
Smith, Charles Martin, *110*, 188, *188*, *189*
Smith, Delos V., Jr., *79*
Smith, Maggie, *63*
Smith, Mel, 134–35, *135*
Smits, Jimmy, *64*, 65
Smoke (Wang, 1995), 238–39
Smythe, Douglas, 129
Snow Leopard, The (novel, Matthiessen), 188
Snow Walker, The (Smith, 2003), 188
Southern, Terry, 29
"spaghetti Westerns," 202
Spano, Vincent, 51
Spielberg, Steven
  Close Encounters of the Third Kind, 229
  Indiana Jones and the Last Crusade, 132–33, *133*
  Indiana Jones and the Temple of Doom, 124–25, *125*
  Indiana Jones series, 106
  Jurassic Park, 231
  Lucas and, 104
  Raiders of the Lost Ark, 103, 118–19, *119*
  The Sugarland Express, 230
Spirit of '76, The (Reiner, 1990), 33
Spock, Judy Wood, 120
Spoor, George K., 13
Sprocket Systems, Inc., 102–103, 105
Sprout (Peterson, 2002), 177, *177*
Squires, Scott, 136
Sragow, Michael, 12–19, 217
Stallone, Sylvester, *178*
Stanford, Leland, 12
Stanton, Andrew, 152
  A Bug's Life, 158–159
  Finding Nemo, 164–65
  Toy Story, 157
Starship Troopers (Verhoeven, 1997), 19, 231
"Star Tours," 105
Star Trek II: The Wrath of Khan (Meyer, 1982), 151
Star Wars: Episode IV A New Hope (Lucas, 1977), 103, *104*, *105*, 105–6, 112–13, *112*, *113*, *114–15*
  sound effects in, 138
  THX 1138 and, 37
  Tippett's work on, 231
Star Wars: Episode V The Empire Strikes Back (Kershner, 1980), 103, 116–17, *116*, *117*, 160, 231
Star Wars: Episode VI Return of the Jedi (Marquand, 1983), 103, 104, 122–23, *122*, *123*
Star Wars: Episode I The Phantom Menace (Lucas, 1999), 106–107, 109, 136–37, *136*, *137*, 138–139
Star Wars: Episode II Attack of the Clones (Lucas, 2002), 35, *101*, 107, 109, 140–41, *140*, *141*
Star Wars: Episode III Revenge of the Sith (Lucas, 2005), 35, 107, 109, 142–43, *142*, *143*, 144–145
Star Wars Trilogy (VHS tapes), 106
Steele, Adrien, *91*

Stern, Daniel, 196, *196*
Sternberg, Tom, 31
Stevens, George, 15
Stockwell, Dean, 17
Stone, Oliver, 192, *239*
Stone, Sharon, *179*
Storaro, Vittorio, 48, 130
Strasberg, Lee, 45
Strasberg, Susan, 17
Sturhahn, Lawrence, *31*
Sugarland Express, The (Spielberg, 1974), 230
Sutherland, Donald, 214, *214*
Sweet Movie (Makavejev, 1974), 237

T

Take the Money and Run (Allen, 1969), 17, 27
Taking Off (Forman, 1971), 87
Tall Guy, The (Smith, 1990), 135
Tan, Amy, 237–38, *239*
Tandy, Jessica, *230*, 231, *231*
Tavoularis, Dean, 48, 59, 71, 130
Taylor, Charles, 186
Tenderloin Action Group (Tenderloin Y Group), 223
Terminator 2: Judgment Day (Cameron, 1991), 105, 173
Thalberg, Irving, 14
Thelan, Jodi, 51
Theroux, Paul, 90
Thin Red Line, The (Malick, 1998), 218
Thom, Randy, 153
Thomas, Kristin Scott, *81*, *94*, 95, *96*
Thompson, Emma, 135
Thompson, J. Lee, 103
Thornton, Billy Bob, 242
Three Warriors (Merrill, 1977), 78–79, *78*
THX 1138 (Lucas, 1971), 29, *30*, 36–37, *36*, *37*, 101, 104, 111
    at Cannes Film Festival, 110
    Coppola and, 30, 31
    dispute with Warner Brothers on, 15
    Lucas's student version of, 102
    Robbins in, 228
Tian Yu (novel, Yan), 192
Tilly, Meg, 88
Tim Burton's The Nightmare Before Christmas (Selick, 1993), 232–34, *232*, *234*
Time of Your Life, The (Potter, 1948), 15
Tin Toy (Lasseter, 1988), 149, 152, *153*, 155
Tippett, Phil, 19, 231
Titanic (Cameron, 1997), 113
Tjader, Cal, 77
Tolkien, J.R.R., 79
Tong, Richard, 29, 221
Torn, Rip, 78–79, 85, *85*
Toys (Levinson, 1992), 173
Toy Story (Lasseter, 1995), 149, *149*, 151, 153, 156–57, *156*, *157*, 173
    Pacific Data Images competing against, 175
Toy Story 2 (Lasseter, 1999), 151, 160–61, *160*, *161*
Tramp, The (Chaplin, 1915), 13
Tron (Lisberger, 1982), 151
Tsui, Michelle, *173*

Tucker, Preston Thomas, 130, *131*
Tucker: The Man and His Dream (Coppola, 1988), 33, 105, 130–31, *130*, *131*
Turan, Kenneth, 153
Turner, Kathleen, *56*, 57, *57*
Twice Upon a Time (Korty, 1983), 103, 120–21, *120*, *121*, 221, 232
Twin Peaks (Lynch, 1989), 192
Twisted (Kaufman, 2004), *213*, 217, *217*
Tyson, Cicely, 220

U

Unbearable Lightness of Being, The (Kaufman, 1988), 77, 80–83, *82*, 92–93, *92*, *93*, 213
Unbearable Lightness of Being, The (novel, Kundera), 92
Unforgiven (Eastwood, 1992), 206–10, *206*, *207*, *208–09*, *210*
United Artists, 214
Universal/Seven Arts, 30, 36, 103, 104
Unkrich, Lee, 162

V

Valentino, Rudolph, 14
Van Sant, Gus, 19
Verhoeven, Paul, 231
Vertigo (Hitchcock, 1958), 16
Viandante del Cielo (wine), 107
Virgin Suicides, The (Coppola, 2000), 35, 68–69, *68*, *69*
Virgin Suicides, The (novel, Eugenides), 68, 69
Visconti, Luchino, 14
Voight, John, 67
Von Stroheim, Erich, 14–15
Von Trier, Lars, 222
Vorkapich, Slavko, 116

W

Waits, Tom, 54
Walker, John, 166
Walsh, Dick, *173*, *174*, 175, 180
Walsh, Raoul, 15
Walt Disney Studios
    James and the Giant Peach, 234
    Lasseter and, 150–51
    Pixar Animation Studios and, 152–53, 173
    Selick and, 232
    Tim Burton's The Nightmare Before Christmas, 232–33
    Toy Story, 149, 156
    Toy Story 2, 160
Walter, Jessica, 204, *204*
Walters, Graham, *173*
Wanderers, The (Kaufman, 1979), 31, 118, 212
Wang, Wayne, 19, 236–39, *237*
Ward, Fred, 212
Ward, Jim, *173*
Warner, Aron, 181
Warner Brothers, 15, 29, 48, 103, 104
Waters, John, 19
Wax, Steve, *31*
Weir, Peter, 80, 81, 90–91
Weiser, Shari, 126
Welles, Orson, 15

Western films, 13
    High Plains Drifter, 205–6
    "spaghetti Westerns," 202
    Unforgiven, 206–10
West Wing, The (television series), 225
Wexler, Haskell, 111
Whalley, Joanne, *129*
What's Up, Doc? (Bogdanovich, 1972), 17
White Dawn, The (Kaufman, 1974), 212
Who Are the Debolts? And Where Did They Get Nineteen Kids? (Korty, 1977), 221
Williams, Cindy, 42, 43, 111
Williams, John, 113
Williams, Robin, 35, 196–97, *197*
Willis, Gordon, 41, 59
Willow (Howard, 1988), 105, 128–29, *128*, *129*
Wilson, Cintra, 55
Wind (Ballard, 1992), 187
wines, 107
Wolfman Jack, 111
Woolvett, Jaimz, 206
Wooton, Patty, *173*, *174*
Wozniak, Steve, 171
Wu, Alice, 193
Wytock, Grant, 15

X

Xiao Hua (Zhang, 1978), 192, *192*
Xiu Xiu: The Sent-Down Girl (Chen, 1999), 192–93

Y

Yan, Geling, 192, 193
Yang, Janet, *239*
Yates, Peter, 16
You're a Big Boy Now (Coppola, 1966), 27, 56
Young Indiana Jones Chronicles, The (television series), 105, 109

Z

Zacharek, Stephanie, 69, 183
Zaentz, Saul, 74, 77, *83*
    Amadeus, 89
    early life of, 77
    The English Patient, 94–95
    as film producer, 79–83
    The Mosquito Coast, 91
    Murch and, 96
    as music producer, 78
    One Flew Over the Cuckoo's Nest, 86
    Payday, 85
    At Play in the Fields of the Lord, 81
    The Unbearable Lightness of Being, 77, 92–93
Zemeckis, Robert, 47, 56
Zoetrope: All-Story (magazine), 32, 35
Zoopraxiscope, 12, 18
Zwigoff, Terry, 16, 19, 79, 240–43, *240*, *242*

PHOTOGRAPHY CREDITS

American Zoetrope
Pages 2–3: *Apocalypse Now.* Photograph Courtesy of American Zoetrope. All rights reserved. Stag Theatre © 2005 Lucasfilm Ltd.

Pages 32, 48–49: *Apocalypse Now.* Photographs Courtesy of American Zoetrope. All rights reserved.

Pages 24–25, 34, 35 (top): © Niebaum-Coppola Estate Winery: Images Courtesy of the Niebaum-Coppola Estate Winery

Pages 29 (top), **31, 35** (bottom): Images courtesy of American Zoetrope Film Library

Page 32: The Sentinel Building. © 2005 Lucasfilm Ltd. All rights reserved. Photo by Michelle Jouan

Page 42: *The Conversation.* Photographs Courtesy of American Zoetrope. All rights reserved.

Kim Aubry
Page 43 (bottom): Photo by Kim Aubry

Joan Chen
Page 192: Courtesy of Joan Chen

Disney Publishing Worldwide
Cover and pages 148, 156–157: *Toy Story* © 1995 Disney Enterprises, Inc.

Page 155: *Mike's New Car* © 2002 Disney Enterprises, Inc./Pixar

Page 155: *Jack Jack Attack* © 2004 Disney Enterprises, Inc./Pixar

Pages 158–159: *A Bug's Life* © 1998 Disney Enterprises, Inc./Pixar

Pages 160–161: *Toy Story 2* © 1999 Disney Enterprises, Inc./Pixar. Original *Toy Story* Elements © Disney Enterprises, Inc.

Pages 162–163: *Monsters, Inc.* © 2001 Disney Enterprises, Inc./Pixar

Pages 164–165: *Finding Nemo* © 2003 Disney Enterprises, Inc./Pixar

Pages 166–167: *The Incredibles* © 2004 Disney Enterprises, Inc./Pixar

Pages 188–189: *Never Cry Wolf* © Disney Enterprises, Inc. Photo page 188 courtesy of Colin Michael Kitchens

Pages 232, 235: *The Nightmare Before Christmas* © Touchstone Pictures

Page 233: *James and the Giant Peach* © Disney Enterprises, Inc.

Pages 236, 239: *The Joy Luck Club* © Buena Vista Pictures Distribution, Inc. All rights reserved.

1492 Pictures
Page 195: Courtesy of 1492 Pictures

Further Films
Pages 66–67: *John Grisham's The Rainmaker.* Courtesy of Further Films

Richard Harris
Page 225 (top): © Richard Harris

John Korty
Page 218: © Korty Films

Page 219 (top left and right): *Crazy Quilt* © Korty Films

Page 219 (bottom): *Funnyman* © Korty Films

Page 220: *The Autobiography of Miss Jane Pittman* © Korty Films

Lions Gate
Page 238: Image taken from *The Center of the World* provided through the courtesy of Lions Gate Entertainment.

Lucasfilm Ltd.
Cover (background) **and pages 4–5, 8–9, 28** (top): © 2005 JAK Films, Inc. All Rights Reserved.

Cover and pages 142–145: *Star Wars: Episode III—Revenge of the Sith* © 2005 Lucasfilm Ltd. & ™. All rights reserved.

Pages 20–21–9, 138 (bottom), **140–141:** *Star Wars: Episode II—Attack of the Clones* © 2002 Lucasfilm Ltd. & ™. All rights reserved.

Page 32 (top right): Reproduced with permission of Toho

Pages 98–99, 106: Skywalker Ranch. © 2005 Lucasfilm Ltd. All rights reserved. Photos by Tom Forster

Page 100: © 2005 Lucasfilm Ltd. All rights reserved.

Page 103: © 2005 Lucasfilm Ltd. All rights reserved.

Pages 105, 112–115: *Star Wars: Episode IV—A New Hope* © 1977 and 1997 Lucasfilm Ltd. & ™. All rights reserved.

Page 107 (top): Big Rock Ranch. © 2005 Lucasfilm Ltd. All rights reserved. Photo by Matthew Porter

Page 107 (bottom): Skywalker Library. © 2005 Lucasfilm Ltd. All Rights Reserved. Photo by Tina Mills

Pages 108, 151: *The Adventures of André and Wally B.* © 1984 Lucasfilm Ltd. and Pixar

Page 109 (top): Photo courtesy of Alvy Ray Smith

Page 109 (bottom two photos): The Presidio. © 2005 Lucasfilm Ltd. All rights reserved. Photos by Tina Mills

Pages 116–117, 231 (bottom): *Star Wars: Episode V—The Empire Strikes Back* © 1980 and 1997 Lucasfilm Ltd. & ™. All rights reserved.

Pages 118–119: *Raiders of the Lost Ark* © 1981 Lucasfilm Ltd. & ™. All rights reserved.

Pages 122–123: *Star Wars: Episode VI—Return of the Jedi* © 1983 and 1997 Lucasfilm Ltd. & ™. All rights reserved.

Pages 124–125: *Indiana Jones and the Temple of Doom* © 1984 Lucasfilm Ltd. & ™. All rights reserved.

Pages 126–127: *Labyrinth.* ™ & © 2005 The Jim Henson Company/Lucasfilm Ltd.

Pages 128–129: *Willow* © 1988 Lucasfilm Ltd. & ™. All rights reserved.

Pages 130–131: *Tucker* © 1988 Lucasfilm Ltd. & ™. All rights reserved.

Pages 132–133: *Indiana Jones and the Last Crusade* © 1989 Lucasfilm Ltd. & ™. All rights reserved.

Pages 136–139: *Star Wars: Episode I—The Phantom Menace* © 1999 Lucasfilm Ltd. & ™. All rights reserved.

MGM
Pages 32 (center left), **46–47:** *The Black Stallion* © 1979 Metro-Goldwyn-Mayer Studios Inc. All rights reserved. Courtesy of MGM CLIP + STILL

Pages 50, 51 (top): *The Black Stallion Returns* © 1983 Metro-Goldwyn-Mayer Studios Inc. All rights reserved. Courtesy of MGM CLIP + STILL

Pages 70–71: *CQ* © 2001 United Artists Films Inc. All rights reserved. Courtesy of MGM CLIP + STILL

Page 193: *Autumn in New York* © 2000 Metro-Goldwyn-Mayer Studios Inc. All rights reserved. Courtesy of MGM CLIP + STILL

Page 214: *Invasion of the Body Snatchers* © 1978 Metro-Goldwyn-Mayer Studios Inc. All Rights Reserved. Courtesy of MGM CLIP + STILL

Pages 240–241: *Ghost World* © 2000 United Artists Films Inc. All rights reserved. Courtesy of MGM CLIP + STILL

Page 242: *Art School Confidential* © 2006 United Artists Films Inc. All rights reserved. Courtesy of MGM CLIP + STILL

Miramax
Cover and page 94: *The English Patient* © Miramax Films

Pages 81 (bottom), **83, 95, 97:** *The English Patient* © Miramax Films. Photos by Phil Bray

Walter & Aggie Murch
Pages 28 (bottom), **51** (bottom), **96:** © Walter & Aggie Murch Private Family Collection

EDITORIAL CREDITS

Most of the book's quotations come from various internal Lucasfilm Ltd. and JAK Films, Inc. interview transcripts, reference books copyrighted to Lucasfilm Ltd., and the personal websites of the studios and featured directors. Additional quote sources are listed below.

American Zoetrope
Page 27: "I left Hofstra as really the top guy..." (Francis Ford Coppola), from *Coppola: A Biography* by Peter Cowie, published by Scribner, 1990, pages 21–22

Page 48: "trials and executions for executives..." (John Milius), from an interview with Kenneth Plume on IGN.com

Page 52: "representative of the youth of America..." (excerpt from librarian's letter), from *Coppola: A Biography* by Peter Cowie, published by Scribner, 1990, page 167

Page 67: "There's so little to choose from..." (Francis Ford Coppola), from *USA Today* article, originally quoted in *New York Times* review by Janet Maslin

The Saul Zaentz Company
Page 72: "She has been able to reinvent..." (Bill Murray), from *New York Times* article, "The Coppola Smart Mob," by Lynn Hirschberg, August 31, 2003

Page 82: "Studios are interested in money..." (Saul Zaentz), from *Variety* article, "Zaentz Addresses Filmmakers," by Mark Woods, November 18, 1997

Page 89: "thanks to Communist inefficiency..." (Milos Forman), from the *Amadeus* DVD

Pixar Animation Studios
Page 149: "It's what you do that matters..." (Ed Catmull), from *Wired Magazine* article, "Welcome to Planet Pixar," by Austin Bunn, June, 2004

Page 154: "If I'm having fun..." (John Lasseter), from Pixar supplemental material on *Toy Story* special edition DVD

Page 154: Randy Nelson quotes from *Wired Magazine* article, "Welcome to Planet Pixar," by Austin Bunn, June, 2004

Page 156: "One of the things we didn't want to do..." (John Lasseter), from Guardian Unlimited Special Report on Regus London Film Festival, November 19, 2001

Page 158: "One inspiring thing we noticed..." (John Lasseter), ibid.

Page 160: "a defining moment" (Ed Catmull), from *Wired Magazine* article, "Welcome to Planet Pixar," by Austin Bunn, June, 2004

Page 166: "over the line" exchange (between John Walker and Brad Bird), from supplemental materials on *The Incredibles* DVD

Page 167: "The purpose of animation..." (Brad Bird), from *The Incredibles* DVD

Pacific Data Images
Page 181: "almost photorealistic..." (Aron Warner), from *Shrek* production notes

Page 183: "I think a lot of challenges..." (Ken Bielenberg), from *Animation World Magazine* article, "What's New in *Shrek 2*," by Ellen Wolff, May 19, 2004

Joan Chen
Page 193: "is a much better place to be unemployed..." (Joan Chen), from *Interview Magazine* article by Franz Lidz, August, 2000

Page 193: "there are only so many roles..." from multiple web sources

Chris Columbus
Page 195: "Making movies is a job..." (Chris Columbus), from BBC interview, November 13, 2002

Page 198: "children of divorce blame themselves..." (Chris Columbus), from Commentary on *Mrs. Doubtfire* DVD

Clint Eastwood
Page 204: "There's a big trap..." (Julie Walters), from *Play Misty For Me* DVD

Philip Kaufman
Page 213: "I don't really ascribe to the theory..." (Philip Kaufman), from *University of Chicago Magazine* article, "Auteur! Auteur!" by Chris Smith, April, 2000

Michael Ritchie
Page 225: "I can say without hesitation..." (Holly Hunter), from a memorial service for Michael Ritchie

Wayne Wang
Page 237: "As Sydney Pollack always says..." (Wayne Wang), from an interview with the Onion AV Club

Terry Zwigoff
Page 240: "Making a feature film..." (Terry Zwigoff), from interview with Daniel Steinhart on Indiewire. July 20, 2001

Page 240: "I don't have a cellular phone..." (Terry Zwigoff), from interview with Roger Ebert in the *Chicago Sun-Times*, May 28, 1995

Page 240: "It's hell down here, I just hate it" (Terry Zwigoff), from interview with Jeffrey M. Anderson for *Combustible Celluloid*, July 19, 2001

Page 240: "one of the last livable cities in America..." (Terry Zwigoff), ibid.

Page 241: "Anything that's authentic..." (Terry Zwigoff), from interview with Travis Crawford in *MovieMaker Magazine*. vol 1.16

Page 241: "I couldn't get him to play his music right!" (Terry Zwigoff), from interview with Marshall Wyatt in *The Old Time Herald*, Fall, 1995

ACKNOWLEDGMENTS

JAK Films, Inc. would like to acknowledge the contributions of the following individuals for their help with photo and other research for this book:

Jeanne Austin, Carroll Ballard, Jeff Briggs, Joan Chen, Richard Chuang, Nancy Eichler, Sarah Garcia, Stephen Gong, Paul Hill, Kathleen Holliday, Christopher Holm, Michelle Jouan, Leslie Kaye, David Kiehn, Colin Michael Kitchens, John Korty, Amy Krider, Tom Luddy, Tina Mills, James Mockoski, Walter and Aggie Murch, Anahid Nazarian, Rosaleen O'Bryne, Cindy Young Russell, Henry Selick, Krista Swager, Wayne Wang, and Terry Zwigoff

Thanks to Random House for their support
and look for Del Rey Book's new *Star Wars: Legacy of the Force* series
launching in June 2006 with BETRAYAL by Aaron Allston.

A very special thanks to Peter Beren for his enormous help.

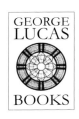

Published by George Lucas Books
An imprint of JAK Films, Inc.
Copyright © 2006 by JAK Films, Inc. ® or ™ where indicated.

Director of Publishing: Lucy Autrey Wilson

Produced and distributed by Welcome Books®
An imprint of Welcome Enterprises, Inc.
6 West 18th Street, New York, New York 10011
(212) 989-3200; Fax (212) 989-3205
www.welcomebooks.com

Project Editor: Katrina Fried
Designer: Gregory Wakabayashi
Editorial Assistant: Maren Gregerson

Library of Congress Cataloging-in-Publication Data

Avni, Sheerly.
Cinema by the Bay / by Sheerly Avni ; introduction by Michael Sragow.--1st ed.
p. cm.
"A welcome book."
Includes index.
ISBN 1-932183-88-4 (hardcover)
1. Motion pictures--California--San Francisco Bay Area. 2. Motion picture industry--
California--San Francisco Bay Area. 3. Motion picture producers and directors--California--
San Francisco Bay Area--Biography. I. Title.
PN1993.5.U718A96 2006
791.4309794'61--dc22
2006001746

ISBN-10: 1-932183-88-4
ISBN-13: 978-1-932183-88-7

First Edition
1 3 5 7 9 10 8 6 4 2

Printed in China by Palace Press International